THE WAY FORWARD FOR
PERENNIALISM

AFTER THE ANTINOMIANISM
OF FRITHJOF SCHUON

REVISED EDITION

Charles Upton

Copyright © 2025 by Charles Upton, All Rights Reserved.

No part of this publication may be reproduced, stored in a retrieval system, or transmitted, in any form or by any means, electronic, mechanical, photocopying, recording, or otherwise, without prior written permission of Divaan E Ishq.

ISBN Paperback: 978-1-990751-33-2

CONTENTS

PART ONE
THE WAY FORWARD FOR PERENNIALISM...7

Introduction...9

Chapter One

The Multiplicity and Unity of Religions according to Guénonian Traditionalism: An Alternative Way of Doing "Comparative Religion"...21

Chapter Two

Entering Houses by their Doors: The Uniqueness and Commonality of Christianity and Islam...29

Chapter Three

Sufism and *Jñana-yoga*: Some Correspondences...47

Chapter Four

The Trinitarian Problem in Christian/Muslim Dialogue...67

Chapter Five
The Question of God's Incarnation as Jesus Christ in Christian/Muslim Dialogue...73

Chapter Six
From a Letter to a Christian Mystic...79

Chapter Seven
The Nature of Ontological Perspectives: A Commentary on Frithjof Schuon's Doctrine of the Relatively Absolute...89

Chapter Eight
For the Intellectual Dark Web, a Letter to Rebel Wisdom on some Contemporary Intellectual and Social Movements Based on, or Compatible with, Traditional Metaphysics...97

Chapter Nine
The Covenants of the Prophet Muhammad as a Valid Exoteric Expression of the Transcendent Unity of Religions: A Call for United Front Ecumenism...107

Chapter Ten
Toward a Brotherhood of Silence: A Response to "Fraternity for Knowledge and Cooperation"...129

PART TWO

THE ANTINOMIANISM OF FRITHJOF SCHUON...149

Introduction..151

Chapter Eleven

The Pivotal Importance of Frithjof Schuon...155

Chapter Twelve

How to Read Frithjof Schuon:
The Importance of a Second Look...163

Chapter Thirteen

Metaphysical Errors in the Writings of Frithjof Schuon:
Their Role in Discernment...175

Chapter Fourteen

Letter to Wolfgang Smith:
On Orthodoxy, Cosmology, Exoterism, Esoterism,
and Frithjof Schuon...327

Chapter Fifteen

Was Frithjof Schuon Really a "Traditionalist"?
A Review of *Keys to the Beyond: Frithjof Schuon's
Cross-Traditional Language of Transcendence*
by Patrick Laude (SUNY, 2021)...331

Addendum

A Last Word?...359

PART ONE

THE WAY FORWARD FOR PERENNIALISM

INTRODUCTION TO PART ONE

The perspective on religion and metaphysics known as Perennialism (also referred to as Traditionalism) has its roots in the writings of Renaissance philosophers like Marcilio Ficino and Pico della Mirandola, as well as in St. Augustine, the Holy Qur'an and the Hindu concept of the *sanatana dharma*. In the twentieth and twenty-first centuries, however, Perennialism has become perhaps the most interesting and useful attempt to deal with the fact of religious pluralism in a globalizing world without relativizing the traditional religions and emptying them of their sacred content. In earlier ages—apart, perhaps, from the syncretistic religion of Manichaeism—Perennialism was an arcane dimension of religious understanding, of interest only to a handful of sages. In our own time, however, it has unexpectedly appeared as one of the necessary defenses of faith in God and the metaphysical order against the assaults of an increasingly secularized world.

I have been studying Perennialism since 1988, mostly from the standpoint of the "Anglo-Swiss-Iranian" branch of

INTRODUCTION TO PART ONE

the Traditionalist School headed by Frithjof Schuon (1907-1998), which was considered by him and others to have been founded by French metaphysician René Guénon (1886-1951) and (secondarily) the Anglo-Indian scholar of metaphysics and traditional art who hailed from Sri Lanka, Ananda Kentish Coomaraswamy (1877-1947), and which has included such writers as Titus Burckhardt (1908-1984), Martin Lings (1909-2005), Marco Pallis (1895-1989), Lord Northbourne (1896-1982), Tage Lindbom (1909-2001), Leo Schaya (1916-1985), Joseph Epes Brown (1920-2000), Whitall Perry (1920-2005), Charles Le Gai Eaton (1921-2010), Alvin Moore Jr. (1923-2005), William Stoddard (1925-2023), Rama Ponnambalam Coomaraswamy (1929-2006), Seyyed Hossein Nasr (1933-), James Cutsinger (1953-2020), and (with reservations) Huston Smith (1919-2016), the last four of whom I was privileged to know personally. The younger generation of the Traditionalist School, which includes such writers as Mark Perry, Harry Oldmeadow, Patrick Laude, Joseph Lumbard, Jean-Baptiste Aymard, Ali Lakhani, Nigel Jackson, John Paraskevopoulos and Michael Fitzgerald must also be mentioned. I have been less directly influenced by a second branch of the Traditionalist School, associated with conservative metaphysical philosopher and Italian political theorist Baron Julius Evola (1898–1974), whose various references to René Guénon as a colleague seem to have transformed Guénon in some people's minds—including Russian political philosopher Aleksandr Dugin and American politico Steve Bannon—into a right-wing political ideologue, based mostly on his book *The Crisis of the Modern World*. Frithjof Schuon's Traditionalism/Perennialism, on the other hand, largely rejects Evola (except for some appreciative references by Rama Coomaraswamy), and presents a more accurate picture

INTRODUCTION TO PART ONE

of Guénon as a metaphysical philosopher largely uninvolved in politics. Schuon in fact derived many of his basic ideas from Guénon, though this is not always made as clear in his writings as it might have been. As for the "Perennial Philosophy" of Aldous Huxley and Gerald Heard, Schuon's school largely dismisses them as second-rate popularizers with little grasp of what Guénon, Schuon and their successors understand to be "the Primordial Tradition." Be that as it may, it is difficult to overestimate how much Frithjof Schuon's Traditionalism/Perennialism meant to those of my generation who had emerged from the 1960s and '70s without becoming either New Age practitioners or materialistic "yuppies" who saw spirituality as a sin of their youth. So much light emanated from the Traditionalist School under Schuon that when we discovered it, usually in the 1980s, we were dazzled by it. We were so grateful to have finally found a school of metaphysics and comparative religion that accepted a plurality of religions as valid (to us an undeniable fact), while strictly respecting the orthodoxy of each, that we couldn't see, or couldn't bring ourselves to see, that the leader of this School, for all his brilliant and sometimes unparalleled contributions to both "pure metaphysics" and the science of comparative religion, did not always strictly adhere to that principle of orthodoxy himself, since he professed Islam and presented himself as a valid Sufi shaykh while placing himself firmly outside of many Muslim norms, and often seemed to situate his own brand of esoterism hierarchically above the orthodox Divine Revelations from which all the Traditional faiths spring, thereby calling into question his "Traditionalist" identity.

INTRODUCTION TO PART ONE

Since this book deals not only with the value of the Perennialist perspective in the contemporary world but the formidable challenges faced by this perspective, a basically metaphysical critique, more than a strictly moral or psychological one, of the doctrines of Frithjof Schuon, as the last generally-recognized leader of the dominant school of Traditionalism/Perennialism in Britain and the United States, forms a necessary part of it. I've attempted to highlight both the strengths of this School, which are formidable, and its weaknesses, which are in some ways subversive to the Perennialist enterprise in its Guénonian Traditionalist rendition. Rather than limiting myself to such a critique, however—which makes up chapters *Twelve, Thirteen* and *Fifteen* in PART TWO—I have given examples (mostly in chapters *One* through *Five*) of how a truly Perennialist form of interfaith dialogue might be carried on from a standpoint substantially free from Schuon's intermittent peevishness in the face of certain orthodox doctrinal formulations, as well as showing (in *Chapter Nine*) how Perennialism might be capable of generating its own socio-political praxis; I have done this by recounting the history of an interfaith peace movement that, while certainly not an aspect of Perennialism per se, is nonetheless entirely compatible with Perennialist principles—namely the Covenants Initiative, which I co-founded with Dr. John Andrew Morrow (Ilyas 'Abd al-'Alim Islam) in 2013, based on his groundbreaking book **The Covenants of the Prophet Muhammad with the Christians of the World** (Angelico/Sophia Perennis, 2013). In the same chapter I have also hopefully demonstrated how true Perennialism is diametrically opposed to the false "Perennialism" of the globalist elites, the goal of which is to co-opt, control, subvert, and ultimately liquidate, the traditional religions of the earth.

INTRODUCTION TO PART ONE

The word "Perennialism" means different things to different people. To some it refers to the understanding that all the world's "transcendental" religions—the religions of Salvation and Enlightenment—and much of its metaphysical philosophy, along with major elements of some of the religions of the "First Peoples," share certain common doctrines and principles. To others it posits the existence of a single "primordial revelation" from which all the world's major religions have sprung. Others simply take it to mean that God has sent more than one true and legitimate Self-Revelation, and that more than one of these Revelations can be spiritually operative at the same time. To still others, Perennialism represents a body of higher doctrine that can potentially provide a deeper realization than any of the revealed faiths, one that consequently transcends these faiths and might perhaps supersede them entirely.

These "perennialisms" may seem to many like various abstract or academic theories of religion, perhaps interesting to those who happen to be interested in them but of little relevance either to the contemporary state of the world or to the needs of anyone struggling to take religion seriously and fulfill the duties of the spiritual life. In most places and times this has been a sound evaluation. In our own era, however, Perennialism in one form or another has assumed a much more central importance due to the fact that globalization has resulted in a condition of enforced religious pluralism. Religions that inhabited their own discrete cultural contexts for centuries or millennia have now been thrown together in an increasingly globalized and homogenized world, both allowing them to learn from one another as never before and bringing them into potentially violent confrontation in new and unexpected ways. Beyond this, the enforced religious pluralism of the contemporary world, particularly when it is interpreted according to the canons of postmodernism, threatens to rob all religions of their legitimacy. Every religion claims in one way or another to speak in the name of Absolute Truth, and yet every religion holds dogmas that conflict with those of the other faiths. This glaring fact has led many to the seemingly obvious conclusions that, 1) only one of these religions is true, this being the position of fundamentalism, or, 2) that there is no such thing as Absolute Truth, this being the position of postmodern relativism. Postmodernism holds that since the divergences between religions are effectively absolute they must lack any Objective Referent outside their own historical experiences, ethnic folkways and shared beliefs. In other words, a True and Living God could not possibly exist, only various tribal notions of "godhood," the kind of collective subjectivities traditionally known as "idols." Only Perennialism, insofar as it can demonstrate that the various religious "languages" are all referring from their different standpoints to one and the same Absolute Reality, can save the theological understanding of God as the Supreme Being, and the faith in that Being, from the apparently obvious conclusion (obvious at least in a religiously pluralistic world filled with competing "absolute" dogmatisms) that any belief in an Absolute Reality can be no more than a pious mirage, and do so without appealing to a potentially violent religious exclusivism. Thus the arguments for Perennialism, once so marginal and irrelevant, have in our own time become unexpectedly crucial in defending the validity of religion itself. (In the writings of Frithjof Schuon, the essence of this argument can be found in his doctrine of the

INTRODUCTION TO PART ONE

"relatively Absolute," for my understanding of which see *Chapter Seven* below, "The Nature of Ontological Perspectives.")

One form of Perennialism, however, is in danger of making itself the enemy rather than the ally of the world's religions, because it makes them vulnerable to the postmodern relativism that rejects any notion of the Absolute. I am referring specifically to the type of Perennialism that sees itself as a higher "esoteric" doctrine superseding the revealed or "confessional" religions—a doctrine Frithjof Schuon has named "quintessential esoterism." To the degree this sort of Perennialism is seen as more complete and elevated than the esoterisms of the God-given faiths, those faiths are relativized, the result being that the uniqueness of a particular religion is viewed only as a limitation, not as a door to the Transcendent that is spiritually effective precisely because it is higher and more essential than any abstract average of the faiths concocted by the human mind. Thus the notion of a supreme, extra-confessional esoterism ultimately alienates the particularities of the unique Divine Revelations from the transcendent dimension, after which they become fair game for the postmodern agenda of absolutizing the relative. This is how, ironically enough, it works against a true understanding of what is sometimes considered to be Schuon's central insight, the Transcendent Unity of Religions (rather than being a valid expression of it, as Schuon apparently believed), since it views those religions as abstractly united in and by an intellectual doctrine rather than as transcendentally, mysteriously, and concretely united in the One God. The forms of the different religions only appear as opposed to one another when the door to the intuition of the Transcendent Absolute is closed, resulting in the false and exclusivist absolutizing of their particular characteristics, considered as representing and communicating with nothing at all beyond themselves rather than as a set of unique and providential keys to that very "Beyond." Nor is this absolutization of particularities in any way compensated for by the supposedly higher esoteric doctrine that has been abstracted from them, simply because the doctrine in question is defined as superseding them, and therefore as more-or-less excluding or abrogating them. It should be obvious that such an ideology could be of interest and use only to a self-styled elite who feel they owe no allegiance whatsoever to any of the world's God-given Revelations, but who nonetheless wish to exercise control over the populations of the world by means of them.

So as to avoid giving aid and comfort to this sort of "anti-religious religion," I have recently taken to calling myself a "minimalist Perennialist." I do not see Perennialism or the Transcendent Unity of Religions as any kind of higher esoteric doctrine, but simply as a perspective that lets us make sense of the religious pluralism that has been created by the globalization process in the postmodern world, a way of understanding the multiplicity of the religions in relation to the Unity of Truth and the Oneness of God. Such a doctrine is illuminating and orienting, but it is in no way spiritually operative in an esoteric sense. If the Transcendent Unity of Religions presents difficulties for many people, this is partly due not to its supposed status as a "quintessential esoterism," but to the fact that there was no need to openly declare it in earlier ages. Furthermore, since the TUR, as an explicit doctrine capable of being accepted (or rejected) by many in the general public, is a strictly postmodern phenomenon, the notion that an understanding of it represents a higher esoterism,

INTRODUCTION TO PART ONE

one potentially capable of producing greater metaphysical sages in postmodern times than any single "confessional" religion operating alone has been able to do in the past, runs counter to the foundational Perennialist/Traditionalist principle (based on the Hindu doctrine of the four *yugas* but also found in many other traditions the world over, including Islam and Christianity, as well as various Greco-Roman and Native American cosmologies) of the inevitable spiritual degeneration of the human collective over the course of a given manvantara or cycle-of-manifestation. As some of Frithjof Schuon's followers apparently believed, the enunciation of the doctrine of the Transcendent Unity of Religions may indeed foreshadow the Golden Age of the next cycle, but in terms of the present one, which is nearing the end of its *kali-yuga* or Age of Darkness, it is in no way a new and spiritually operative Revelation, simply a viewpoint useful to correctly orient us to the unique qualities of our time. That Schuon posited the TUR as a perspective that transcends the revealed religions, but nonetheless never claimed (at least openly) that he had received any new Revelation from God, is one of the major contradictions in his teachings. And in terms of the "primordialism" that is closely associated with the Transcendent Unity of Religions in Schuon's writings, with its nostalgia for older and more spiritually elevated times, it is in no way possible for any human soul to pass from the Dark Age of one cycle to the primordial Golden Age of another except through the door of death: a foreshadowing is not a restoration. Suffice it to say that true spirituality, true esoterism, true sainthood is a far higher station than a mere acceptance of the truism that every valid religion emanates from the same Divine Source—a concept which, for all the difficulty that many intelligent people of good will have in understanding

INTRODUCTION TO PART ONE

and accepting it, remains nothing more than a preliminary orientation for the spiritual Path in postmodern times. This is another point on which I differ from Frithjof Schuon.

In my book *The System of Antichrist* (2001), I said the following:

According to the Traditionalist doctrine of The Transcendent Unity of Religions, all true revealed religions are renditions of the one Primordial Tradition which is as old as humankind. This Tradition, however, cannot be accessed directly, but must be approached via one of the major world religions—otherwise one will probably encounter one of the many attempts at a kind of "generic" metaphysics, drawing upon fragments of many traditions, some system which represents itself as universal but remains cut off from the Wisdom and Grace of God, the only power which can make either a sage or a saint. Although Truth is One, and the esoteric or mystical centers of all true religions point directly to this same Divine Truth, "primordialism" cannot be a viable form in itself; the nourishing fruit grows on the branches of the tree, not the trunk . . . [furthermore], the distinction between the Transcendent Unity of Religions on the one hand, and that syncretistic "world fusion spirituality" which is the hallmark of Antichrist on the other (a collection of fragments entirely postmodern in its nihilism) is simply too subtle to be understood by everyone attracted even to Traditional metaphysics. (Schuon himself seems to have suspected as much in *The Transcendent Unity of Religions* (1948), when he characterized his open revelation of esoteric doctrines as an abnormal response required by an abnormal situation, and expressed his belief that "the harm which might in principle befall certain people from contact with the truths in question is compensated by the advantages others

INTRODUCTION TO PART ONE

will derive from the self-same truths.") The satanic shadow of the Transcendent Unity of Religions, in other words, is precisely the pseudo-esoterism of the Antichrist. Therefore to invoke primordial spirituality in the latter days of the cycle, before the second coming of Christ invokes it definitively, is to further the agenda of both good and evil, both Christ and Antichrist. It is to make virtually present, along with the primordiality of the Edenic state, the entirety of the human *karma* for this cycle, and in so doing serve the final polarization, that separation of the Sheep from Goats which will climax at the battle of Armageddon.

Furthermore, if it turns out (as certain evidence indicates) that some aspects of Schuon's teachings are beginning to prove useful to the globalist elites, it becomes necessary to subject them to the most rigorous possible criticism. In any case, it is my belief that the notion that the Transcendent Unity of Religions is a "higher esoterism" is of no conceivable spiritual use to any believer in any of the Traditional religions; it could in no way make a Muslim a better Muslim, a Christian a better Christian, a Hindu a better Hindu, a Jew a better Jew, except perhaps by preventing them from wasting their time and their precious spiritual attention in hating the other God-given faiths. Its only potential function as a doctrine with "esoteric" pretensions would be to provide the globalist elites with spurious theological backing for their projected One-World Religion, while defining and promoting the exact kind of inverted "spiritual" elite (those whom René Guénon called the *Awliya al-Shaitan*, "the Saints of Satan") that is best fitted to control and enforce such a religion, to rule a "church" that is destined to form an integral part of the regime of *al-Dajjal* or Antichrist. This is the second point on which I differ from certain tendencies apparent today among Schuon's followers, notably Patrick Laude in his book ***Keys to the Beyond: Frithjof Schuon's Cross-Traditional Language of Transcendence*** (see *Chapter Fifteen* below).

As I see it, the true and valid use of the doctrine of the Transcendent Unity of Religions in the spiritual life is to support the intuition of the Unity of Truth and the Oneness of God, a truth that is accepted in one form or another by every God-given faith but which is being threatened and eroded in the postmodern world by the religious pluralism enforced by globalization as well as by the various violent "extremist" reactions against this pluralism. Likewise, one proper "exoteric" use of the TUR in the socio-political dimension would be—God willing—to organize the revealed religions to stand against the invasive and hegemonic actions of the globalist elites. This is what, in ***The System of Antichrist***, I named "united front ecumenism"; it is a perspective which has the virtue of directing the attention of the interfaith movement away from any form of heterodox syncretism based on the homogenization of doctrines (a tendency which could only work to weaken and undermine the Traditional faiths) and toward practical mutual defense against common enemies (see *Chapter Nine*). In view of the fact that the ever-more-clearly-emerging agenda of the globalist elites is to co-opt, manipulate, and possibly even liquidate the Traditional religions of the earth, or at least to federate them under some form of global secular control, united front ecumenism must become the keynote and *raison d'être* for the global interfaith movement in the twenty-first century.

CHAPTER ONE

The Multiplicity and Unity of Religions according to Guénonian Traditionalism: An Alternative Way of Doing "Comparative Religion"

In this chapter I will do my best to give the student or researcher in the field of religious studies a clear idea of how the principle that the religions are both intrinsically one and necessarily multiple—a principle central to the Traditionalist or Perennialist School—might work as a paradigm to open new and fertile perspectives in the field of comparative religion, avoiding both the syncretism of the usual universalist approach and the fragmentation of postmodernism.

The practice of medicine presupposes that the states called health and disease actually exist. The discipline of anthropology is based on the certainty that there are such things as human beings, all of whom belong to a single species. The study of history is built on the assumption that, in the past, certain things actually occurred. The science of physics is based on an acceptance of the existence of space, time, matter and energy, that even though random indeterminacy may be posited at a certain point, these things nonetheless obey natural laws, and that it is possible to discover at least some of these laws. Therefore one would think that such disciplines as theology or religious studies could not be carried on without a belief in the existence of God, or at least in a supernatural order. Would you put yourself in the hands of a physician who didn't believe in health and disease? Would an institution of higher learning hire someone to teach anthropology who didn't believe in the existence of human beings? Could an historian who held the opinion that nothing ever really happened be expected to make a useful contribution to the study of history? Could a physicist who believed that there was no such thing as physical reality, or that the behavior of this reality is completely random, be capable of advancing the science of physics?

The answers are obvious. And yet we are routinely asked to believe it is possible to study religion in the absence of a belief in the reality of the Object of that study. If you wouldn't patronize a doctor who didn't believe in health and disease, why would you listen to anyone who purported to practice theology or teach religion but didn't believe in God? Would a competent astronomer make an exhaustive comparative study of all the discoveries of astronomy, past and present, yet never once look at the stars themselves because he believed that stars do not exist? Practicing medicine without a license is a danger to society; practicing theology without a license—the license being Faith—is a danger to the soul. Religious studies conducted by atheists, by which I mean the habit of investigating belief rather than the Object or objects of this belief, necessarily puts theology, religious studies and comparative religion on the same level as the study of abnormal psychology; if you believe someone's ideas are delusional, it will be very difficult for you to do a serious study of them.

The common justification for the practice of studying belief without in any way entertaining it is the conviction that those who have no faith are necessarily more "objective" than those who do, because faith is a subjective delusion. When I consider such a belief, however, I find it is based on the unproved (and likely unprovable) assumption that one's knowledge of something is never enhanced, but only compromised, by any direct experience of it. This is obviously not true in the fields of medicine, law, martial arts, music, athletics, sexuality—so why should it be true in the field of religion? The fact is, it is not. You can't study yoga or kung fu or body-building or musical performance from the outside; if you aren't *doing* it, you don't *know* it. And the same is certainly true of religion: even a competent theoretical grasp of a given faith requires at least a beginner's familiarity with its actual practice. Consequently, as with any art or science (religion being both a science and an art), if fully-trained practitioners of a given religion, past or present, are not available to be studied and consulted, no concrete experiential knowledge of that religion is possible.

The idea that faith is delusional immediately runs into a serious difficulty. As is well known to anyone with a sense of history, the great world religions, most of which began as revelations received by single individuals or small groups, have been the founding principles of whole civilizations, principles that permeate their art, philosophy, architecture, social structure, and methods of character-formation; these religious have consequently produced many of what are almost universally recognized to be the greatest civilizational achievements of the human race. The notion that such achievements could have been based on the delusions of imbalanced individuals suffering from mental illness stretches credulity to the breaking-point.

A "comparative religion" that treats the various religions as isolated, self-contained and self-referential "belief systems" whose object is not the realization of God or the conformation of the group psyche or the individual soul to the supernatural order but simply the maintenance and defense of a given group identity—this being the essential approach of postmodernism—will largely fail of its purpose. Yes, it may come to certain true perceptions on the level of sociology, but it will certainly miss the main point—actually, a number of main points—on the level of religion itself. If a religion is nothing more than a belief system, if it refers to nothing beyond itself, if it has no true Objective Referent, then it is not a religion at all but simply a case of atheism whose adherents do not realize that they are atheists. This is not meant to imply, however, that the differences in belief and practice between the various religions are of little or no significance; nothing could be further from the truth. Since Absolute Reality is inexhaustible, its Self-manifestations are endless, no two being identical. Thus the researcher seeking a multitude of perspectives will in no way be hampered in his or her search by an acceptance of the reality of God. On the contrary, he or she will gain access to a potentially infinite field of varying forms and colors and qualities of religious knowledge—all of which, however, are ultimately united through orientation to a common Center. From the Traditionalist/Perennialist perspective, this opening to religious knowledge will include the understanding that God is the Source of all true religions—that is, of all religions which teach certain fundamental metaphysical principles. Among the most basic of these principles is that Absolute Reality is both transcendent and immanent: transcendent in the sense that it lies beyond any limitation imposed by sense-experience, scientific experiment, emotion, imagination, logic, or intellectual intuition; immanent by the simple fact that Its transcendence of limitation by any form of existence we can define or conceive of means that It must necessarily permeate all forms of existence, expressing Itself and revealing Itself by means of them.

The reader who wishes to get a better idea of the nature and implications of the doctrine of the unity and multiplicity of religions according to the Traditionalist School should consider the following seven points, which together constitute the first principles of that School:

1) God, Absolute Reality—whether we conceive of this Reality as personal or transpersonal—has sent more than one valid Revelation, more than one version of the spiritual Path by which humanity can understand Him, experience Him, and return to Him. By following the principles and practices of one of these paths, which are to be found for the most part in the world's great religions and wisdom traditions, we may realize and actualize our knowledge of, and union with, Absolute Reality.

2) More than one of these paths may be valid and in operation at the same time.

3) These paths, no matter how different their doctrinal starting-points and their methodologies may be, all ultimately lead to the same goal. Absolute Reality lies at the end of each path, because the Truth is One. This is the basis of the intrinsic and *transcendent* unity of the religions.

4) Nonetheless, which path one chooses is not a matter of indifference, since the paths are designed for different character-types and cultural frameworks and spiritual capacities. Consequently, though the Goal is ultimately the same for all, the fact that more than one version of the spiritual Path exists is necessary and providential. However, not everything that presents itself as a valid spiritual way is necessarily what it claims to be: pseudo-religions, psychic or magical belief-systems, even new "religions" created as social engineering experiments, represent a grave danger to be discerned and avoided.

5) The metaphysical philosophies and mystical theologies of the various religions are much closer to unanimity than are the exoteric aspects of these religions, though differences will always remain; therefore a study of the metaphysical doctrines of one religion can often illuminate certain aspects of the analogous doctrines of another. That the religions come closer and closer to doctrinal unanimity as their mystical centers are approached is evidence of their fundamental unity. That they never in fact attain this unanimity in the world of form is proof that this unity is not of this world: since it transcends the dimension of form, it cannot be expressed in terms of any social or political unification on the terrestrial plane. The paths are one only in the One—only in God.

6) The fact that God has sent more than one valid revelation does not mean that a unification of these revelations into a single "one-world religion" would represent a more complete vision of the Truth and a more effective Path for the realization of It than any of the revelations taken separately. As we have said, such a worldly unification is impossible—and even if it were possible, it would be destructive to the cause and purpose of true religion. Syncretism, then, does not lead to the same intimacy with the Truth as does one of the several Divine revelations lived to the fullest extent in its own terms. Since each religion, each path, is complete and sufficient unto itself, mixing them only adulterates them and renders them chaotic and ineffective.

7) A central metaphysical principle is that an Absolute Unity transcending form must express itself on the plane of form as a multiplicity. If the Absolute were to limit Its expression to a single form in this world, that form would imprison It and replace It, thereby destroying any sense of the necessary transcendence of the Absolute and replacing the human intuition of It with the idolatrous worship of this or that "absolutism." As it is, however, the Self-revelation of God in terms of a multiplicity of forms serves to *triangulate* the Transcendent Absolute without imprisoning It. Just as the true distance of a star can be determined by *parallax* (the difference between that star's apparent position when viewed from two different points in the earth's orbit around the sun), so both the actual reality and the necessary transcendence of God can be triangulated, as it were, through the realization that the religious traditions, from their radically different perspectives,

are all referring to the same Transcendent Absolute, seeing that a "plurality of Absolutes" is impossible both logically and actually.

Any student of comparative religion who thoroughly assimilates the Traditionalist perspective of the necessary unity and multiplicity of religions, according to these seven principles, will be treated to virtually inexhaustible new vistas of the Self-revelation of God to the human race.

CHAPTER TWO

Entering Houses by their Doors: The Uniqueness and Commonality of Christianity and Islam

The image of the "Judeo-Christian tradition" commonly held by post-Christian western society often includes the view, or feeling, that Islam is a relatively alien faith. The Bible, made up of Old and New Testaments, certainly demonstrates many points and lines of continuity between Judaism and Christianity; however, from the self-enclosed Judeo-Christian perspective, though the Muslim Qur'an gives the appearance of having been largely derived from the Bible, it often seems like a lesser scripture, one pieced together out of poorly understood scraps of Biblical narrative and moral teaching. This narrowly prejudicial viewpoint is the modern successor to the Medieval Christian view that Islam was either a kind of paganism, or else a heretical Jewish sect. Those familiar with the Holy Qur'an, however, well understand that the Book speaks with its own authority, and that its often abbreviated references to well-known Bible stories partly stem from its use of these incidents as symbolic examples of various spiritual principles. The acceptance of the Qur'an as a revealed scripture in its own right, one considerably less altered from its original form by human editors than much of the Bible, is reflected in a great deal of twentieth-century religious scholarship. This scholarship has laid a solid groundwork for a comparative study of the three Abrahamic faiths, which, when taken together, present the picture of a relatively integrated Judeo-Christian-*Islamic* tradition.

In reaction to the growing plague of interfaith violence in our time—or rather of political strife that hides its origins and agendas by falsely presenting itself as interreligious, expressing itself either through the actions of variously ethnically- or nationally-centered quasi-religious movements or through various conflicts engineered by the global elites to turn the religions against each other in order to better undermine and control them—there has been an understandable push to reach greater understanding of the doctrinal common ground between Christianity and Islam. This approach is not without its dangers, however. The various revealed religions are much more than accidental, culturally- and historically-conditioned variations on a few common "spiritual" themes. They are specific, particular, unique and—on certain levels—incomparable. If Christianity were induced to deny the Divinity of Christ so as to "make the Muslims happy," or Islam tempted to downplay the revealed and uncreated nature of the Qur'an to "make the Christians happy," friendship between the faiths would be relatively meaningless, since there would effectively be no faiths left to befriend each other. If each religion did not have an irreducible element, uniquely willed by God, they would have no reason to exist as distinct Divine revelations. That said, there are actually more points of doctrinal similarity between Christianity and Islam than may be apparent on the surface.

The common ground between the Abrahamic religions is attested to by the Holy Qur'an itself, in the following verses:

> *He has revealed unto you (Muhammad) the Scripture with truth, confirming that which was (revealed) before it, even as He revealed the Torah and the Gospel.* [3:3]

> *Say (O Muhammad): 'O people of the Scripture: Come to a word that is just between us and you, that we worship none but God, and that we associate no partners with Him, and that none of us shall take others as lords besides God.'* [3:64]

> *And do not dispute with the followers of the Book except by what is best, except those of them who act unjustly, and say: We believe in that which has been revealed to us and revealed to you, and our God and your God is One, and to Him do we submit.* [29:46]

> *Verily! Those who believe and those who are Jews and Christians, and Sabians, whoever believes in God and the Last Day and does righteous good deeds shall have their reward with their Lord, on them shall be no fear, nor shall they grieve.* [2:62]

The "family ties" between Islam and Christianity were explicitly defined by Muhammad in his covenants with the Christians of the world. The covenants or treaties of the Prophet with various Christian communities of his time uniformly state that Muslims are not to attack peaceful Christian communities, rob them, stop churches from being repaired, tear down churches to build mosques, prevent their Christian wives from going to church and taking spiritual direction from Christian priests and elders. On the contrary, the Prophet commands Muslims to actively defend these communities from their enemies "until the coming of the Hour," the end of the world, as well as to help them repair their churches as an act of pious solidarity with their Christian brothers. In the language of the Covenants, which Muhammad declared were given him by direct inspiration of Allah, the Prophet refers to Christians as members of his community, and calls them by the name *mu'minin*, "the faithful." When, in his later years, the Algerian Sufi and freedom-fighter against the French colonialists, Emir 'Abd al-Qadir al-Jazairi, defended the Christians of Damascus from massacre at the hands of the Druzes, he was following the Prophet's Covenants to the letter.

On the other hand, though the Qur'an exalts Jesus as a prophet and characterizes him as a "spirit from Allah," it rejects the identification of Jesus of Nazareth or anyone else as the Son of God, as well as disallowing—at least apparently—any sort of Trinitarian conception of the Godhead. Muhammad certainly knew that the Eastern Orthodox Christians he encountered were Trinitarians and incarnationists, the first of his covenants having been granted to the monks of the Monastery of St. Catherine in the Sinai, which was and is under the jurisdiction of the Greek Orthodox Church—and yet, even though Trinitarianism and incarnationism (*hulul*) are specifically condemned in Islam, the

CHAPTER TWO

Prophet extended his protection to the Christians, and included them in his growing community. This was certainly in line with the Qur'anic injunction *There is no compulsion in religion* [2:256]; and the fact is that the Prophet made covenants even with pagan communities. This however is not enough to explain the great liberality and cordiality of the Prophet's Covenants with the Christians, which give the definite impression that he recognized in them the followers of a kindred Way. And when the Muslims conquered Mecca, and Muhammad commanded that the pagan idols be cast out of the Kaaba, he either excluded from his edict an icon of Christ and the Theotokos—"the Mother of God"—which he ordered returned to the Christians, or else, according to a different version of events, he allowed such an icon, which had been painted on the inner walls of the Kaaba, to remain; the image only finally disappeared when the Kaaba was burned by Mu'awiya in 683 A.D. Was Muhammad guilty in this case of placing worldly diplomatic concerns on a higher plane than theology? Had he allowed his personal gratitude to the two Christians who had recognized his prophethood—the Syrian Christian monk Bahira and the (likely) Nestorian *hanif*, Waraqah ibn Nawfal—to lead him to ignore the teachings of the Qur'an itself, not to mention his great appreciation (according to Christian chronicles and Bedouin legend) for the monks of St. Catherine's monastery, who asked him to grant them a covenant of protection when he made contact with them as a caravan leader, even before the Qur'an descended upon him, as well as for the Monophysite Christian Negus, king of Abyssinia, who had extended his protection to the Muslim "emigrants" fleeing persecution on the Arabian peninsula? Or does this apparent inconsistency on his part conceal a deeper mystery? As for the

Prophet's toleration for (though not acceptance of) Christian incarnationism, it is true that the Sufis often speak of a *shaykh* (spiritual master) or a *wali* (saint) in terms suggesting divinization, as when Mansur al Hallaj issued the ecstatic utterance *ana l'Haqq*—equivalent to "I am God"—for which he was martyred and/or executed, depending on one's evaluation of him. Orthodox Sufism, however, is careful never to cross the line into *hulul*, as *al-Hallaj* may or may not have done; Allah is present in the shaykh or the *arif* (gnostic) by virtue of theophany, not incarnation. The reason for this distinction is that, while the central manifestation of God to humanity in Christianity is the *body* of Christ, in Islam it is the *word* of the Qur'an. According to a prophetic hadith, the Prophet once said: "Whoever has seen me has seen Allah"—a saying nearly identical to Jesus's statement in John 14:9: "Whoever has seen me has seen the Father." Yet both the Qur'an and the *ahadith* make it crystal clear that Muhammad never claimed Divinity—as Jesus apparently did when he said "Before Abraham came to be, I am." [John 8:58] Nonetheless it is reported that the Prophet also said: "I was a prophet when Adam was still between the water and the clay" (the soul and the body). Here we can see how the fundamental constituting doctrines of Christianity and Islam as distinct revelations, even as they draw closer and closer together, more so than many of us may have suspected, never actually meet.

According to a tradition recounted by Virgil Gheorghiu in his book ***La vie de Mahomet***, referenced also by Maqrizi (1363–1442 AD) and Muhammad Hamidulluh (1908–2002), the Prophet met with Jewish and Christian ambassadors in the guest-house of Ramlah bint al-Harith in the neighborhood of Najdariyyah in the year known as *am al-wufud*, "the year of ambassadors" (630/631 A.D.), during which he received various delegations. The leader of one of them was Abraham, the Armenian abbot from the Monastery of St. James in Jerusalem and the Monastery of Zion, who was the ambassador of the Katholikos of Armenia, residing in the oldest abbey in the world, Etchmiadzin, founded in 285 A.D. in the foothills of Mount Ararat on the site where St. Gregory the Illuminator received a revelation from God by means of an illumination reputedly identical to the one Saint Paul received on the road to Damascus. Muhammad questioned him:

> "In Jerusalem there is a (monotheistic) Christian sect that worships Sirius, the dog-star; what does that dog and that star symbolize?" Abraham answered: "The star symbolizes the illumination that Saint Gregory the Illuminator received on Mount Ararat. This night star has sixteen rays; the one of Dikpala represents the Vanatur of Mount Ararat[1] . . . both the morning and evening stars have eight rays Together, they symbolize the manifestation of God by means of illumination. The dog represents the *tariqah* which signifies a Spiritual Path; it is the guide of those who submit to God [and is] revealed by the evening star." Muhammad was pleased to see that Abraham submitted to God

---

1 The meaning of the phrase "the one of Dikpala represents the Vanatur of Mount Ararat" is unclear. The Dikpala are the Hindu gods of the eight directions, and in the pre-Christian Armenian religion, Vanatur according to some scholars was the god of the North, though he was sometimes identified with the chief god Aramazd, connate with the Persian Ahura Mazda. Was an ancient Armenian monastery founded on the site of an earlier shrine to Vanatur? If Vanatur represented the North, the holy Mount Ararat most likely stood for the Center.

in his monastery in Jerusalem. "Submission to God is my tradition," he replied.

If this tradition is accepted as valid, we can see how Muhammad was entirely willing to credit a religious form that many a narrow-minded Muslim zealot might have viewed as nothing but Pagan idolatry—if not as an example of the cardinal sin of *shirk*, the act of attributing partners to God—a version of Christianity that expressed itself through esoteric symbols that in no way compromised the fundamental monotheism of the Christian revelation. Is it possible that the Prophet viewed the Trinitarian doctrine of the Christians in a similar light—as heretical if taken literally but highly illuminating if understood symbolically? Any answer to this question must remain speculative. Nonetheless, this was more or less the position expressed by the great Algerian Sufi master Shaykh Ahmed al-'Alawi on the occasion of a dialogue between him and a European Christian physician, as presented in **A Sufi Saint of the Twentieth Century** by Martin Lings. In addition, a form of "Islamic trinitarianism" appears in the teachings of Ibn al-'Arabi, the Shaykh al-Akbar or "greatest (Sufi) shaykh," a doctrine distinct from the Trinitarianism of the Christians though exhibiting certain similarities. In the famous epitome of his doctrines, the **Fusus al-Hikam** or **Bezels of Wisdom**—most particularly in the chapter dedicated to the Prophet Salih—Ibn al-'Arabi presents us with a trinity of the Lord, the Servant (or the Cosmos), and the Reality: Allah is Lord of the Worlds, but—because He is the One, the Only Reality—He is also the Essence of the Servant, or of the Cosmos, in relation to which Allah functions as Lord, as well as being the Reality in which the polarity of Lord and Servant, or Lord and Cosmos, is resolved; according to this conception, it is the very Unity of Allah which makes it necessary for Him to appear according to these three different "presences." However, we need not rely upon Sufi esoterism to find exceptions to Islam's apparent absolute and blanket rejection of Trinitarianism; certain verses that suggest a more nuanced view of the matter may be found in the Qur'an itself.

The Christian idea of the Trinity is nonetheless one of the major points of disagreement between Christianity and Islam. The Christian doctrine does not appear explicitly in the New Testament, though it does appear "iconically" in the account of Christ's baptism by St. John in the Gospel according to Matthew 3:16. Furthermore, since Jesus made references to God as His "Father" and implied His own divinity in the words "before Abraham came to be, I Am," as well as speaking of the "Paraclete" (Comforter) who would come after Him—a prophecy fulfilled at Pentecost as recounted in the Acts of the Apostles but which Muslims sometimes see as a prediction of the future advent of Muhammad—Christian Trinitarianism has a firm scriptural basis. As for the disagreements as to the true nature of the Trinity that developed later, the chief of these was the controversy between the Western and Eastern Churches over the addition of the Latin word *filioque*, "and the Son" to the Nicene Creed, indicating the Western view that the Holy Spirit proceeds from both the Father and the Son, as against the Eastern doctrine that the Spirit proceeds from the Father alone.

The Qur'an appears to explicitly deny the Trinitarian nature of God, in such *ayat* as:

> *They surely disbelieve who say: Lo! Allah is the third of three; when there is no God save the One God* [5:73],

and:

> *And they say: The Beneficent hath taken unto Himself a son. Assuredly ye utter a disastrous thing. Whereby almost the heavens are torn, and the earth is split asunder and the mountains fall in ruins, That ye ascribe unto the Beneficent a son, When it is not meet for (the Majesty of) the Beneficent that He should choose a son. There is none in the heavens and the earth but cometh unto the Beneficent as a slave.* [19:89-93]

In the face of these tremendous rejections, it certainly seems as if no kind or degree of Trinitarianism could ever be acceptable to orthodox Islam—and certainly, even in Christian terms, Jesus spoke as a servant or slave when he said: "Why do you call me good? No one is good except God alone" [Mark 10:18], and "Not my will but Thine be done" [Luke 22:42], and "My God, my God, why have You forsaken me?" [Matthew 27:46]. Nonetheless, this may not be the end of the story because, in point of fact, traditional Christian doctrine nowhere declares that God is "one of three"; rather, all three Persons of the Trinity are considered to share the same Divine Substance and Unity. Eastern Orthodox theology, perhaps more explicitly than the theology of Rome, considers the Father to be "God per se," yet the Son and the Spirit are no less God than the Father is. The Father is God in His own unknowable Essence—this is why no icon can be made of Him; nonetheless, both the Son and the Spirit, like the Father, contain the fullness of the Godhead. The notion of God as one of three is closer to the Arian heresy, which accepts the Father alone as God, sees the Son as a creature of the Father who nonetheless conferred Godhood upon him, and the Holy Spirit as the impersonal power of the Father rather than as a distinct Person. Likewise, the doctrine that God has "taken to Himself a son" is found nowhere in orthodox Christian theology; rather, it constitutes the recognized heresy of "Adoptionism." According to Orthodox doctrine, the Son is not God because the Father has adopted Him but because He is "begotten" by the Father from all eternity; this is why in the Book of Apocalypse He is called "the Lamb slain from the foundation of the world" [13:8]. Certainly this act of begetting does not imply that the Father had a wife, that He begat the Son through a literal act of sexual intercourse with a female partner, in either material or spiritual terms, in this world or any other. The metaphor of "begetting," and thus of Sonship itself, is chosen to demonstrate that the Son is not a creature of the Father (as the Arians believed) but intrinsically shares with Him the same Uncreated Essence. Consequently no doctrine that God has a celestial wife, or that the Father begets the Second Person of the Trinity in some Divine version of sexual intercourse with a female consort, is anywhere stated or implied in traditional Christian theology. However we look at it, to say "God is one of three" or "God has taken unto Himself a son" are both heresies from the point of view of Christian orthodoxy. I certainly don't mean to imply that Islam secretly accepts the view that Father, Son, and Holy Spirit, considered as three separate Persons, are all equally God; obviously it does not. Yet if Muhammad had not in some sense understood Trinitarian Christianity as not fundamentally compromising God's Unity, how could he have called Christians "the faithful"? Were the condemnations of Trinitarianism and Incarnationism in the Qur'an God's way of cautioning Christians, through Muhammad His last Prophet, against literalizing or concretizing the doctrine of the Trinity until it finally descends into polytheism? I have often heard Evangelical Protestant ministers speak of "God and Jesus"—and Pope Francis himself in an interview for Vatican Radio has declared that "God does not exist," though the Three Persons of the Trinity do, thus heretically defining Christian Trinitarianism as tri-theism in direct contradiction to the Nicene Creed, which states: *Credo in Unum Deum*, "I believe in One God." The Qur'an certainly does not preach orthodox Christian theology, but it is still a lot closer to Christian orthodoxy than Pope Francis is! In reducing the Blessed Trinity to a trio of pagan gods, Francis—for all his truly hopeful and ground-breaking *diplomatic* overtures to Islam as a valid Divine Revelation—has placed his Roman Catholic Church at a greater *theological* distance from Islam that it has occupied at any time in its history.

As Ibn al-'Arabi implies, it is possible to apply Sufi forms of metaphysical speculation and expression to the Christian Trinity, as long as these are never granted dogmatic authority in Christian terms. One version of such speculation might go something like this: The Christian dogma of a Trinitarian God only compromises the truth of God's Unity if the Deity is conceived of as an external Object that is somehow both three and one, an Object capable of being contemplated by a limited human subject. The source of this externalization was the historical need to transform a relatively esoteric/metaphysical principle, accessible only through *gnosis*, into a dogmatic formulation, which thereafter became the object not of direct knowledge but rather of accepted belief on the part of the faithful who, for the most part, were not expected to understand it.

On the level of esoteric *gnosis*, the Threeness of God is an inescapable consequence of His Unity. If God were One in the sense that nothing "other-than-God" could possibly exist, then there would be no universe, no angelic beings, no human race, nothing whatsoever but the Divine Essence eternally communing with Itself with no creative effect. But since the universe, both celestial and terrestrial, does indeed appear, a universe that includes human beings who are designed to know God and submit to His Will, then the existence of "other-than-God" must somehow be accounted for without falling into *shirk*, without positing a pluralistic theology with God conceived of as only one among the several factors constituting the universe, albeit the most important and the most powerful.

Speaking in Islamic terms, if God, and the human subject capable of contemplating Him, both truly exist, then Unity is replaced by duality. God is no longer One-without-a-second; he now has a "son" whom He has created and who is capable of knowing and serving Him—namely, humanity. The sign of this created human sonship within Christianity is the fact that Jesus called himself both "Son of God" and "Son of Man." However, a God Who is capable of compromising His own Unity, in more-or-less Arian mode, by sharing it with His creatures, or who eternally begets the Son as the orthodox Christianity of both the East and the West teaches, is not the God Who can be truly characterized, in the words of the *Sura al-Ikhlas* of the Qur'an, as *He (who) neither begets nor is begotten, and there is nothing to which He might be compared.*

Ibn al-'Arabi solved the problem of the apparent existence of other-than-God for Islam by declaring that each created thing has two faces: that of Servanthood and that of Lordship. Humanity defined as Servant, considered strictly in its own terms apart from God, has no self-existence. Whatever existence the human race exhibits is derived from the One Real Existent, which is God. Thus humanity, when it does not claim self-existence but recognizes its nothingness in the face of God, has realized its Servanthood and thus become the locus-of-manifestation for God's Lordship. The sign of this Lordship is the fact that no Servant can encompass his or her Lord in knowledge because only God can know God. Yet God in the Servant does indeed contemplate, and know, God as He Is in Himself, though the Servant when considered strictly as himself, apart from God, can never attain such Knowledge. Nonetheless, we now have an apparent duality: a "Father" and a "Son"; God-as-He-is-in-Himself, and God-within-the-Servant. Yet there is no possible or conceivable distinction-in-Essence between God-in-Himself and God-in-the-Servant, since God is One; therefore this principle posits a third necessary term. The truth that the Lord-Servant polarity does not and cannot constitute a duality within God is what Ibn al-'Arabi calls "the Reality," which is realized in the contemplative life precisely by the experiential annihilation of the polarity between the Divinity in man and Divinity per se. Thus the Reality is analogous to, though not identical with, what the Christians call the "Holy Spirit," the upshot being that even though the Shaykh al-Akbar's Trinitarianism does not satisfy the standards of traditional Christian dogma, it can nonetheless be seen as a kind of esoteric commentary on certain aspects of that dogma.

We can only know God by virtue of the God within us. Our knowledge of Him, though necessarily limited from our subjective point of view, is continuous, in its deepest nature, with God Himself—Who, in ultimate terms though not in terms of our limited human form, is our true Essence. As Meister Eckhart put it, "My truest 'I' is God." God as the Known, the Knowledge, and the Unity of the Known with the Knowledge, is analogous—though not identical—to what the Christians, speaking in mythopoetic language, call "the Father, the Son, and the Holy Spirit." Thus the Threeness of God is strictly implied by His Unity according to the necessary form of the act of cognition—though when cognition is transcended, this Trinity no longer appears—a truth that St. Dionysius the Pseudo-Areopagite expresses in his *Mystical Theology*. And this act of cognition is not limited to or dependent upon the existence of a limited human subject; it eternally pre-exists within God Himself as the form of His own Self-knowledge. If it did not, there is no way it could manifest in terms of God's relationship with His cosmos and His servants. Consequently we can say from the standpoint of Sufi Islam that God is not a Three-in-One Object Who can be contemplated as He truly is by a limited human subject—which is not to deny that the Christian dogma of the Trinity, accessible to belief, can function as an effective and orthodox sign of the real Trinity, accessible only to *gnosis*, to God's knowledge of Himself within us, a Knowledge that subsists beyond the subject/object duality. The Absolute Transcendence of God, His total freedom from the limitations of His creation, which implies the impossibility of His being compared to anything other than Himself (an attribute that Islam calls *tanzih*, "incomparability") is in some ways analogous to God the Father. God's Immanence in His creation (the Islamic *tashbih*, "comparability")—and most particularly His Immanence in me, which allows all things to function as signs of His Action and His Nature, and which establishes the Human Form, the epitome of God's creation, as the bearer of what the Qur'an calls the *Amana*, the Trust [cf. Q.41:53]—is analogous to God the Son. And the fact that His Immanence in no way compromises His Transcendence, and that His Transcendence in no way precludes His Immanence, due to the fact that He is Immanent in all things precisely by virtue of His Transcendence of them, is suggestive of God the Holy Spirit, seeing that the power of that Spirit to transfigure us and take us beyond all limitations is based precisely on the realization of the identity of God-within-us and God-as-He-Is-in-Himself. This is the consummation of all sacrifice, all meditation, all prayer.

The above rather convoluted piece of metaphysical speculation can be taken as a sample of how the Sufis sometimes talk—at least before God reminds them that, even though speech is silver, silence is golden. If human words could command faith and grace, the above words might prove useful; such "interfaith" speculation is at least interesting to those who are open to it.

Nonetheless, in terms of practical spirituality—the only kind of spirituality that can save our souls—a Muslim must approach Allah strictly in terms of His Unity, while a Christian's Way must be based on God's Unity-in-Trinity. No matter how ingenious our metaphysical speculations may seem, there is no way they can obviate the irreducible divergences between the Way of the Qur'an and the Prophet, and the Way of Christ; and this is as it should be. We may be granted the light to see deeply enough into each other's religions to accept that God may have given different mysteries to different nations, a truth Jesus alluded to when he said "I have other sheep that are not of this fold" [John 10:16]. Nonetheless, as the Qur'an teaches, *If Allah so willed, He could make you all one people* [16:93], indicating that the manifest diversity of the religions is as much in line with the Will of God as is their hidden unity; if we understand this principle, then as soon as we remember that the only purpose of religion is to lead us to God by the Ways He has chosen for us, we will lose no time in returning to our own discrete Paths. As the Prophet Muhammad put it: "Enter houses by their doors."

BIBLIOGRAPHY

Chittick, William. *Imaginal Worlds: Ibn al-'Arabi and the Problem of Religious Diversity*: State University of New York Press: Albany, 1994.

Clément, Olivier, *The Roots of Christian Mysticism*. New York: New City Press, 2013.

Ibn al-'Arabi. *The Bezels of Wisdom*, translated by Ralph Austin: New York: Paulist Press, 1980.

Morrow, John Andrew: *The Covenants of the Prophet Muhammad with the Christians of the World*. New York: Angelico Press/Sophia Perennis, 2013.

CHAPTER THREE

Sufism and Jñana-yoga: Some Correspondences

[This essay first appeared in *The Mountain Path*, Oct. 2016, Jan. 2017 and April 2017 issues, the journal of the Sri Ramanashramam, Tiruvannamalai, India]

I: Advaita Vedanta and Tasawwuf; *Jñana* and *Ma'rifa*

Jñana, the Path of Knowledge, is universal. *Jñana-yoga* as a *marga* within the context of the Yoga and Vedanta traditions is one manifestation of it, but signs of it can be found in every world religion—if you know how to look. Meister Eckhart, who succeeded St. Thomas Aquinas in his chair at the University of Paris, and whom Perennialist writer Wolfgang Smith sees as the one who revealed the esoteric dimension of Aquinas' Scholastic Philosophy, expressed the essence of Christian *jñana* when he said, "The eye through which I see God and the eye through which God sees me are the same eye," and "my truest 'I' is God." Likewise the Prophet Muhammad, peace and blessings be upon him, was undoubtedly alluding to *jñana* within the context of Islam when he said, "He who knows himself knows his Lord."

The inner exegesis of this hadith belongs almost exclusively to the mystics of Islam, the Sufis. In rather gross but nonetheless useful terms, Sufism or *tasawwuf* can be described as a *marga* (*tariqah*) whose effective force is *bhakti* (*mahabbah*), whose goal is *jñana* (*Ma'rifa*), and whose principle though not exclusive method is *japam* (*dhikr*). On one level, "He who knows himself knows his Lord" means: He who knows his *nafs* (literally "soul")—his passions, his ego, his habit of obsessive self-definition and world-definition—knows what controls him, until he becomes free of it. On a deeper level, it means: He who recognizes his dependence upon God, his need for God, his insufficiency in the absence of God, thereby recognizes the reality of God. On the deepest level it means: He who recognizes his own intrinsic nothingness realizes God as his Essence.

Sri Ramana Maharshi's version of *jñana-yoga* is, of course, his well-known method of "self-inquiry," by which we progressively realize that "I am not the body; I am not the feelings; I am not the thoughts; I am not the thought of 'I'," etc., etc., but that, ultimately speaking, "I am the Self, the *Atman*." According to Sri Shankaracharya, the ego or I-sense arises when the *Atman* identifies with—or rather is identified with—the various sheaths of the *Atman*, the *koshas*: the physical sheath or *annamaya-kosha*, the energy-sheath or *pranamaya-kosha*, the mental sheath or *manamaya-kosha*, the wisdom-sheath or *vijñanamaya-kosha*, and the bliss-sheath or *anandamaya-kosha*. Self-enquiry progressively breaks these identifications.

To say "I am the Self," however, has certain dangers; it either removes the final veil, or sets up the subtlest and most impenetrable veil of all. "I am the Self" is properly a realization, not an identification. It can become an identification, however, if the *jñana-yogi* falls into the trap of identifying with a subtle mental concept of the *Atman* rather than realizing the *Atman* itself. "I am the Self" is not an identification because it is not based on a union of two terms, one of which (the ego) identifies itself with the other (the Self). Rather, it is the end of all identification; it is the very Reality. To say "I Am the Self" is not to identify oneself with God, but to assert that "the Self (God) is the only I Am"; thus it is strictly equivalent to the first part of the Muslim *shahada* or testimony of faith, *La Ilaha illa 'Allah*, "there is no god but God," which the Sufis interpret as "there is no reality but The Reality." Likewise the Vedantic *Tat Twam Asi*, often translated into English as "That art Thou," does not mean: my self-concept is God, but rather: God is the actual Reality of what I mistakenly consider to be myself.

On one occasion the famous Sufi Mansur al-Hallaj cried out in an ecstatic state, *Ana l'Haqq!*, "I am the Truth!"—*Al-Haqq* being one of the Ninety-Nine Names of God in Islam—an indiscretion for which he was tried and executed. Jesus Christ almost suffered the same fate when he said "Before Abraham came to be, I Am" [John 8:58]. "I Am" is the English translation of what was likely the first syllable of the Hebrew Name for God, a Name often translated as "I Am That I Am." This Holy and Unspeakable Name of God, known as the *Shem ha-Mephorash*, was never to be pronounced except by the High Priest on the Day of Atonement in the Holy of Holies of the Temple in Jerusalem. The exoteric Muslims who heard the "blasphemy" of al-Hallaj believed that he had deified his self-concept, which is a sin in any religion. The Sufis, however—or some of them—believe that al-Hallaj was annihilated at the moment he spoke, and consequently that the one who said *Ana l'Haqq!* was really Allah, who of course had the complete right to say it.

The **Upanishads**, the **Brahma Sutra**, etc. are directed primarily to the mystics, and are consequently explicit about the doctrines of the Advaita Vedanta—though we must not ignore the fact that the entire collective of traditional Hinduism is more open to the mystical perspective than is the collective of traditional Islam. The Qur'an, on the other hand, is directed to the entire Muslim *ummah*, which is why the mystical doctrines can only be isolated through a *batini tafsir*, an inner exegesis, of the Holy Book—and of the *ahadith* as well, especially the *ahadith qudsi* (those in which Allah Himself speaks through the Prophet)—which are largely understood, and put into practice, by the Sufis alone, whether or not they go by that name. Likewise it is normative for most Sufis to be "householders," involved in the common day-to-day pursuits of the Muslim community; as the Prophet stated, "there is no monasticism in Islam." The upshot is that the Sufi spiritual "states" and "stations" are virtually innumerable; they are rarely reducible to a handful of definable and recognizable types of *samadhi*. Every aspect of daily life, every human encounter, can be the occasion for a particular spiritual insight, based on the operation of a particular Name of God. Consequently, the whole realm of personal and collective morality and social interaction, as well as ritual obligation, is not taken as simply preparatory to the mystical Path; instead, it is seen as providing a set of practical supports and symbolic insights for the actual traversing of that Path. And the purely inner states experienced in contemplation are also virtually innumerable, though certain states or stations, such as Expansion and Contraction or Annihilation and Subsistence, are recognized by nearly all Sufis. And yet, given that God is One, the essence of self-transcendence is also One, in Islam as in Hinduism, and throughout all the sacred traditions. Nor are the spiritual methodologies of Islam and Hinduism as dissimilar as they might appear at first glance. It is often said that Islam comprises three levels of understanding and practice: *islam* proper, which is satisfied by obedience to the *shari'ah*; *iman*, which has to do with the development of real faith; and *ihsan*, which means "excellence" or "perfection." According to the esoteric meaning of these terms, *islam* would roughly correspond to *karma-yoga*, *iman* to *bhakti-yoga*, and *ihsan* to *jñana-yoga*.

II: Is God the Doer or the Witness?

One of the effects of the applicability and availability of the Qur'an to all Muslims is that the spiritual Path or *tariqah* is conceived of more in terms of the will than of the contemplative Intellect, at least to begin with. The sacred law or *shari'ah* applies to all Muslims, consequently the fundamental virtue is *taslim*, "submission," which is understood by the Sufis to imply that only God is the Doer, that to claim for oneself the power to conceive and carry out action apart from the will of God is to deny Him. In the Hindu Vedanta, on the other hand—in line with its more intellectual and contemplative point of departure—God is most commonly seen not as the Performer of action, but as the Witness of it.

Islam shares with the other Abrahamic religions the emphasis on God as Performer of Action. Like the Hindu Brahma, the creator, or like the gods Indra or Ishvara insofar as they may be taken as different guises of the One as Governor and Administrator of the universe, God is most often conceived in Judaism, Christianity and Islam as pre-eminently active rather than contemplative. God is omnipotent, and one of the not-always-elaborated but nonetheless inevitable implications of His omnipotence is, not simply that He can do anything He desires, but that all action, whoever the apparent actor may be, ultimately flows from Him. If "It is not I who live but Christ lives in me" [Galatians 2:20], it must also be true to say that "It is not I who acts, but Christ acts in me." Outside of Sufism, the most explicit expression of the doctrine that only God is the Doer in the Abrahamic religions is to be found in the Asharite school of Islamic *kalam* (theology) which denies secondary causes (comparable in some ways to the *gunas*) and attributes everything—all forms, all events, even all choices—to the sovereign will of God as the First Cause, operating in this moment—even going so far as to assert that events are not even proximately attributable to natural law, or secondary causes within the realm of creation, but are produced directly by God through His continuous re-creation of the entire universe, instant by instant: the famous doctrine of "occasionalism."

On the other hand, according to the Advaita Vedanta of Sri Shankaracharya, God is no doer, He does not act. Likewise, from the standpoint of the Samkhya philosophy, God as Purusha is the Witness, but all actions are performed by Prakriti, universal

CHAPTER THREE

Substance, through the interaction of the *gunas*. In the words of the **Bhagavad-Gita**,

> Who sees all action
> Ever performed
> Alone by Prakriti,
> That man sees truly:
> The Atman is actless.

Likewise, in Shaivite terminology, all action is performed by *Shakti*, the Power of Shiva, while Shiva Himself is the impassive adamantine *Shaktiman*, the Power-holder, who holds the totality of *Mahamaya*, universal manifestation, as his *Shakti* by virtue of His absolute transcendence of it. He transcends it precisely through total non-identification with it; that is to say, by witnessing the totality of it. Here *Shakti* dances while Shiva looks on. However, as we all know, Shiva Himself is also the consummate Dancer, and it is a central tenet of Shaivism that Shiva and *Shakti* are one in essence. And Sri Ramakrishna, like the Sufis, teaches that "only God is the Doer"—not surprisingly, since he knew God primarily as *Shakti*. Likewise Allah tells Muhammad in the Qur'an, referring to the moment at the Battle of Badr when the Prophet threw a handful of pebbles in the direction of the enemy, after which the tide turned in favor of the Muslims: *It was not you who threw when you threw, but God threw* [Q. 8:17]. So does God act, or does He simply witness action? Or are these nothing but two different ways of seeing and describing the same thing?

In the **Bhagavad-Gita**, Krishna tells Arjuna: "Act, but dedicate the fruits of the action to Me." This is the classic definition of *karma-yoga*. The essence of this dedication-of-action, however, involves the ability to recognize God's pre-existing title to all action. If we believe that we are the authors of a given action, we will be hard-pressed to totally dedicate it to God; some trace of the sense that God owes us something in return for our good deeds will always remain, and this is one of the attitudes the Sufis recognize as a mark of the *zahiri* or outer/exoteric perspective. Only if we see all actions as coming *from* God will we be able to perfectly release all actions *to* God. Just as our very being is a gift from His Being, so all our actions are echoes of His Action; in the words of the Qur'an: *You cannot will unless Allah wills* [Q. 76:30]. And to see all actions as both coming from God and returning to Him is to transcend the sense that you are performing them, but simply to witness them. The effect of this is to lift the veil from the Heart, the *hridayam*; to disclose the *Atman*; to reveal God as the Indwelling Universal Witness. So we can see here that to understand God as the only Doer, and to understand Him as the uninvolved Witness of all action, as no doer at all, ultimately comes down to the same thing. Given that God is the Only Being, how could it be otherwise?

"In Hinduism it is not only possible but normative to say *Tat Twam Asi*— "That art Thou"—God is Who you really are. In Islam, given that it is based on human obedience to Divine law (though this is certainly also an integral part of Hinduism in the form of the *dharmas* of the various *varnas*), "God is Who you really are" is a doctrine rarely heard so explicitly, even among Sufis. When al-Hallaj said "*Ana l'Haqq*" and was executed for it, even many of his fellow Sufis condemned him. I believe that this radical difference in perspective between Islam and Hinduism has partly to do with a difference in the collective configuration of the human ego. Given the more intellective orientation of Hinduism, the ego or phenomenal self is conceived more archetypally or transparently than it is in Islam, where the individual is seen more in terms of the will, which will tend toward either rebellion or submission. Consequently the Sufi *adab* (etiquette) toward Allah is not to say "I am God" ("*Jiva* is Shiva"), but "I am not; God alone is." This, however, is virtually identical with Ramana Maharshi's method of self-enquiry, based on the question "Who am I?" and resulting in the progressive realization that I am not the body, I am not the feelings, I am not the mind, I am not the I-sense (since even the I-sense can be witnessed by Something deeper), but that the "I" is nothing other than the One who asks this question, and Who is also its sole and final Answer. The points of departure are different, but the Goal is the same. When the Self is realized, when the I-thought is dissolved, God alone is. I believe it is even possible (at a stretch) to identify *La ilaha* ("there is no god") with "I am not this or that object, whether body, feelings, mind or I-sense," and *illa 'Allah* ("but God") with *Tat Twam Asi*—as long as "That art Thou" is not taken on the mental level, as if it described the identification of the phenomenal ego with the Self, but rather as representing the final End of all identification: the Self abiding alone.

Nonetheless, self-enquiry remains a quintessentially Hindu approach to God-realization, and surrender a quintessentially Islamic one; the word "Islam" itself means "surrender." Both, however, were recognized as *margas* by Ramana Maharshi, who taught that self-enquiry and self-surrender ultimately lead to the same Goal. And the two methods may actually be more similar in actual practice than is often realized.

CHAPTER THREE

In almost every rendition of the Sufi path (and such renditions are nearly innumerable), the final two "stations" are *fana'* and *baqa'*: Annihilation (in God) and Subsistence (in God). The self-referential ego is annihilated; the *fitra*, the essential human nature as Allah created it, remains. And, in terms of *fana'* and *baqa'*, self-surrender opens to the same realization as self-enquiry, because what is surrendered are precisely the various layers of the ego, the identifications of the *Atman* with the five *koshas*. The essence of surrender is the surrender of self-will. To surrender self-will in the realm of action, to give up the notion that "I can do what I want", is to renounce ownership of the body and recognize Allah as the body's Lord: *it was not you who threw*. To surrender self-will in the realm of the feelings is to renounce the right to invoke them and repress them and indulge in them at will, turning all power over one's emotional nature to Allah by recognizing Him as the ultimate Source of it, and of all the changes it undergoes; in the words of the hadith, "God holds the Heart between His two fingers, and turns it however He will." (We must always remember, however, that the spiritual Heart, *al-Qalb*, is not just the seat of the feelings, but the site of the Knowledge of Allah.) To surrender self-will in the realm of thought is to allow one's thoughts to be conformed to objective Reality, to Allah, and thus to begin opening the Eye of the Heart. To surrender self-will on the levels of Wisdom and Bliss is to renounce the identification of one's Knowledge of Allah, and even one's rapturous Love of Allah, with Allah Himself, thereby fully opening the Eye of the Heart and overturning the last idol. After that, all that had once been identified as "me" is annihilated (*fana'*) and God is recognized as the only Reality ("there is no god but God"). Yet the phenomenal self, body, speech and mind, all that had once been identified as "me", is still walking, talking, thinking, etc. Nonetheless if only Allah is, then no-one is really walking, talking, thinking but He. In the words of a famous *hadith qudsi* (prophetic tradition in which Allah Himself is the Speaker) often quoted by the Sufis, "And when I love him [My servant], I become his ears with which he listens, and his eyes with which he sees, and his hands with which he strikes, and his feet with which he walks." This is *baqa'*. The Maharshi was annihilated as a self-identified individual—yet he could still eat, talk, intelligently answer questions, write, compose devotional hymns, direct the affairs of the ashram, circumambulate Arunachala, fully play the part of a sentient human being. In reality, however, no-one was doing any of these things but God.

In my own Sufi lineage, which springs from the great Sufi saint Ahmad al-'Alawi of Algeria, himself part of the Shadhili-Darqawi *silsila*, we are taught that there are two levels of *Ma'rifa* (*jñana*): the *Ma'rifa* of Allah and the *Ma'rifa* of the *Nafs*, the second being higher and more complete. In Hindu terms, these are probably more-or-less identifiable with *Brahma-vidya* and *Atma-vidya*. How can we understand the difference between these two stations?

It's likely that I never would have grasped the essence of Rama Maharshi's teaching if it weren't for the following passages by Frithjof Schuon:

> For the "volitional" or "affective" man [the *bhakta*] God is "He" and the ego is "I," whereas for the "gnostic" or "intellective" man [the *jñani*], God is "I"—or "Self

"—and the ego is "he" or "other" [from *Language of the Self*].

When the perception of the Object is so intense that the consciousness of subject vanishes, the Object becomes Subject, as is the case in the union of love; but then the word "subject" no longer has the meaning of a complement that is fragmentary by definition; it means on the contrary a totality which we conceive as subjective because it is conscious" [from *Survey of Metaphysics and Esoterism*].

Likewise C.F. Kelley, in *Meister Eckhart on Divine Knowledge*, distinguishes between a "relational" mysticism, such as that of Francois de Sales or St. John of the Cross, based on "a gazing at, a looking at" its Divine Object, and the *jñanic* mysticism of Eckhart, who could say: "My truest 'I' is God."

I believe that what Schuon calls "*bhaktic*" is what Kelley calls "relational"; I would only add that relational mysticism can be based either on devotion to the Divine Object, or on the desire to know that Object, or both. So when we make distinctions between relational and *jñanic* mysticism, we should be very careful not to define relational mysticism as love without knowledge, or *jñanic* mysticism as knowledge without love. As Ramana Marshi expressed it, "*Bhakti* is love for God with form; *jñana* is love for God without form." According to Frithjof Schuon in *Spiritual Perspectives and Human Facts*, "The love of the affective man [the *bhakta*] is that he loves God. The love of the intellectual man [the *jñani*] is that God loves him; that is to say, he realizes intellectually—but not simply in a theoretical way—that God is Love." (We should also remember that the Hindus speak of a *parabhakti* in which the subject/object duality is transcended.)

When the Divine Object (*Ishvara, Saguna Brahman*) becomes the Divine Subject or Self (*Nirguna Brahman, Atman*) through the annihilation of the limited human subjectivity—which is to say, when the *Atman* is unveiled—then all that was once under the sign of that limited subjectivity is transformed into the direct radiant manifestation of the Self. This, in Sufi terms, is *baqa'*, Subsistence in God. Ibn al-'Arabi, the Shaykh al-Akbar or "greatest shaykh" of Sufism, says of this station:

> The recipient sees nothing other than his own form in the mirror of Reality. He does not see the Reality Itself, which is not possible, although he knows that he may see only his [true] form in it. If you have experienced this you have experienced as much as is possible for created being, so do not seek to weary yourself in any attempts to proceed higher than this, for there is nothing higher. He is your mirror and you are His mirror in which He sees His Names and their determinations, which are nothing other than Himself. [from the **Futuhat al-Makiyya**, quoted in **The Sufi Way of Knowledge** by William Chittick]

Meister Eckhart says precisely the same thing: "The eye through which I see God, and the eye through which He sees me, are the same eye"—the Eye of the Heart.

The entire story of the path leading from relational mysticism through annihilation in God to the unveiling of the Absolute Witness is told in the famous *hadith* of the Prophet Muhammad, peace and blessings be upon him: "Pray to God as if you saw Him, because even if you don't see Him, He sees you". According to the esoteric meaning of this *hadith*, "Pray to God as if you saw Him" denotes relational mysticism, "because even if you don't see Him" posits Annihilation in God, *nirvikalpa samadhi*, and "He sees you" defines *sahaja samadhi*, Subsistence before the face of the Absolute Witness. In terms of a spiritual Way that begins, as Sufism does, with submission to God conceived of as the Absolute Other, *jñana* or *Ma'rifa* starts as the intuition that God sees and knows us, in this very moment, infinitely better than we can ever know either ourselves or Him; and to know that you are known is to know the Knower. In the words of the Qur'an, *I will show them My signs on the horizons and in their own souls until they are satisfied that this is the Truth. Is it not enough for you, that I am Witness over all things?* [Q. 41:53]. This intuition develops into the understanding that God's knowledge of us is in fact our essential reality, that we do not exist in our own right, but only as a projection of one of His infinite Names.

Ultimately we realize that what we call "me" is fully objective to the Divine Witness within us, Allah as *Al-Shahid*, Who (in Eckhart's words) is "our truest 'I'", given that (in Muhammad's words) "he who knows himself knows his Lord."

III: *Japam* and *Dhikrullah*

On one occasion Ramana Maharshi said, in answer to a question: "Whoever practices *japam* gets realization." The Hindu method of *japa-yoga* is strictly equivalent to the Sufi *dhikrullah* and the Christian Hesychast *mnimi Theou*, both of which mean "remembrance of God". The practice is to invoke the Absolute

CHAPTER THREE

Reality by the constant pronunciation (sometimes vocally but more often silently) of a Name of God.

The Invocation of the Name of God usually begins as a simple recognition of God's reality on the part of the devotee, combined with the ongoing work of dispelling the habitual distractions that veil this recognition, and consequently interrupt the Invocation. It may also take the form of a petition directed to God, a prayer that He unveil His Presence, that He grant his devotee the Beatific Vision of His Face.

This level of Invocation is based on the perception of God as "He" and the devotee as "I"; it is built upon the common assumption that ego is real, and that this ego—humbled, purified, fervent, but still assumed to exist—can witness God, at least partially and intermittently. Whatever "God" the ego sees, however, is inseparable from the ego; this is what Ibn al-'Arabi calls "the god created in belief." It is a projection of that ego, and consequently a veil, but it is also the beginning of the realization that there is Something more real than the ego, Something that does not depend upon the I-sense or exist in relation to it, Something that continues to be real whether the I-sense appears or disappears. Consequently the worship of God with form (*Saguna Brahman*) is usually an indispensable prelude to the realization of God beyond form (*Nirguna Brahman*); this is the inner meaning of the saying of Jesus, "None come to the Father but through Me" [John 6:44].

Dhikr or *japam* encompasses both *bhakti* and *jñana*. On the *bhaktic* level, I invoke God's Name, hoping He will unveil His presence. On the *jñanic* level, God speaks His own Name within me. And in the course of the Invocation of that Name, the inversion of subject and object described by Frithjof Schuon may take place—if, that is, the *dhakir* (the *japa-yogi*) is destined to attain the station of *baqa'*, of Subsistence in God, by virtue of the unveiling of the Self, the Absolute Witness. From the standpoint of that Self the devotee is not I but he; the Self is the Witness and the human form the thing witnessed; the psycho-physical individuality is fully objectified before the Eye of the Heart. Here I am no longer striving to remain aware of God's presence or petitioning Him to unveil that presence. I am not invoking God; rather, the Self within the Heart is witnessing the Invocation itself *as* God; this is the true meaning of the traditional formula "God and His Name are One". The human form itself is God's Name in a certain sense; through the Heart of the human being who remembers Him, and is consequently remembered by Him [cf. Q. 2:152], God names all things in manifest existence as Names and Signs of Himself.

In the Vedanta, this transition from *bhakti* to *jñana* is presented in terms of four stages of realization:

1) *The universe is unreal, Brahman is the Real.* Here the universe includes the human subject, which still "exists", though it is recognized as illusory—in Buddhist terms, devoid of self-nature; in Sufi terms, too "poor" to claim self-existence.

2) *There is only Brahman.* At this point both the human subject and the universe it perceives are annihilated; this is the esoteric meaning of the first part of the *shahada*, *La Ilaha illa 'Allah*, "there is no god but God."

3) *I am Brahman.* The "place" vacated by the human subject is now "occupied" by the Witness, Allah as *Al-Shahid*, the *Atman*. This is the station Mansur al-Hallaj was speaking from when he declared *Ana l'Haqq*, "I am the Truth."

CHAPTER THREE

4) *All this is Brahman.* Here the Witness witnesses all things as Itself; as the Sufis teach, "Allah sees only Allah."

From one perspective this progression from *bhakti* to *jñana* can be seen as a motion from duality to Unity, but it cannot thereby be strictly considered as a motion from Love to Knowledge. Rather, it is a motion away from the illusion of separation between Love and Knowledge and toward the realization of their intrinsic Union. In the words of Ramana Maharshi, "Imperfect *jñana* and imperfect *bhakti* are different; perfect *jñana* and perfect *bhakti* are the same."

Dhikrullah can be understood as combining the way of Surrender and the way of the Witness. Though *dhikr* takes many forms in Sufism according to which the Name of God is used, the most common—and, according to the teachers of my lineage, the most spiritually effective—is the first part of the *shahada*: *la ilaha illa 'Allah*. With *la ilaha*, "there is no god", the *dhakir* releases attachment to and identification with all the "idols"—not just the lower passions, but every variation and incarnation of the I-sense, including even the highest conceptions of God, seeing that these are still related to the I-sense as projections of it, thereby realizing that the conception—the "god created in belief"—is not the Thing Itself. This is the way of Surrender. Then, with *illa 'Allah*, "but God", the very Presence of the Absolute Reality is invoked and recognized: necessarily so, since "God and His Name are One". And to the degree that the entire self-concept is surrendered, leaving no sense of "me" behind, no limited subject that could pretend to know God to any degree, God Himself necessarily becomes the only Knower, the Universal Witness.

Dhikr/japam recollects the mind so that it becomes able to ask the question recommended by Ramana Maharshi: "Who am I?" The answer to this question is not any of the imaginable replies, not even "I am the Self"—since to affirm "I am the Self" is simply to produce one more idea, one more refinement or modulation of the I-sense. The only true answer to "Who am I?" is: "I am the One presently asking this question." And who but God can really ask this, and answer it?

IV: *Ma'rifa* of the *Nafs*, or *Atma-vidya*

The ego—in Sufi terms, the *nafs*—is most often considered to be a veil of ignorance concealing the reality of God. Yet Sri Shankaracharya teaches that the essence of the ego, the habitual feeling "I am myself", is also a sign of the *Atman*, of the presence of God within the spiritual Heart. As the Sufis of my lineage express it—at least according to my own understanding of their teachings, and I am certainly open to correction—the dissolution of the ego-as-veil relates to the *Ma'rifa* of Allah, while the recognition of the ego-as-sign, though from a point deeper than the ego, relates to the *Ma'rifa* of the *Nafs*. The perfection of the *Ma'rifa* of Allah is *fana'*, annihilation in Allah as the Formless Absolute; in yogic terms, this is undoubtedly equivalent to *nirvikalpa samadhi*. In what sense is the *Ma'rifa* of the *Nafs* a higher station even than this? As long as the human person remains self-identified, immersed in the I-sense, the *nafs* appears in one of two states: the *nafs al-ammara bi'l su* ("the soul commanding to evil") or the *nafs al-lawwama* ("the accusing soul"). The first is the ego as the familiar "lower self" that teaches us to totally identify with our impulses and do our best to live them out; the second is the ego as the troubled, but impotent, conscience. In both cases the *nafs* is still "me"; it is the very incarnation of the I-sense. But when the I-sense is transcended, when self-identification comes to an end, when the human person is objectified before the face of the Absolute Witness, then the *nafs* is transformed into something else entirely. All the familiar human faculties continue to operate, but they do so without identification, without in any way constituting "me." This is the station of *baqa'*, Subsistence in God. In the *Ma'rifa* of Allah, the human form disappears; all is Allah, no longer veiled by His manifestation on lower levels than the Formless Absolute, but revealed in His naked Essence—even though there is no longer anyone else there to witness It. In *Ma'rifa* of the *Nafs*, however, all these lower levels of manifestation come back again; the difference is that they have lost the ability to veil the Absolute, but now fully manifest It, on all levels, and in a single form: the human form. This is the esoteric meaning of the second part of the *shahada*, *Muhammadun rasulu Allah*, "Muhammad is God's prophet," who consequently stands as a representative of the Human Form per se; consequently it alludes to the *Ma'rifa* of the *Nafs*—though we must always remember that, in Islamic terms, the Prophet is the site of the manifestation of Divinity not because his humanity has become literally Divine, but strictly by virtue of his annihilation in Allah.

In his poem "Auguries of Innocence", the English poet William Blake describes the difference between the *Ma'rifa* of Allah and the *Ma'rifa* of the *Nafs* both accurately and succinctly, by presenting the Human Form in the light of God as the most complete manifestation of the Divine:

CHAPTER THREE

> God appears and God is Light
> To those poor souls who dwell in night,
> But does a Human Form display
> To those who dwell in realms of Day.

The complete unveiling of the *Atman*, with the Human Form as the site of this unveiling, is the essence of the spirit of Guidance, whose name in Hinduism is *Satguru*, and in Islam, *Murshid*. The Guide who has transcended self-existence exists only to guide others to this same Transcendence. He has no form of his own, but—like a perfect mirror—he takes on the form of the one contemplating him, according to the precise outlines of that person's state, while remaining entirely free of any identification with it. He does this—or to be strictly accurate, this occurs—so as to demonstrate the fundamentally illusory, apparitional or *Maya*-like nature of the form so reflected. Once again, in the words of Ibn al-'Arabi,

> The recipient sees nothing other than his own form
> in the mirror of the Reality. There is nothing higher.

That form may dissolve and pass away in the state of *fana'*; it may also return, in the state of *baqa'*, so that it seems to exist once again on the basis of its own self-nature. This, however, is not the case; such "seeming" is merely an apparition of the All-Merciful, for the sole purpose of extending the Mercy of Allah to all who contemplate it. *La ilaha illa 'Allah*: there is no god but God; *Tat Twam Asi*: there is no self but the Self.

CHAPTER FOUR

The Trinitarian Problem in Christian/Muslim Dialogue

Christian Trinitarianism is not tri-theism. The Persons of the Trinity are not three gods, or three "parts" of God. No traditional Christian is anything but a monotheist; the Trinity is the specific mode in which *tawhid*, the Unity of God, was revealed to the Christians. Ibn al-'Arabi in the *Fusus al-Hikam*, in his chapter on the Prophet Salih—as we have seen above—presents an esoteric Islamic "trinitarianism" as the deployment of the Unity of Allah: The Lord, the Servant (or the Cosmos) and the Reality. All are equally and wholly Allah because Allah is their Essence, as he is indeed the Essence of all things, no thing ultimately possessing any Essence or Being but His. This is the true, radical and absolute *tawhid*.

And this *batini* (inner) conception in no way compromises the doctrine of Unity of Allah, but rather protects it and confirms it. The Nestorians, and other Christian sects who remained closer to

CHAPTER FOUR

Judaism (the Ebionites; the Church of James) undoubtedly had a conception of Jesus that was closer to Judeo-Islamic prophetology. Yet the central doctrine of orthodox Christianity has always been Trinitarianism, which is inseparable from the doctrine of God's incarnation in the person of Jesus Christ. Though this doctrine was certainly made more explicit by later Church councils, it was not simply a later invention. In the Gospels Jesus speaks of both the Father and the Paraclete, the Spirit of God, Who is identifiable on one level with the Muslim *Ruh* (Spirit) or the *Nafas al-Rahman* (the Breath of the Merciful), and who might also, on another level, actually represent a foreknowledge of the coming of the Prophet, as some Muslims maintain. Nonetheless the Spirit who overshadowed the Apostles on Pentecost was certainly not identifiable as the man known as Muhammad. And the theophany of the Trinity appears explicitly in the Gospel of Matthew in the account of Jesus's baptism by John the Baptist, as the voice of the invisible Father, the person of Jesus, and the Dove of the Holy Spirit. The Gospels, we must remember, are the later crystallizations of an oral tradition going back to the Apostles, and to Jesus Himself.

According to Islamic teaching, Allah cannot appear in His Essence, at least without annihilating the witnessing believer and his world; He can only appear in terms of His Attributes, His Names and His Acts. In Muslim terms, to say "every Name of Allah contains all the Names"—because otherwise the Names would be "parts" of Allah, and Allah is indivisible, one of His Names being *Al-Ahad*, "the One"—is equivalent to saying, in Christian terms, that the Persons of the Trinity are "fused but

CHAPTER FOUR

not confused": each of the Persons contains the fullness of the Godhead, Who—according to the Nicene Creed—is One.

One of the many things that it is very difficult to conceive about Allah is expressed in the *hadith qudsi*, "I am according to My servant's opinion of Me," something that cannot be said of anything other than Allah. In the world of nature, society, and history—which are the ensemble of the *ayat al-zahir*, the outer signs of Allah—the nature of things is NOT based on our opinion of them. They are not what we imagine them to be; they are what they are. Our opinions about things are only valid if they conform to the objective reality of those things.

It is otherwise with Allah, because Allah is infinite, and one of the implications of His infinity is the fact that every opinion any of His servants holds of Him necessarily represents one of His actual Names—each containing all the others—given that His Names are not parts of Allah but His specific relationships with the many and varied objects, entities and conscious beings whom He has created. He is so far beyond and so totally free of every conception of Him, according to the principle of *tanzih*, His Transcendence or "Incomparability"—*there is nothing to which He can be compared* says the *Fatiha*—that any conception of Him will draw upon one of His real Names or Attributes. And because He is the Infinitely Generous, *Al-Karim*, and the infinitely Merciful, *Al-Rahman*, He pours His Reality into each of these conceptions of Him to the total extent of their capacity: which is precisely why—according to *tashbih*, His Immanence or "Comparability"—He is also comparable, in a certain sense, to this or that: he is like a *Lord (of the worlds)*, like an *Owner (of the Day of Judgment)*, etc. In the words of the Qur'an, *Allah's is the Sublime Similitude* [Q. 16:60], a verse also translated as *God is to be likened to whatever is loftiest*. And this is precisely how various divine revelations with irreducible differences between them can still all be sent by Him, seeing that the Qur'an also says [Q. 16:93], *If Allah had so willed He could have made you all one people*. The differences between the religions, irreducible on the plane of form, are thus providential and necessary, because Allah is jealous of His Unity, and will not allow this Exclusive Unity to appear in its perfection anywhere in the created world.

It is hard for many, even many Christians (Pope Francis included), to understand how the Trinity could be the guarantee of God's Unity, not a violation of it. But since God is not just Absolute Being but also Absolute Self-knowledge—there being nothing outside Himself for Him to Know—this Self-Witnessing (the Father) and the Object of it (the Son) would constitute a duality within the Godhead, if it weren't for the absolute identity of the Knower with the Known in the Unity in the Spirit. The third term unites the first two, thus returning them to the Unity of the Godhead of which all three are expressions. The problem with this Trinitarian conception of God when it is expressed in dogmatic terms is that it is an esoteric conception, and thus always in danger of being misunderstood and consequently of becoming a stumbling-block or an idol; the same thing can probably be said of the theosophy of Ibn al-'Arabi. Frithjof Schuon called Christianity an "eso-exoteric revelation," an esoteric doctrine preached openly to the masses. This is confirmed, interestingly enough, by the Mandaeans of Iraq, thought by many to be descended from the Essenes, who name John the Baptist as their founder but hate Jesus because, they claim, he openly revealed their esoteric secrets to the masses. And Christian Trinitarianism can certainly degenerate into tri-theism. Nonetheless any traditional Christian Trinitarian would entirely agree with the Qur'an that God is not *the third of three* [Q. 5:73]. As for the divinity of Jesus Christ, this can in some ways be compared with the *ana l'Haqq* ("I am the Truth") of Mansur Hallaj—but here we have to stop, having reached the level where the differences between the revelations really are irreducible. At this point all we can say is "and Allah knows best," stop comparing Islam to other revelations, and fully concentrate upon the revelation by which Allah has called us to Him, whether this be Christian Trinitarianism or strict Islamic Unitarianism. To use our piety and our energy-of-attention to disagree with other religions—or even to agree with them—is to remove that attention, to one degree or another, from Allah, who demands, deserves, and requires our undivided vigilance in His Presence. Nonetheless, to the degree that Christian Trinitarianism has actually degenerated into an implicit tri-theism, the Islamic revelation can act to reinstate and confirm the original Unitarianism of the Abrahamic faiths, which no traditional Christian has ever denied; this is one of the senses in which the Holy Qur'an is the *Furqan*, the Criterion.

The esoteric doctrines of Sufis like Ibn al-'Arabi or Mansur al-Hallaj—who also said "To assert that Allah is One is thereby to set up another beside Him"—are of little use in either legitimate interfaith dialogue—except in the case of rare and providential meetings between *batinis* or pneumatics—or united front ecumenism, defined as the mutual defense of the traditional religions in the face of common enemies, where such notions could only muddy the waters. I have expressed them here only to justify my contention—which is certainly also justifiable in purely strategic terms—that for Muslims to imply that Trinitarianism does not represent the original, pure Christian doctrine of the Unity of God is to lose all the Christians, or at least the best and most traditional of them, at a single stroke. Muslims would do better to understand Trinitarianism as a way of expressing the Unity of God that prevents His Transcendence (*tanzih*) and his Immanence (*tashbih*) from being falsely seen as opposed, thus guaranteeing the doctrine of *Wahdat al-Wujud*, the Transcendent Unity of Being. To the degree that Muslims are capable of understanding Trinitarianism in this way, they may even be able to save some Christians from falling into the heresy and the delusion of tri-theism that always threatens Trinitarian believers—at least in the realm of the imagination, if not in the realm of explicit dogma. We must accept that certain central doctrines of Christianity and Islam will always contradict each other, and consequently base our interfaith dialogue on the Qur'anic principle that *unto Allah ye will all return, and He will then inform you of that wherein ye differ* [Q. 5:48]. As Jalaluddin Rumi said:

> When has religion ever been one? It has always been two or three, and war has always raged [even] among coreligionists. How are you going to unify religion? On the Day of Resurrection it will be unified, but here in this world that is impossible because everybody has a different desire and want. Unification is not possible here. At the Resurrection, however, when all will be united, everyone will look to one thing, everyone will hear and speak one thing. [Jalalluddin Rumi, ***Signs of the Unseen (Fihi ma-Fihi)***, Threshold Books edition, 29].

CHAPTER FIVE

The Question of God's Incarnation as Jesus Christ in Christian/Muslim Dialogue

Inseparable from the Christian doctrine of the Trinity is the dogma of the Incarnation: that Jesus Christ was and is the "only-begotten Son of God." This Islam denies, defining the belief in *hulul*, "incarnationism," as a major error. But do we know exactly what Islam means by *hulul*? This is a hard question to answer in view of the fact that Islam had no need to explicitly define the nature of Jesus Christ in dogmatic terms, except to number him among the prophets and call him *a spirit from Allah* and *a word which He (Allah) cast into Mary* [Q. 4:171]. Nonetheless, according to Islam, Jesus is not literally Allah in any sense, a position Jesus himself seemed to agree with when he said "Why do you call me good? There is no-one good except God alone" [Mark 10:18].

Nonetheless he also said, "Before Abraham came to be, I Am" [John 8:58], applying to himself an element of the Divine Name

CHAPTER FIVE

"I Am that I Am" revealed by God to Moses at the Burning Bush; the Jews recognized the allusion and attempted to stone him for blasphemy. Furthermore, as Ibn al-'Arabi teaches, the ultimate Essence of all things is precisely Allah, a doctrine that nonetheless does not constitute pantheism, defined as the belief that the totality of the existing entities that make up the universe actually constitute or "add up to" God—for the simple reason that, as the Shaykh al-Akbar teaches, all things have two faces, one of Allah and one of themselves. With respect to themselves they are nothing, while with respect to Allah, they are Allah.

Muslims deny that God can become man. Yet orthodox Christianity, in its doctrine of the Two Natures of Christ, the human and the Divine, also denies this in a certain sense, seeing that it is necessary to assert that Christ has both a human and a Divine nature precisely because his human nature is not Divine, and never becomes Divine. Nonetheless his two natures do not remain separate, but exist in a Hypostatic Union. This mysterious formulation was necessary to refute the various Christological heresies which claimed that Jesus Christ is a created being who was raised to Divinity by the Father (Arianism; Adoptionism); or that he was a Divine apparition, not a man (Docetism); or that his human nature was completely subsumed and dissolved into his Divine Nature (Monophysitism). As such, the Hypostatic Union, for all its awkwardness and seemingly hybrid nature, is the dogmatic formulation closest to the actual truth of the matter, which is what makes it orthodox and necessary in a Christian context.

But perhaps there is a bridge between the Christian and the Muslim conceptions of the nature of Jesus. The Sufis interpret

CHAPTER FIVE

la ilaha illa 'Allah, "there is no god but God," the first half of the shahadah, to mean that there is no Real Existent except the One Real Existent—namely, God. And if this is true, then the ultimate Essence of all beings and forms must be Allah and nothing else—though no being, considered according to the limitations of its formal existence, can ever be or become Allah. Meister Eckhart for one, in saying "my truest 'I' is God," seems to accept this doctrine.

But if this is true, then what becomes of the preeminence of Jesus Christ as the unique "only-begotten," Son of God, the only being to whom the doctrine of the Hypostatic Union can be applied? What becomes of him as the *exclusive* Incarnation of God as man? Once again, Jesus himself appears to deny this exclusivity when he says, in John 10:34, "ye are all gods, and sons of the Most High." This statement is usually explained according to the doctrine that Jesus came to give men the power to become sons of God [John 1:12], thus making them co-heirs with Christ of the Kingdom of Heaven [Romans 8:17]—and yet the scripture Jesus was quoting when he made that statement, Psalm 82, was written down long before he appeared on earth.

We must accept that the Muslim and Christian views of the nature of Jesus can never be fully reconciled. If they could, Christianity and Islam would lose their status as discrete Divine Revelations, and this is contrary to the will of Allah, as expressed in Q. 5:48: *If Allah had willed, He would have made you one nation*. Christians must approach God through the doctrines of the Trinity and the Incarnation, otherwise they are no longer Christians. Likewise, Muslims must approach Him through His unmediated Unity, as One Who neither begets nor is begotten, otherwise they are no longer Muslims. But how is this possible? How can two clearly opposed conceptions of God both be true? The answer to this question is as deep a theological mystery as any we will encounter, a mystery alluded to by Allah when He tells us, in the *hadith qudsi*, "I am as my servant sees me." (See *Chapter Seven*, "The Nature of Ontological Perspectives".)

However, after retreating several steps from the awesome majesty of this mystery, and turning from the realm of Incomprehensible Certainty to that of mere individual opinion, it may also be possible to say that, though the ultimate essence of every human being is Allah, since He is the Only Being, Jesus is the one pre-eminent Divine Incarnation within the framework of the three Abrahamic religions by virtue of the fact that only he kept the unbroken memory and certainly of his Human Divinity that was his before his Incarnation, when he was strictly identified with the Second Person of the Trinity, the Archetype of Man *in divinis*; retained it while in the womb of Mary; and continued to be conscious of it throughout his earthly life. The only other figure in the Abrahamic universe about whom this might conceivably be said is Melchizedek, the spiritual master of Abraham, who was "without father or mother," and to whom Jesus is compared in Hebrews 7:17: "You are a priest forever after the order of Melchizedek"—but this is only speculation, and speculation has no spiritual efficacy. And certainly, Jesus was superior to Melchizedek in terms of his spiritual power and the universality of his ministry. The only other fully Divine Incarnations recognized among the traditional revealed religions are the Ten Incarnations of Vishnu, among which some Hindus number Jesus Christ. Be that as it may, Jesus is unique in being the only Incarnation or Avatar who was sent to suffer and die for the sins of humanity, and then to rise again, thereby—in the Eastern Orthodox phrase—"trampling down death by death."

Muslims, however, deny that Jesus was crucified—and this divergence between Christianity and Islam is apparently irreducible. Muslims know Jesus as born of the Virgin Mary—Maryam—and as the one who will return at the end of time to slay the Antichrist, but they do not accept the Crucifixion and the Resurrection. Christians, on the other hand, must accept salvation and sanctification only through "Jesus Christ, and Him crucified" [1 Corinthians 2:2]. Here we can see how even the most esoteric ecumenism, to the degree that it attempts—in spite of itself—to define a mid-ground or average between two quasi-Absolute Revelations, can only lead us into a state of Limbo where we will not be able to draw spiritual sustenance from either one of them. In light of this, the only recourse for Muslims who wish to befriend the Christians—to defend them "until the coming of the Hour" as the Prophet Muhammad commands all Muslims to do in his Covenants with the Christians of the world—is, in the words of the Holy Qur'an, not to struggle with them over questions of dogma but rather to "compete in good works":

> *We have appointed a law and a practice for every one of you. Had God willed, He would have made you a single community, but He wanted to test you regarding what has come to you. So compete with each other in doing good. Every one of you will return to God and He will inform you regarding the things about which you differed.* [Q. 5:48]

CHAPTER SIX

From a Letter to a Christian Mystic

It was not for nothing that the Virgin Mary appeared in a town in your homeland [Portugal] named after Fatima, the daughter of the Prophet Muhammad (peace and blessings be upon him)—Fatima who in Muslim veneration is second only to Mary, and who, if it had not been for Mary herself, would have been the closest thing to her equivalent in the Islamic tradition. In Shi'ism she has almost become a Queen of Heaven in her own right. And as Mary is slighted in certain places in the Gospels—"woman, what have I to do with thee?"—so Fatima was seemingly treated unfairly by her father the Prophet, who did not let her inherit the Fadak Oasis, and perhaps also by the first Caliph, Abu Bakr, whose election by the community over her husband Ali (whom the Shi'ites and the Sufis consider to be the Prophet's spiritual heir, though the Sufis take this in a *batini* or initiatory sense while the Shi'a also see him as Muhammad's proper *zahiri* successor) placed her in a difficult position. And then, like Mary, in later years Fatima became exalted to near-divine status. All this, in my opinion, has something to do with the mystery of the feminine reflection of Divinity, which is a secret that must be kept until the last days. Look at all the problems, from the Gnostics to Soloviev, which grew out of attempts to make "sophianic" spirituality explicit within Christianity. Where is Mary as hypostasis to be placed? As a fourth person of the Trinity? And yet there is a mystery in her that is incomparably exalted—the mystery of perfect *islam*, of the pure, self-annihilating receptivity-to-God of the perfected soul, which thereby becomes host to the Divinity. As the Sufis say, the soul does not become God, but is annihilated in His presence; then there is only He. But when there is only He, there is nothing that does not reflect Him or participate in His nature, and so the soul paradoxically remains—annihilated in its separateness but remaining forever as a pure gift, to nothingness, of God's own Being. And so, in a certain sense, all things are names of God. I am in no way God— but God is most certainly me. I am nothing but His veil; He is entirely my Being. The veil, the hijab, imposed (intermittently) upon women after the Prophet's time, can certainly be an abuse. Yet there is a secret in the feminine nature that must be kept at all cost. Mary is the deepest secret of creation; when this secret is finally told in its completeness, the Hour will come. That is when the veil of the Temple will really be torn in two—not just in the inner chamber, but for the whole world.

The equivalent of Mary in Islam is the Prophet Muhammad; his receptivity to the Qur'an is compared to Mary's receptivity to the Holy Spirit. Just as in Christianity the Word is made flesh, so in Islam the Word is made book—and both events were announced by the angel Gabriel. The coming of the Word of God in Christianity is an Incarnation, and in Islam a Theophany. When the Eucharist is received, it becomes part of the living body of the recipient. When the words of the Qur'an are recited, they strike like lightning on a dark night. And then go out. And then come again. In the same way, God, by his Word, creates and re-creates the world in each separate instant.

Muslims usually consider the Christian Trinity to be a kind of tritheism, which is a misunderstanding of Christian theology, but a very accurate critique of Christian idolatry. When the Qur'an says "He neither begets nor is begotten, and there is nothing to which He can be compared," it announces the Divine Transcendence in tones easily found in Christianity as well; the *Mystical Theology* of Dionysius the Pseudo-Areopagite comes immediately to mind. And passages in the Gospels such as "why do you call me good? There is no-one good but one, that is, God" are not lost on Muslims. When the Qur'an speaks of Jesus as a word of God and a spirit from Him, but not a Son, what is being asserted is simply that God cannot beget a second God like Himself, as a human father can beget a son who, in turn, can also become a father. When Eastern Orthodox theologians assert that Christ proceeds from the Father, not the other way around—which is why the Father is called Father—they are saying that the Father is Origin and the Son is second in procession, being a Word spoken by, and (by the Holy Spirit) a spirit proceeding from, the Father. (When Catholic theology asserts that the Holy Spirit proceeds from the Father and the Son, this simply means that, without the Son, there would be no "point of destination" for the outflow of the Spirit, Who would therefore never be deployed as a distinct hypostasis.)

CHAPTER SIX

So Christ is a Word of God and a Spirit (breath) proceeding from Him, not a separate or second God. When we speak a word, that word reveals us; it does not become us. Yet Christian theology asserts that the Son is equal in divinity to the Father, for all that he emptied Himself and took on the form of a servant. Christ is a Word of God, not a second God….and yet when that Word is spoken in eternity, when It is co-eternal with the Speaker….what then? Islam will never accept the literal divinity of Jesus; yet in Sufi metaphysics, notably that of Ibn al-'Arabi of Andalusia—who felt himself to be under the special tutelage of the Prophet Jesus—Being can legitimately be attributed, as an intrinsic essence, only to God; all other things exist as gifts freely given by that One Being to nothingness, since everything that is apart from Him, in its own essence can only be nothingness. So even though nothing that can be attributed to me as a creature is or can ever become God, nonetheless my Being and Essence are God Himself, and nothing else. "Ye are all gods, and sons of the Most High"—not in our separate forms, which can no more attain to or be united with God than a flashlight can shine its light on the face of the sun, but in our essence, which is already and only Him. If there is no God but God, as in the Muslim testimony of faith, then there is no Being but the One Being; this is the essence of the Sufi message.

As for its denial of the Crucifixion, the Qur'an does so partly in line with its conception that every prophet sent by God is virtually perfect—a far cry from the Old Testament view of Moses, for example, or Jonah, or King David, all three of whom are considered prophets in Islam. (This sense of the perfection of every prophet, though they differ in mission, capacity, and degree of "success," some of them having been martyred by the people to whom they were sent, gives the Muslim conception of Jesus as among the greatest of the prophets a nuance not entirely transmitted simply by saying "Muslims deny the divinity of Christ.") The Qur'an is saying that the Jews were not able to degrade or destroy God's prophet Jesus—for did he not walk free of all their schemes? This, of course, can never be fully reconciled with the doctrine of the Crucifixion and the Resurrection. But if God did indeed send Muhammad, peace and blessings be upon him, then He could not have sent Him with a doctrine identical to that of Christianity; if the Prophet had preached such a doctrine he would have been a Christian, and in no way a law-giving prophet (*rasul*) sent by God, which is precisely what he was. As is said in many places in the Qur'an, in the next world Allah *will enlighten them as to wherein they differ.*

And yet—is the Qur'an's assertion concerning Jesus, *they killed him not, nor crucified him*, as direct a contradiction of the Gospel story as it appears to be, or does it exist on a different plane where contradiction does not apply, since two truths that abide in different worlds can never come to blows because they can never meet on the same field? The Qur'an says:

> *That they said (in boast), "We killed Christ Jesus the son of Mary, the Messenger of Allah"; but they killed him not, nor crucified him, but so it was made to appear to them, and those who differ therein are full of doubts, with no (certain) knowledge, but only conjecture to follow, for of a surety they killed him not: But Allah raised him up unto Himself; and Allah is Exalted in Power, Wise.* [Q.4:157–58]

Martin Lings maintains that the phrase *"they killed him not"* should be seen in light of Q. 2:154: *"And call not those who are slain in the way of Allah "dead." Nay, they are living, only ye perceive not."* And certainly the perfidious among the Jews had no cause to boast that they had killed Jesus, seeing that—according to the Christians at least— he "trampled down death by death" by rising from the dead. The Qur'an may simply be saying that the Jews thought they had gotten rid of Jesus, but were sorely mistaken; and *Allah raised him unto Himself* may simply be a shorthand way of referring to the Resurrection and the Ascension. I believe, however, that it is more to the point to consider Q. 4:171, where Jesus is described as a messenger of Allah, and His word which He projected unto Mary, and a spirit from Him. It is from this perspective that the Qur'an asserts that *they killed him not*, since no spirit nor word can ever be killed. We may destroy an enemy in anger, but we can never destroy a *truth*.

I believe that the Qur'an, here, is directing Muslims not to relate to Jesus through dependence upon and participation in his self-sacrificial act, otherwise they would be Christians; they must relate to him through his reality as a deathless spirit, as an immortal prophet like Idris (Enoch) or Ilyas (Elijah) or the Khidr of the Sufis. To Muslims, Jesus is the Christ of the Transfiguration, not of the Crucifixion; this is because the Muslim Way is based not on sacrificial atonement for the sin of Adam but on overcoming Adam's—that is, humanity's—*ghaflah*, our congenital forgetfulness. (Nonetheless, Islam does embrace the path of self-sacrifice in a more sublimated way, through the Annihilation-and-Subsistence of the Sufis, which can be accurately epitomized as: "He who seeks to keep his life will lose it, but he who loses his life, for My sake, shall find it" [Matthew 16:25].) The case could be made that the divergence of Christianity and Islam regarding the death of Jesus is not primarily a disagreement on matters of fact, but rather a divergence between two operative spiritual Ways, each with its own uniquely necessary doctrinal standpoints and methodological requirements. Jesus as Christianity defines him, a mortal man who was host to the Divinity with Which He was hypostatically united, died and rose again. Jesus as Islam defines him, as a spirit from Allah, an immortal prophet, did not die and could never die. And these two definitions, though they are widely divergent, are not fundamentally opposed—unless we place them in opposition by attempting to logically reconcile them—any more than a view of a mountain from the southeast and another view from the north are opposed. God is vast, and—in the words of the *hadith qudsi* (Prophetic tradition in which Allah Himself speaks), "I am as my servant sees Me," which does not mean that each individual invents his or her own "god" according to the eccentricities and limits of that individual's subjectivity, but that every perceiver's mode of perception on a given occasion is an objective factor that reveals a different aspect of the infinite reality of God. It is obvious that "Jesus Christ, and Him crucified" and *they killed him not, nor crucified him* are mutually exclusive on the level of historical fact—but this does not mean they contradict each other on every level. In terms of the necessary divergence (on one level) of operative spiritual Ways, their divergence simply requires that the Christian and the Muslim avail themselves of two different aspects of the comprehensive reality of the Divine Self-manifestation, just as two mountain climbers climbing different faces of a mountain must negotiate their own unique sets of topographical features on their way to the Summit.

CHAPTER SIX

Perhaps the limits of the ability of the human mind to grapple with this question were plumbed by Frithjof Schuon in the following passage from ***Christianity/Islam: Essays in Esoteric Ecumenism***:

> Religious oppositions cannot but be, not only because forms exclude one another . . . but because, in the case of religions, each form vehicles an element of absoluteness that constitutes the justification for its existence; now the absolute does not tolerate otherness nor, with all the more reason, plurality. . . . To say form is to say exclusion of possibilities, whence the necessity for those excluded to become realized in other forms.

On the plane of the direct knowledge of God, however, this formulation—while undoubtedly ingenious, and certainly true on its own level—is profoundly unsatisfying; in contemplating the Divinity we do not seek "an element of absoluteness" but the Absolute Itself. To expend our piety and our energy-of-attention in viewing various religious forms from the outside, in order to agree or disagree with them, is to remove that attention, to one degree or another, from Allah, who demands, deserves, and requires our undivided vigilance in His Presence. Therefore I will end by returning, gratefully, to what can be known and accepted in practical terms for the spiritual life:

> *We have appointed a law and a practice for every one of you. Had God willed, He would have made you a single community, but He wanted to test you regarding what*

CHAPTER SIX

has come to you. So compete with each other in doing good. Every one of you will return to God and He will inform you regarding the things about which you differed. [Q. 5:48]

CHAPTER SEVEN

The Nature of Ontological Perspectives: A Commentary on Frithjof Schuon's Doctrine of the Relatively Absolute

Frithjof Schuon's doctrine of the Transcendent Unity of Religions is based, in my view, on the principle that while we human beings can compare, contrast, and evaluate realities lower than we are on the Great Chain of Being, we cannot do so when it comes to those that are higher. Religious revelations are higher than our individual humanity because they are sent by God, which is why they have a right to command our allegiance; and because they are higher than us, we cannot encompass them or pass judgment upon them on their own plane of being.

Facts are objective realities that occupy a lower ontological plane than human beings; we can evaluate them, but they cannot evaluate us; this is why we can pass judgment as to the truth or falsehood of statements presented as factual. Lee Harvey Oswald was either a lone assassin or a member (or dupe) of a conspiracy whose aim was to assassinate President Kennedy. One of these statements must be true, but both cannot be true; there is no way that these two contradictory statements can be resolved in some higher unity.

Religious revelations, on the other hand, are objective realities that occupy a higher ontological plane than we do; there is no way we can place them, as it were, on the table in front of us so as to compare, contrast, evaluate, or judge between them. They are not laboratory specimens; we will never be able to construct an experiment capable of exhaustively determining their actual properties. It would be truer to say that we are their experiment. Though we will never be able to exhaustively test them, they are already testing us.

Religious revelations might be characterized as "ontological perspectives"—God-given perspectives that allow us to entertain certain valid views as to His nature. But since God is Absolute Reality, no single view can encompass Him; in the words of the Qur'an [6:103], *Vision comprehendeth Him not, but He comprehendeth (all) vision.* And because He is Infinite Reality as well, no number of valid views, even if they are revealed by Him, can "add up" to a complete understanding of Him. Nothing other than He can encompass Him in knowledge, which is why all theological formulations must fall short of defining Him—even if, in relation to the particular ontological perspective we occupy, they are necessarily true, and therefore (in Schuon's phrase) "relatively Absolute."

CHAPTER SEVEN

Ontological perspectives are not subjective beliefs or impressions, but objective realities. They are not views we choose to adopt on our own authority, or are influenced to adopt by social or psychological or biological factors: they are views that God Himself both permits us and commands us to adopt, as ways of knowing Him. We are used to thinking of "views" as collective or individual opinions. And it is true that when speaking of beliefs, impressions, or conclusions based on human experience—rather than of the necessary conclusions of logic that partake of the objectivity of the Transcendent, as both Schuon, in **Logic and Transcendence**, and C. S. Lewis, in **Miracles**, conclusively demonstrate—we are dealing with perspectives on Reality that, though they may attain a certain degree of objectivity, can never entirely escape from the subjective bias of those entertaining them. Ontological perspectives, on the other hand, are not based on belief or experience; they are not dependent upon psychology, or history, or culture, either individual or collective; they are not opinions. Like the view of a stationary object from a given distance while facing a given point of the compass, each is entirely objective—as real as (or rather, much more real than) the rocks on the hillside or the stars in the sky. And since they have radiated directly from Absolute Reality, they are ontologically superior to us. We can never encompass them; they have already encompassed us. Consequently, though we can compare certain reverberations of them as they appear in psychology, or history, or culture, or the discipline of metaphysics, we cannot compare them to one another on their own plane of being, because each Divine revelation, each act of God, is incomparable—unique. Realities superior to us on the Great Chain of Being are in fact more unique, and thus more fully incomparable, than the realities of our human world; this is what St. Thomas Aquinas was alluding to when he taught that each individual angel is a species unto himself. (Furthermore, what appears as a doctrine or system of ideas in this world may in fact be a conscious, living entity in another world; as the Shi'ite theosophers teach us, the Platonic Ideas, in that higher spiritual world which is proper to them, are, precisely, angels.)

Lee Harvey Oswald cannot have been both a lone assassin and a member (or dupe) of a conspiracy; logic is logic, and facts are facts. But when it comes to questions like "Was Jesus Christ the Son of God (the Christian view), or was he only a prophet, though among the greatest of them (the Muslim view)?", exclusionary logic no longer applies. Such logic can certainly be applied to facts that are ontologically lower than us; we can compare them with each other, and evaluate them in relation to one another, because we transcend them. But it cannot be used to evaluate perspectives that are ontologically higher than we are.

Consequently, as soon as we admit that more than one Divine revelation is true and valid, we can no longer compare one revealed religion with another on the plane of essence. And we cannot accept one Word of God and reject another without denying God's veracity, and consequently destroying the very basis upon which we claim to invoke His authority, even insofar as it validates the particular Word we are willing to accept. Nor can we stand outside of two Divinely-revealed propositions—"Jesus is the Son of the God" and "God has no son," for example—so as to compare, contrast, evaluate, and judge between them, since to do so could only be based on the false belief that we can encompass the revelations of God with our human understanding, which clearly we cannot. And we can't say "Jesus both is and is not the Son of God" either, since to do so would be to place in a false relationship two unique Divine revelations which, on the plane of form, "quasi-absolutely" exclude each other. Formal reverberations can be compared; transcendental essences cannot.

This seemingly insoluble dilemma is only resolved by an intuition of the overwhelming vastness of God. We agree that God is "Absolute, Infinite, Perfect, the Sovereign Good"—and then we treat Him as if He were like the king in a game of chess, moving in response to our own will and intelligence on a board of 64 squares we can survey in a single glance. But that is not how it is. I have said that we cannot encompass the reality of God—but we can encompass the necessity for this very inability. God is not fully intelligible to us, but His unintelligibility is—and this, precisely, is our point of intimate contact with the Divine Transcendence. As Abu Bakr said (peace and blessing be upon him), "To know that God cannot be known is to know God." And the resulting certainty that God is infinitely beyond our power to encompass Him is the root of the further certainty that every perspective upon His nature that has in fact been revealed by Him, not concocted by human cleverness, is objectively real, necessary in its own terms, superior to us, and incomparable in essence to any other such perspective. No two religions are "equivalent" to one another, any more than two human individuals can be equivalent, or an eagle equivalent to a lion. If more than one religion is true—just as the lion and the eagle are both beautiful, both awe-inspiring, both sublime—this is because all Divinely-revealed religions are unique and incomparable, and because God's Truth, which is a Name of His Essence, is Infinite. Infinite Truth has the power to *make* true (and therefore spiritually efficacious), every idea we may entertain about It, though on vastly different hierarchical levels, stretching from self-serving and/or paranoid delusions that are disastrous to those entertaining them and so manifest God's Wrath, to objective perspectives upon Its Reality that It has granted us of Its own volition, and which consequently, as what Schuon calls "saving illusions," manifest God's Mercy—even if from our limited, subjective perspectives (a limitation in no less necessary than is God's Infinity), they contradict each other; as William Blake put it in *The Marriage of Heaven and Hell*, "Everything possible to be believed is an image of Truth." If God's unknowability imposes, at one level (though certainly not all), a necessary quality of paradox upon all statements made about Him, this same unknowability also makes His Self-revelations necessarily contradictory, to one degree or another, on the plane of form. In His own Essence, God cannot contradict Himself—but the incapacity of form to fully embody the Formless Absolute makes contradiction a necessary element—though certainly not the only one—in His cosmic Self-revelation; as Ibn al-'Arabi expressed it, "there is war between the Names of God." If we are unable to accept this truth, we are in effect demanding that the world of form encompass God, or actually *be* God—something that is both impossible in reality and idolatrous in effect.

From a different but equally-valid perspective, however, two things that cannot be compared with one another cannot contradict each other; they can never come to blows because they can never occupy the same field. A Divinely-revealed ontological perspective is a saving ray of Light that, if we truly and existentially enter into the stream of it, will sweep all other perspectives away, and concentrate us upon God Himself, upon the Divine Reality from which it flows. The two propositions that "Jesus is the Son of God" and "God has no son" can never be resolved on the plane of form; no degree of human ingenuity can make peace between them. They are, however, truly resolved in a higher Unity—the Unity of God Himself. And so, if we wish to avoid the seemingly inevitable conflict between two objective, ontological perspectives on the Divine Nature that contradict each other, the only way is to renounce comparisons entirely, and follow the stream we have chosen (and that therefore must necessarily first have chosen us) to its ultimate Source—in the understanding that a unique, incomparable, Divinely-revealed, "relatively absolute" perspective on the nature of God has no other purpose in the Divine economy than to lead us back to that Source. Once our initial orientation is complete, such a perspective is not to be speculated upon or theorized about; it is to be put to work.

All I have said here, however, does not mean that God is simply opaque to us, absolutely unintelligible. He is, in fact, the only completely intelligible Reality precisely because He is the Only Being; His intelligibility, however, is contingent upon our annihilation as limited subjects capable of entertaining "propositions" and making "judgments." Because, in God, Knowledge and Being are One, God can be known only by God. But to the degree we are annihilated as limited subjects we become host to this Knowledge, which subsists within us, in a seamless unity with That which is Known. In the words of the *hadith qudsi*, "Heaven and earth [head and body, the human mind and the material universe] cannot contain Me, but the heart of my believing slave can contain Me." The Essence of this Unity cannot be described in terms other than Itself: Its Presence is Its sole and sufficient definition and description and exegesis. When God said to St. Catherine of Sienna, "I am He who Is, you are she who is not," He annihilated abstract speculation and replaced it with concrete Realization.

CHAPTER EIGHT

For the Intellectual Dark Web, a Letter to Rebel Wisdom on some Contemporary Intellectual and Social Movements Based on, or Compatible with, Traditional Metaphysics

Dear Rebel Wisdom:

Greetings: I am contacting you because I believe I have identified two areas of serious discourse that deserve to be integrated into what you call the Intellectual Dark Web, or are *de facto* already part of it without being generally recognized as such. The first is the recovery of Traditional Metaphysics, which is part of an intellectual turn of some in the younger generations, in reaction against postmodernism and the regime of political correctness, toward a more traditional worldview; this turn is affecting Christians, Muslims, the religiously unaffiliated, and even agnostics. The second is the reality of the marginalization if not persecution of the religions, including both Christianity and Islam, in contemporary Europe and North America, apparently according to the agenda of the global elites, but certainly in line with the postmodern ethos, leading both to social oppression and the loss of profound traditional worldviews that have much to teach us about the nature of reality and the place and function of the human form within it.

A large and growing body of sophisticated philosophical speculation and social analysis is being generated to serve and express this turn toward Tradition, a universe of vital insight that is routinely either suppressed or caricatured by the dominant liberal media, who see it either as an unfamiliar brand of religious fundamentalism or else as some kind of "New Age occultism" that has unexpectedly found a place within the Alt Right. The shadow side of this traditionalist renaissance is indeed reactionary fundamentalism, which those informed by Traditional Metaphysics reject—something that is not hard for us to do since the religious fundamentalists also reject us, in some cases marking us out for their own brand of persecution, were they ever to gain political power.

In the "Our Vision" section of your website you say: "When our existing assumptions and ways of thinking break down, it's rebels and renegades, those who dare to think differently, who are needed to reboot the system . . . a new counterculture is filling the void, driven by a great intellectual awakening . . . the new is struggling to emerge. In a time where truth has become whatever you want it to be, we believe in the rebellious, transformative power of genuine Truth." I would respond: "Yes, the new is struggling to emerge, but the primordial is also being reawakened; both are happening at the same time. The postmodern absolutization of the relative and rejection of genuine objective Truth cannot be effectively countered without incorporating, as one element in the spectrum of critical responses to the postmodern ethos, the worldview of Traditional Metaphysics and religion, a worldview based on eternal archetypal principles rather than historical contingencies, and therefore capable of responding to the chaos of our times from a stable foundation. Postmodernism, however, rejects every aspect of this worldview as embracing the kind of 'metanarratives' that must be suppressed at all cost. The true rebellion is not against *Tradition* but against *convention*—and since the conventional postmodern wisdom of our time rejects and suppresses Tradition, religion, and metaphysics, the sophisticated critique of postmodernism that is presently being produced by the exemplars of Tradition, religion, and metaphysics definitely deserves a hearing."

According to postmodern ideology, "tradition" is a set of moribund received ideas that are not only passé but dangerously irrelevant, while "metaphysics" is a limiting, constrictive, and paralyzing meta-narrative imposed on the human collective only so as to establish social dominance for its proponents—one which, due to its abstraction and its separation from the concrete conditions of life, is generally incapable of making sense of the massive changes that characterize our time. And "religion" is commonly thought of as a more-or-less isolated and in-turned set of special interest groups, vulnerable to abusive practices, exhibiting various cult-like elements, maintaining an attachment to outworn mythic worldviews, and tending to reject well-established scientific truth. All these characterizations are in some ways true to the shadow of tradition, metaphysics, and religion, but in no way true to their essence. They are a kind of caricature. A good caricature will capture certain real aspects of its subject, but once it is mistaken for a comprehensive view of that subject, it becomes a slander.

Much important work is now being done to recover Tradition and employ it in new and relevant ways; traditional metaphysics is being applied to the scientific understanding of the natural world, to psychology, to social analysis and social action, and to the work of re-defining the place and function of religion under present postmodern conditions. If the Intellectual Dark Web fails to take into account the widespread turn of well-informed and intellectually sophisticated young people toward Tradition, I fear it will be unable to avoid the kind of narrowing-of-focus that must eventually lead to its petrification and irrelevance.

Tradition, metaphysics, and religion, narrowly defined as a mass of conventionally-transmitted ideas, sentiments, and beliefs, demonstrated some obvious shortcomings in the twentieth century, if not as early as Nietzsche's "death of God" and Kierkegaard's critique of bourgeois Protestant Christianity. Postmodernism's response was to insist that there be NO OVERARCHING PARADIGMS, and thus to atomize the intellectual life of humanity, reducing it to a chaos of supposedly equally-valid individual perspectives, with no hierarchy of values or insights available to orient the human intellect, affections, and will toward any true goal. Furthermore, mostly in the past decade, this postmodern tendency to pulverize our perception of reality by placing all world-views on the same level has called up its inevitable shadow and counterforce in the form of a new and militant "orthodoxy," complete with an inquisitorial oppression of all opposing views, in the form of the "Woke" ideology, based primarily on Cultural Marxism. The Perennialism of the Traditionalist School, however, has taken the opposite tack. Diagnosing the malaise of contemporary religion as based on the loss of its intellective dimension, it has sought the eternal metaphysical principles, the true archetypes underlying all the world's religions and metaphysical philosophies, and thereby gained the ability, at least in general terms, make perfect sense out of any form or event in the realm of cosmic manifestation as well as any historical development affecting the human race, without thereby dismissively imprisoning them in this or that narrow dogmatic box—though it has not been able to do this without invoking, from time to time, the lore of collective eschatology. Ever since Hegel, Darwin and Marx—not to mention Rudolf Steiner and Alfred North Whitehead and Sri Aurobindo and Teilhard de Chardin—we have defined all collective change as "evolution," no matter how devolutionary it has often appeared to be; consequently, we can't imagine any rationale for principled action unless we define it as "helping evolution along"; if the earth and the human race are generally devolving rather than evolving—at least according to certain criteria—we think this could only mean that all social action is futile. Perennialism, contrary to both Marxism and liberal secular humanism, sees history as essentially devolutionary and entropic, in line with the Hindu doctrine of the *manvantara* (cycle of manifestation) and the eschatologies of Islam, Christianity, and even Buddhism—but this is in no way meant to imply that all social action, under devolutionary conditions, is useless: far from it. Nor does it necessarily posit any kind of militant, reactionary "return to the past," both because the traditional worldview considers this impossible and because the degeneration of the cosmic environment in the later phases of the manvantara, for all its dangers and tragedies, is considered to be entirely lawful according to the will of God, who thereby challenges us to remain true to Him under the most difficult circumstances of all, and thereby form a "faithful remnant" who will be of great use to Him under apocalyptic conditions. The question is, can there be a true dialogue between the perspective that recognizes the possibility of collective social action to improve human life and the one that sees history as a collective devolution, though nonetheless punctuated by various "renewals," "redresses," and "revivals"? I, for one, believe that such a dialogue is certainly not easy, but definitely possible.

In the face of the loss of Tradition, "the death of God," Nietzsche invoked the duty of the individual spiritual/intellectual hero to create his or her own myth and live by it; the drawback of this approach, however, is that any myth created by the individual will tend to become a myth of that one individual and no other, a dramatization of the ego rather than a new and fertile approach to the Self. But if the quest of the hero is redefined in terms of the lonely struggle to find, return to, and actualize the Metaphysical Order, as a battle to recover the depth of Tradition that shallow dogmatic, social, or sentimental religion, as well as modernist secularism and postmodernist nihilism, had obscured or betrayed—a quest symbolized by the recovery of the Magic Bird, the Imprisoned Princess, or the Water of Life that the Grimms' fairy tales and so many other mythopoetic sources speak of—then I believe Nietzsche's challenge can be embraced and lived out without the kind of self-contradiction and self-sabotage

CHAPTER EIGHT

that reduced him, at the end of his life, to a demented madman being publicly exhibited by his sister as a kind of circus freak version of the Great Philosopher.

So, the first question is: "Can traditional religion and metaphysics enter into serious intellectual dialogue with other perspectives without descending into dogmatism and invective?" I believe the answer is "yes." And the second question is: "Can the Intellectual Dark Web deal with the socio-political dimension in a world as seriously polarized as ours is today without lapsing into ideological gang warfare?" Here too I believe that the answer is "yes"—but neither of these "yesses" is an easy one, neither is a foregone conclusion, nor can either be arrived at without a certain amount of creative suffering and honest conflict—though it's hard to remember the last time that anyone caught sight of these mythic animals. Some more specific answers to these two questions are as follows:

In terms of the first question, I can point you to two areas where Traditional Metaphysics has engaged with a wider intellectual world, namely physics and psychology. For physics, I refer you to the work of physicist, mathematician, philosopher, and metaphysician Wolfgang Smith [*he passed away in this year of 2024*] and his Philos-Sophia Foundation (https://philossophia.org), whose major contribution outside his many books, notably **The Quantum Enigma,** has been the film "The End of Quantum Reality." In his 80s, Dr. Smith entered into extensive dialogue with younger freelance Traditionalist intellectuals who have serious problems with establishment physics as represented by figures such as Stephen Hawking; they call themselves the "Wolfgangsters" and maintain a page on Facebook.

CHAPTER EIGHT

For psychology, you might familiarize yourselves with the work of Dr. Samuel Bendeck Sotillos, who is more or less identified with the school of Transpersonal Psychology and has extensively critiqued both Freudianism and Behaviorism from the standpoint of Traditional Metaphysics. My own contribution to the reconciliation between psychology and metaphysics are my books *The Science of the Greater Jihad: Essays in Principial Psychology* and *Day and Night on the Sufi Path*.

As for the second question, related to social action, my theoretical approach to such action from the standpoint of Traditional Metaphysics can be found in my essay "Principles of Sacred Activism" (dedicated to Andrew Harvey), which is Part II of *Chapter Seven* of my book *Dugin against Dugin: A Traditionalist Critique of the Fourth Political Theory*. Much more to the point, however, is the Covenants Initiative, which I co-founded with Dr. John Andrew Morrow in 2013, based on his groundbreaking book *The Covenants of the Prophet Muhammad with the Christians of the World*. The Initiative takes as its foundation the Prophet's Covenants with the Peoples of the Book—Christians, Jews, Zoroastrians, etc. I believe the Covenants Initiative, which more-or-less went into suspended animation when Covid hit, can be accurately characterized as a global movement entirely in line with Traditional Metaphysics, one that incorporates a *theoria* and *praxis* of social justice and social responsibility in no way based on the liberal, atheistic "rights of man" ideologies derived from the French Revolution, but rather on the Mercy and the Justice of God as transmitted by the Judeo-Christian-Islamic prophetic tradition. (The history of the Covenants Initiative, along with its relevance to Perennialism, is laid out below in *Chapter Nine*:

CHAPTER EIGHT

"The Covenants of the Prophet Muhammad as a Valid Exoteric Expression of the Transcendent Unity of Religions: A Call for United Front Ecumenism.")

In the summer of 2020, the Covenants Initiative revealed itself to be highly relevant to the present social upheaval in the United States. While we entirely supported the demand for police reform being advanced by Antifa and Black Lives Matter, the movement associated with these groups soon went far beyond this legitimate grievance in the direction of a widespread anarchism that threatens to destroy civil society, which actually appears to be one of the goals of the movement. Not only that, but one of the elements in this rage to destroy is a growing characterization of Christianity as the enemy. An episcopal church in Washington D.C. was torched by the demonstrators; statues of Christian saints have been attacked in many parts of the country, and the Christians trying to protect them have been assaulted. Furthermore, one of the greatest dangers in this anti-Christian violence is that it could well appeal to those misguided American Muslims who identify with ISIS, people who could too easily be led to see the toppling of Christian statues as no different than the overthrow of the idols inhabiting the Kaaba when the Prophet Muhammad conquered Mecca, even though he reverentially returned to the Christians an Eastern Orthodox icon that was found among them. Those unnamed social engineers who may well be behind the BLM/Antifa uprisings (George Soros has been named as one of their sponsors), the ones who would apparently like to see not only a race war but a war between Christians and Muslims in the United States, may already have thought of that angle. In view of this clear and present danger, it is vital that the Prophetic

CHAPTER EIGHT

Covenants be inserted as a divinely-sanctioned shield between U.S. Christians and their enemies, which is why we are now pressing for the widespread publicizing of the existence, provenance, and rulings of the Prophetic Covenants with all deliberate speed. In view of the evidence suggesting that the global elites are now moving to co-opt, control, and even possibly liquidate the Traditional religions of the earth, a "united front ecumenism" of the religions against their common enemies, based partly on the Prophetic Covenants, should seriously be considered by all who both believe in God and oppose the hegemony of these elites.

July, 2020

NOTE: Rebel Wisdom was a media company/podcast that acted as a platform for psychologically and spiritually-based social critics like Jordan Peterson; it folded in 2022.

CHAPTER NINE

The Covenants of the Prophet Muhammad as a Valid Exoteric Expression of the Transcendent Unity of Religions: A Call for United Front Ecumenism

In 2013 I made the acquaintance of Dr. John Andrew Morrow (Ilyas 'Abd al-'Alim Islam)—a meeting that, as the saying goes, "changed my life." Dr. Morrow is known for his profound, detailed, and ground-breaking research work on the Covenants of Prophet Muhammad with the Christians of his time, and other "peoples of the book." These Covenants, a number of which he has either newly discovered or rescued from obscurity, are treaties that the Prophet concluded with various Christian communities of his time; they uniformly forbid all Muslims to attack or rob or damage the buildings of peaceful Christians—or even prevent their Christian wives from attending Divine Liturgy and taking spiritual direction from their Christian elders—"until the coming of the Hour," the end of the world. The bulk of Dr. Morrow's research to date on these documents appears in his seminal book *The Covenants of the Prophet Muhammad with the Christians of the World* [Angelico/Sophia Perennis, 2013], as well as a three-volume anthology edited by him and entitled *Islam and the People of the Book: Critical Studies of the Covenants of the Prophet* [Cambridge Scholars, 2017]. This much-needed scholarship has gone a long way toward resurrecting the Prophetic Covenants from obscurity, and throwing light on the just and equitable norms the Prophet laid down governing how Muslims were to treat Peoples of the Book and other religious minorities within the growing Islamic State. It has also struck a new chord in interfaith relations, one that is not dependent upon the world-view of secular Liberalism, but springs directly from the Abrahamic tradition itself, as well as providing a powerful ideological weapon to de-legitimize ISIS and other Takfiri terrorist organizations.

Out of Dr. Morrow's scholarly efforts grew an international Muslim/interfaith peace movement known as the Covenants Initiative, whose goal has been to combat terrorist ideology and protect persecuted Christians—a movement which, as of 2019, became the Covenants of the Prophet Foundation. The Initiative (which I initially conceived of) invites Muslims from all walks of life to accept these Covenants as legally binding upon them today. It has been signed by many prominent Muslim scholars, including a representative of al-Azhar University, and has been endorsed by such dignitaries as Ayatullah Khamenei, Supreme Leader of Iran, Pope Francis (through intermediaries such as the

CHAPTER NINE

Caux Round Table) and Bartholomew, Ecumenical Patriarch of the Eastern Orthodox Church.

Islam has a clear doctrine of the nature, goals, and limits of the Lesser Jihad, the intellectual or social or military struggle to defend religion in the outer world; the Catholic tradition too has its equivalent in the doctrine of the "just war." In our own time, however, the war to defend religion must be conceived of not only in terms of the defense of particular religions, but of the struggle for survival of religion itself, in view of the mounting evidence supporting the conclusion that the global elites are implementing a long-term agenda to co-opt, control, and/or destroy all the Traditional religions of the earth.

As I see it, the most accurate picture of the proper relationship between the revealed religions, based on the acceptance of the principle that more than one religion based on a Divine Revelation may be spiritually operative at the same time, is the *relatively* esoteric doctrine that Traditionalist/Perennialist Frithjof Schuon, following René Guénon, called "the Transcendent Unity of Religions," which forms the conceptual center of what has come to be known as the Traditionalist or Perennialist School of traditional metaphysics. The Transcendent Unity of Religions accepts all the great world religions as valid spiritual paths based on Divine Revelation—as indeed the Holy Qur'an allows Muslims to believe, according to the following passages:

> *Verily! Those who believe and those who are Jews and Christians, and Sabians, whoever believes in God and the Last Day and does righteous good deeds shall have their reward with their Lord, on them shall be no fear, nor shall they grieve.* [2:62]

CHAPTER NINE

He has revealed unto you (Muhammad) the Scripture with truth, confirming that which was (revealed) before it, even as He revealed the Torah and the Gospel. [3:3]

Say (O Muhammad): O people of the Scripture: Come to a word that is just between us and you, that we worship none but God, and that we associate no partners with Him, and that none of us shall take others as lords besides God. [3:64]

Say (O Muhammad): We believe in Allah and that which is revealed unto us and that which was revealed unto Abraham and Ishmael and Isaac and Jacob and the tribes, and that which was vouchsafed unto Moses and Jesus and the prophets from their Lord. We make no distinction between any of them, and unto Him we have surrendered. [3:84]

And do not dispute with the followers of the Book except by what is best, except those of them who act unjustly, and say: We believe in that which has been revealed to us and revealed to you, and our God and your God is One, and to Him do we submit. [29:46]

I need to make it clear at this point, however, that I do not consider the Transcendent Unity of Religions to be any kind of Muslim or crypto-Muslim doctrine; if one Revelation is given intrinsic and eternal precedence over the others—in line with the interpretation of the Transcendent Unity of Religions apparently held (for example) by certain "Neo-Traditionalists"—then the essence of that Transcendent Unity is compromised. Nor do I accept this doctrine as positing any kind of superior religious universalism or "quintessential esoterism" (Schuon's phrase) that places the TUR on a level that "transcends" the Divine Revelations—a position taken by Patrick Laude in his book ***Keys to the Beyond: Frithjof Schuon's Cross-Traditional Language of Transcendence*** (see *Chapter Fifteen*). To believe this is to reject Guénonian Traditionalism in favor of the sort of Counter-Traditional Perennialism presently sponsored by the globalist elites.

But does the inner, more-or-less "esoteric" doctrine of the Transcendent Unity of Religions, when it is accepted as in no way exclusively Islamic in nature, also have an outer or "exoteric" expression that is proper to it? Is it a *theoria* capable of generating a valid social *praxis*? In my view, the answer is yes; the reason I can say this is because I have watched the Covenants Initiative, over the course of its development, begin to define a true outward expression and context for interfaith action that is entirely in line with the TUR. Certainly, the Covenants Initiative is inspired by the Prophet of Islam, demonstrating that Muhammad, peace and blessings be upon him, exhibited a more explicit interfaith orientation than the founder of any other revealed religion, except perhaps the archaic Hinduism that could legitimately synthesize the indigenous religions of the Indian subcontinent with the Vedic religion of the Aryan invaders. Nonetheless, the Covenants Initiative claims no intrinsic superiority as a Muslim movement over any compatible ecumenical effort that might emerge from another Traditional faith. Nor has it always been useful to explicitly present the Initiative as a direct manifestation of the Transcendent Unity of Religions, since this term is meaningful only to those who understand and accept the Traditionalist/

CHAPTER NINE

Perennialist perspective. On an official level, the Covenants Initiative is not a Perennialist movement; our founder, Dr. John Andrew Morrow, does not particularly identify as a Perennialist. Nonetheless, if it had not been for my own prior understanding of the TUR, according to the specific interpretation of it that rejects both its identification as a strictly Muslim manifestation and its characterization as a higher doctrine that transcends the "confessional" faiths, seeing it only as a recognition that the revealed religions spring from a common Source and presently face a common challenge—I would never have recognized the Prophetic Covenants as capable of generating an international peace movement that treats all the Traditional religions as distinct and equally valid Divine Revelations, and which can therefore envision a true alliance between them for mutual protection against the Anti-Traditional and Counter-Traditional forces of the secular world.

If the Unity of Religions is truly Transcendent, if the paths of the revealed faiths and primordial wisdom traditions only finally meet at the Center from which they all have emanated—that is, only in God—then any form of interfaith dialogue or secular ecumenism that tends toward a homogenizing of doctrine, that places the discernment of "common ground" between the faiths (certainly a valid ground to define, as long as the strict limits of orthodoxy are preserved) above a recognition of the providential differences between them, is disallowed from the outset: each Divine Revelation is an incomparable expression springing from the Divine Uniqueness. But if this is true, is there any way the faiths can legitimately express their solidarity? Must their intercourse be limited to a simple factual understanding of each

CHAPTER NINE

other's doctrines based on an "agreement to disagree," coupled with a "tolerant" willingness to simply let each other alone?

Since the Transcendent Unity of Religions, though it discerns certain metaphysical principles common to all the faiths, resists any horizontal doctrinal unification, reserving full Unity for the Day when all the Paths return to their origin in the One God, it is necessarily opposed to syncretism; consequently it sees all hopes and plans for world unity based on a One World Religion as both unrealistic in practical terms and either dangerously naïve or spiritually subversive in conceptual terms. In my book *The System of Antichrist: Truth and Falsehood in Postmodernism and the New Age* (Sophia Perennis, 2001) I called for a "united front ecumenism," according to which the world religions, putting aside various increasingly barren attempts to define a doctrinal common ground—while agreeing to disagree (or, as Dr. James Cutsinger phrased it, "disagreeing to agree")—would come together to defend themselves and each other from the forces of false religion and militant secularism that now threaten to destroy them all. I thought I would never have a chance to see such a movement in action until, in 2013, I realized that the Covenants Initiative was a perfect example of the united front ecumenism I had called for in 2001, and that it was in fact a legitimate outer expression of the Transcendent Unity of Religions, in a way that most Liberal ecumenical and interfaith initiatives, with their syncretistic tendencies and their poorly-understood though not entirely clandestine sponsorship by the globalist elites, could never be.

Satan hates all the revealed religions because he recognizes them as emanating a single Divine Source, this Source being the prime Object of his loathing. Thus the Darkness of This World, by that very hatred, testifies to the truth of the Transcendent Unity of Religions, and challenges the religions to form alliances to oppose it. In light of this principle we can begin to see how traditional metaphysics and eschatology could conceivably generate a viable socio-political *praxis* on their own, independent of any Liberal, Libertarian, Fascist, Marxist, Militant Religious Exclusivist, Islamicist, or Globalist ideology, or any permutation or combination thereof. The theoretical foundation of this *praxis* would include the recognition of certain eternal metaphysical Principles, and the vision of history as the working out of these Principles in the dimension of time, largely within the context of a set of unique Divine Revelations. To the degree a person recognizes and understands such Principles, and works to actualize them according to the norms of one of these Revelations, he or she is "in the world but not of it," and consequently is not hampered by an unconscious identification with the realm of relative and ever-changing conditions. Only someone who is not identified with the conditional world, and is therefore free of all partiality, can see that world as it really is. This sort of transcendental objectivity would allow the one who has achieved it to hear and obey the will of God in all his or her dealings with this world, and consequently to formulate strategic initiatives that take into account the entire situation he or she confronts, rather than simply reacting to a limited view of that situation based on belief, obsession, or ideology.

One of the historical ancestors of this kind of metaphysically-based social action is the *praxis* of the Prophet Muhammad, peace and blessing be upon him, as expressed in his Prophetic Covenants, which Muhammad tells us were inspired by Allah

CHAPTER NINE

Himself. As we have already seen, these Covenants, as well as the famous Constitution of Medina, comprise the treaties Muhammad concluded with Christians, Jews, Zoroastrians, and others—and one of their most striking aspects is that they exhibit a nearly seamless union between theocracy and democracy. They are announced and written in the name of Allah and claim divine inspiration as their origin; likewise, they posit the Prophet Muhammad and his legitimate successors as the ultimate authority. On the other hand, they contain God-given laws and norms that even the Prophet had no authority to change or revoke, including what is perhaps the first "universal declaration of human rights" in human history, written down more than a full millennium before what we, looking back to the French and American revolutions, might consider to be "its time." The rights of women and minorities are clearly spelled out; the socio-political implications of the Qur'anic principle of *no compulsion in religion* [Q. 2:256] are fully expressed and defined.

The re-appearance of the Prophetic Covenants in this darkest hour of human history is nothing short of providential. There is no denying that we live in apocalyptic times—which certainly does not mean that we must now "seize the apocalypse" and turn it to our own ends; such a course of action would be both impossible to accomplish and fatal to attempt. In the terminology of the Book of Revelations and the Holy Qur'an, a Third World War (for example) between polarized human collectives such as the United States, the European Union, Russia, or China, would be the final expression of the barren, titanic struggle between the Biblical Gog and Magog—the Qur'anic *Yajuj* and *Majuj*—and would consequently spell the end of the human race. The war between the worldly forces represented by these two titans, a war we are presently immersed in on many levels, is nothing less than the satanic counterfeit of the true eschatological conflict between the Prophet Jesus and *al-Dajjal* (the Antichrist) that figures so prominently in the eschatological *hadith* literature of Islam, or that between the Word of God called Faithful and True—the Rider on the White Horse—and the armies of the Beast in the nineteenth chapter of the ***Apocalypse***. This falsely-conceived imitation of the ultimate eschatological conflict is the archetypal source of the many ideological "imperatives" we are confronted with today—hotly defended intellectual, cultural, or political positions that may seem like true alternatives, but that in reality are all working together to separate humanity from the common vision of our Creator. It is the Devil who draws the sides in our time—and, as Rama Coomaraswamy liked to say (son of the co-founder of the Traditionalist School, Ananda K. Coomaraswamy), "the Devil doesn't care which side of the horse you fall off of." Satan labors to falsely define the various worldly positions we are induced to adopt, and by so doing makes sure that any stance we take will be essentially skewed, and will therefore lead, by the path of self-contradiction, to our ultimate destruction. Only those who have died to this world can know God's true will for the earth, and obey it; only they can tell the difference between the true and false wars.

The re-appearance of the Prophetic Covenants this late in the day, in this darkest of times, is truly mysterious. If adopted by Islamic authorities in the context of present-day conditions they would present nothing less than a blueprint for the fundamental renewal of Islam after the ravages of colonialism, the fall of the Caliphate (and its successor, the Ottoman Sultanate), and the depredations of the Takfiri terrorists and their western and Muslim-national sponsors. In addition—to turn aside for a moment into the more arcane reaches of esoteric historical research—it is even possible that they relate to René Guénon's belief that the Knights Templars were in touch at one point with representatives of the "Primordial Tradition" in Jerusalem, though these holy warriors may later have descended into worldliness and corruption, and that they consequently must have recognized and practiced some form of the Transcendent Unity of Religions. In Dr. John Andrew Morrow's chapter "The Covenant of the Prophet Muhammad with the Armenian Christians of Jerusalem," which appears in ***Islam and the People of the Book: Critical Studies in the Covenants of the Prophet***, he quotes French researcher Bernard Falque de Bezaure as follows:

> These firmans [Covenants of the Prophet] would become ahadith in the Muslim corpus known as the Sunnah and would later be transcribed in the houses of wisdom in Baghdad and Damascus. They later passed into the hands of the Umayyad, 'Abbasid, and Fatimid Caliphs....These are also the documents that were given, in the eleventh century, by Michael, monophysite bishop and patriarch of Antioch [that is, Michael the Syrian (d. 1199 CE), the Armenian Patriarch of Antioch, who was in office from 1166–1199 CE.], to the dynasty of Armenian kings, the Rupenids, and to Mleh, [Prince of Armenia r. 1170–1175 CE], the Master of the Templars of Armenia, in particular, at the same moment that the 'Alawi-

CHAPTER NINE

Hashashin-Nusayri documents entered the chain of Armanus in Sicily. These [latter] documents concern the mysteries of illumination of the ancient Christian and Jewish prophets as well as Muhammad. They represent the foundations and the basis of the secret spiritual meditations that were given by Hugues de Payens, the ordained priest of the Saint Sepulcher, to the thirty-one proto-Templars cited in the Armenian chronicles of the aforementioned Michael the Syrian.

Dr. Morrow goes on to say: "Bernard Falque de Bezaure advances another astonishing and audacious theory; namely, that the secrets granted, and jealously guarded, protected, and transmitted by the Knights Templar and other secretive Christian societies, consisted of the Covenants of the Prophet Muhammad. Since the Dome of the Rock [occupied by the Templars during the Crusades] contains some of the most ancient examples of early Arabic and Islamic writing, it is also likely that the complex contained precious documents from the dawn of Islam, including, apparently, copies of the Muhammadan Covenants." If true, this would certainly go a long way toward corroborating Guénon's belief that the Templars were in some sense the "guardians of the Primordial Tradition," earlier exponents of one version of the Transcendent Unity of Religions.

According to Islamic tradition, a "renewer of the religion" is destined to appear at "the head of every century"—and certainly the Covenants of the Prophet continue to spread widely through the Muslim world, often eliciting a heart-warming and enthusiastic response. However, from the practical, worldly point of view of cultural analysis and *realpolitik*, the prospects for a total renewal of

CHAPTER NINE

Islam at this late date (for nothing less is required) do not look very promising. All the Traditional religious collectives are in a state of retreat due to the "degeneration of the cosmic environment" discerned and predicted by René Guénon for the latter days of the cycle, and the Islamic *ummah* is no exception. Nonetheless we must always remember that things that are difficult or impossible for us are easy for God: if He wills a renewal of Islam at this late date, then it will come to pass.

However, two other possible goals, one moral, the other eschatological, may be discerned for God's clear command that the Prophetic Covenants reappear in our time. The first would be to give individual Muslims a chance to repent of the hatred of the other God-given religions that has been instilled in them by the kind of corrupt and treacherous religious scholars that the *hadith* literature warns us against. The second would be to prepare a Remnant from Islam—not necessarily limited to the Shi'a—to actively await the coming of the Mahdi, who will establish justice and true religion, and for the Prophet Jesus, who will slay *al-Dajjal* the Deceiver, the Antichrist.

Some Christians have been understandably suspicious of our rediscovery of the Covenants of the Prophet; it seems to them as if these documents might represent a covert attempt to re-introduce the notion of an Islamic Empire under which Christians would be relegated to *dhimmi* (protected minority) status once again. Our position, however, is that the Covenants possess a relevance and a force-of-law that transcends dhimmitude, since the Prophet declared them to be in force and incumbent upon all Muslims "until the coming of the Hour," not simply until the fall of the Ottoman Empire, the last Muslim political entity that took the

CHAPTER NINE

Covenants as the basis of official policy toward non-Muslim religious minorities. And it is clear that the Covenants of the Prophet incarnate Muhammad's great love and respect for the Peoples of the Book—Christians in particular—which is entirely in line with the teachings of the Noble Qur'an. On the basis of these documents, the signatories of the Covenants Initiative, as Muslims, offer the following pledge to Christians:

> *We the undersigned hold ourselves bound by the spirit and the letter of the covenants of the Prophet Muhammad (peace and blessings be upon him) with the Christians of the world, in the understanding that these covenants, if accepted as genuine, have the force of law in the shari'ah today and that nothing in the shari'ah, as traditionally and correctly interpreted, has ever contradicted them. As fellow victims of the terror and godlessness, the spirit of militant secularism and false religiosity now abroad in the world, we understand your suffering as Christians through our suffering as Muslims, and gain greater insight into our own suffering through the contemplation of your suffering. May the Most Merciful of the Merciful regard the sufferings of the righteous and the innocent; may He strengthen us, in full submission to His will, to follow the spirit and the letter of the Covenants of the Prophet Muhammad with the Christians of the world in all our dealings with them. In the name of Allah, Most Gracious, Most Merciful. Praise be to Allah, the Cherisher and Sustainer of the worlds.*

CHAPTER NINE

This pledge, which forms the heart of the Covenants Initiative, has been signed by many Muslim scholars and religious leaders from around the world. We believe that the Initiative, as well as our ongoing scholarship related to the Covenants of the Prophet Muhammad which continues to bring new ancient documents to light, can serve to powerfully validate and support such allied initiatives as the Amman Message issued by the Kingdom of Jordan in 2004, as well as the collective *fatwa* of the "International Conference on Who are the Ahl al-Sunnah," promulgated in Grozny, Chechnya, in August of 2016, and the "*Fatwa* on Dangerous Sects" of The Council of Muftis of Russia, issued at the same time, both of which make it abundantly clear that the Salafi-Takfirists, including Da'esh—the so-called "Islamic State," otherwise known as ISIS—al-Qaeda, Boko Haram, and similar extremist groups, are firmly outside the Islamic fold.

An unbiased study of the Prophetic Covenants, as well as of the Constitution of Medina, should make it clear that it was the intent of the Prophet Muhammad, peace and blessings be upon him, to found a federation of the Peoples of the Book as an act of united front ecumenism for mutual defense against that federation's common enemies: the Byzantine Empire (insofar as it attacked Islam and oppressed various marginalized Christian communities), the Persian Empire, and the pagan Quraysh of Mecca. And as in the Prophet's time, so in ours: Judaism, Christianity, and Islam, as well as Hinduism, Buddhism, and other traditional religions, are presently under attack from many directions—cultural, ideological, socio-political, terroristic, and military. It is certainly common knowledge that these attacks are taking place—but do we know exactly who is behind them in every case? We assume (correctly) that some are based on hereditary feuds between the Traditional faiths, that others are the result of anti-religious policies by governments like that of Communist China, and that still others are the work of "lone gunmen." But do we actually have a theoretical basis for these assumptions backed up by a sound body of research? For example, assuming we are willing to admit that some attacks on churches in the West are carried out by Satanists, are we willing and able to investigate exactly who these so-called "Satanists" might be, their ideological histories, their sources of funding? And what about the possibility that some attacks against houses of worship are really false flags designed to turn one religion against another, possibly under the ultimate sponsorship of the globalist elites? Do we ever even ask if this might be so, much less carry on any serious research into this possibility?

When the Covenants Initiative made its debut at the Bilal Mosque in Lexington, Kentucky in 2013, I expressed my belief that forces exist in the world today that are actively attempting to foment conflict between the religions in order to weaken them. In response, a Muslim from the Indian sub-continent told the story of those nights in his native city when pig carcasses were thrown into mosques and slaughtered cows dragged into Hindu temples, predictably resulting in Muslim/Hindu riots the next day; needless to say, it was quite obvious to him that such actions were not planned for the same nights by Hindus and Muslims working in unison, but were perpetrated by unknown third parties. This and many other indications suggest that the likely meta-strategy of the global elites is to co-opt and neutralize ALL the religions. After all, why should an elite cadre of oligarchs backed by global

CHAPTER NINE

finance who aspire to world domination sit back and do nothing when the beliefs and aspirations and moral standards of billions of people are determined by "outmoded" religious institutions that those oligarchs do not control?

Evidence exists that the globalist elites are now subjecting the traditional religions of the earth to a two-pronged attack: on the one hand, they are sponsoring a global interfaith movement that subtly pressures the faiths to de-emphasize any "divisive" doctrines in the name of interfaith friendship, even if these doctrines are foundational to the faiths in question, thereby weakening their doctrinal and moral fabric; on the other hand, by both military action and false flag terror operations, they are turning the faiths against each other and so setting them up for mutual destruction. A Muslim leader who wishes to remain anonymous reported to us that, at a meeting at the Obama White House in 2016, a delegation of Muslim leaders was told the following by the National Security Adviser: "ISIS is now losing territory in Syria and Iraq, therefore ISIS fighters will be coming *home* to the United States. Muslim leaders, we want your help in *reintegrating these fighters into U.S. society*, for which Federal grant funds are available." On hearing this, the Muslim leader in question said to himself: "Doesn't this woman realize that ISIS has a hit list of U.S. Muslim leaders, some of whom are in this room right now?" It is clear from this and many other indications that at one point the U.S. government was sponsoring terrorist mercenaries under the banners of al-Nusra, the Free Syrian Army, and Da'esh in Syria and Iraq, just as it had trained and armed the Salvadoran death squads in the 1980s. Given that no actual record (as far as we know) of that White House meeting exists,

CHAPTER NINE

we began scouring the web for evidence of a government plan to reintegrate ISIS fighters into U.S. society; our findings appear in Dr. John Andrew Morrow's article "Welcome Home ISIS! The Obama Administration's Plan to Reintegrate Foreign Terrorist Fighters": [https://www.globalresearch.ca/welcome-home-isis-the-obama-administrations-plan-to-reintegrate-foreign-terrorist-fighters/5563476]

A lesson drawn from my own experience may further illustrate this two-pronged strategy: at the very same time the U.S. Obama Administration was providing funding, training, and logistical support to terrorist organizations such as al-Nusra and the Free Syrian Army, as well as elements of ISIS, in an attempt to bring down the Assad regime and menace Iran—organizations that have massacred countless Christians, Yezidis, Sufis, Shi'ites, and traditional Sunni Muslims—the Christian/Muslim Dialogue in my home town of Lexington, Kentucky was hosting speakers from the FBI, the Federal Attorneys' Office, Homeland Security, and the State Department, all preaching the eternal virtues of interfaith friendship!

In any case, we are all well aware by now of the growing number of attacks on churches, mosques, and synagogues around the world, including North America. In view of the uncertain origin of many of these attacks, and the possibility that at least some of them are being carried out by forces dedicated to subverting all the traditional faiths, I believe a vigorous response based on united front ecumenism is clearly called for. The virtue of this kind of ecumenism, as opposed to the more familiar form of Liberal ecumenism, is that it leaves the foundational doctrines of the different religions intact, concentrating instead on the practical work of mutual defense against common enemies. And the metaphysical implication here is that because the forces inimical to religion, whether or not they are working together on a given occasion, all recognize a common threat to their various agendas in the Traditional religions of the earth, these religions must possess a mysterious unity-of-standpoint that transcends their obvious doctrinal differences. In other words, rather than attempting to establish a conceptual unity of religions, united front ecumenism posits their existential unity on a plane transcending form. It is precisely this orientation that makes such ecumenism a proper outward expression of the Transcendent Unity of Religions.

Nonetheless, whether or not the doctrine of the Transcendent Unity of Religions ultimately forms part of a comprehensive theoretical response to the spectrum of anti-religious attacks we are seeing today, we believe that the religions should begin, with all deliberate speed, to develop plans for the establishment of a united front ecumenism for mutual aid and defense, while at the same time intensively investigating the possibility that outside forces might be acting to infiltrate religious organizations, co-opt them, and turn them against each other. The established interfaith movement, heavily sponsored by the globalist elites (see ***False Dawn: The United Religions Initiative, Globalism and the Quest for a One-World Religion*** by Lee Penn) operates according to the paradigm that the religions should concentrate on dialoguing with one another, not one that directs them to investigate the motives and funding-sources of those non-religious third parties—national governments, extra-governmental foundations, and think-tanks, etc.—who often support such dialogue. Likewise, today's interfaith world does not seem overly willing to expend

CHAPTER NINE

much time or energy in determining whether the various groups who espouse anti-religious ideologies in today's world might actually be practicing what they preach by secretly mounting physical attacks against the faiths they so openly despise. In this age of anti-religious violence, due diligence in these areas is obviously called for—especially in view of the fact that the tactic of creating conflict between religions in order to control populations has a long and well-documented history. Joachim Hagopian, in "Divide and Conquer: The Globalist Pathway to New World Order Tyranny", speaks of:

> ....the retention of power by utilizing a deliberate strategy of causing those in subordinate positions to engage in conflicts with each other that weaken and keep them from any unified effort to remove the status quo force from power. . . . This divide and conquer stratagem was frequently repeated by European colonial powers, typically pitting competitive tribal, ethnic, and religious factions against each other to ensure they would not conspire to revolt against the ruling imperialists. In Asia the British took full advantage of Muslims versus Hindus in India as well as creating conflict between Indians and Pakistanis. [Entire article available from Global Research, October, 23, 2015: https://www.global-research.ca/divide-and-conquer-the-globalist-pathway-to-new-world-order-tyranny-from-a-geopolitics-perspective/5483935]

If such tactics are indeed being practiced on a global scale, with the goal of reducing nearly the entire population of the

CHAPTER NINE

earth to quasi-colonial status, the doctrine of the Transcendent Unity of Religions could function as the guiding principle around which a true united front ecumenism to oppose this universal re-colonialization might develop. Such an ecumenism would only succeed, however, if this Unity were understood as truly Transcendent, not as a worldly doctrinal or political unification of the religions on the horizontal plane to establish some version of a One-World Religion, an *ecclesia* that would inevitably fall into the hands of the globalist elites, if it was not in fact established by them in the first place. This, unfortunately, is one of the more common misunderstandings of the Transcendent Unity of Religions, an inversion-of-meaning that is likely being promoted—according to the principle of *corruptio optimi pessima*, "the corruption of the best is the worst"—by the globalist elites themselves. According to the metaphysical relationship of the Many and the One, the manifestation of the Transcendent One in the relative world is necessarily multiple, since this is the nature of relativity itself. The clear implication of this is that an enforced unification of the Many is impossible, since the One is truly Transcendent, and also unnecessary, since the One is Immanent in all things. If this principle were fully grasped, then the Transcendent Unity of Religions, God willing, could become the Pole Star around which the constellations of God's several Divine Self-revelations to humanity, for this cycle of manifestation, might continue to turn, shedding their saving Light on the human race, until the consummation of the age.

> *Those groups or individuals who wish to know more about the Covenants Initiative, the Covenants the of the Prophet Muhammad, and how these Covenants*

CHAPTER NINE

might be used in an interfaith setting to further united front ecumenism, may be interesting in taking the self-administered "Covenants of the Prophet Training Course": https://covenants-oftheprophet.org/the-covenants-course/

CHAPTER TEN

Toward a Brotherhood of Silence: A Response to "Fraternity for Knowledge and Cooperation"

[This article first appeared in *Dilatato Corde*, Volume XI, Number 1 the journal of Monastic Interreligious Dialogue, 2021]

Having been born and raised a Roman Catholic, during which time I spent 14 years in Catholic school (my only formal education) in a basically pre-Vatican II church—a church which I left, or which possibly left me, in the 1960s—and having embraced Islam and Islamic Sufism in 1988, the publication in 2019 of the highly significant document "Fraternity for Knowledge and Cooperation"—produced under the direction of Shaykh Yahya Pallavicini of the Comunità Religiosa Islamica Italiana, a major "civic shaykh" of Italy as well as a follower of René Guénon—

CHAPTER TEN

has left me with a vivid spectrum of feelings, some radiant and harmonious, others filled with uncertainty and foreboding.

The document in question is a response to the unprecedented rapprochement between the present Catholic Pope, Francis, and Ahmed el-Tayeb, the Grand Imam of Al-Azhar, the highest authority in traditional Sunni Islam after the fall of the Caliphate, and the later fall (in 1922) of its partial successor, the Sultanate of the Ottoman Empire. This reconciliation resulted in the signing of a truly ground-breaking agreement, "Document on Human Fraternity for World Peace and Living Together," which has taken the interfaith world by storm, not to mention the world of religion as a whole.

"Fraternity for Knowledge and Cooperation" can be understood as a commentary on the "Fraternity for World Peace" from a more metaphysical, more spiritual standpoint, and thus as a necessary complement to the latter document. "Fraternity for World Peace" deals with the outer, socio-political world—in Arabic, the *zahir*—while "Fraternity for Knowledge" has more to do with the inner world, the theological, metaphysical, and contemplative dimension—in Arabic, the *batin*. As Allah declares in the Holy Qur'an, *I am the First and the Last, the Inner and the Outer* [Q. 57:3].

That the Catholic Church, or at least a portion of it, has apparently reached the point of concluding a near-alliance with traditional Sunni Islam—a religion often considered, not without reason, to be the hereditary enemy of Christendom—is both a radiant sign and a grave omen—but a sign or omen of what? What does this apparent rapprochement portend for the two religions, both of them Divine Revelations, of Christianity and Islam?

CHAPTER TEN

Since the birth of Christianity, two thousand years ago, the Church has survived by clearly distinguishing itself from the paganism of late antiquity and its numerous cults; from the many competing theological doctrines of those theologians who came to be classed as heretics, most having to do with the nature of Christ and the Holy Trinity; from later theological separatist movements such as the Albigensian/Bogomil counter-church of the Middle Ages and the Protestant Reformation; from the subversive infiltration of anti-clerical Freemasonry and atheistic Communism; and from This World in general. It was only by standing aloof—though far from perfectly!—from the Darkness of This World and the Rulers of it, however these forces may have been conceived, that the Church was able to save herself from destruction at the hands of its many enemies, both within and without, according to the promise of Christ in the Gospels that "the Gates of Hell shall not prevail against it" [Matthew 16:18].

This attitude of deliberate and principled aloofness, though radically compromised on many occasions by various geopolitical involvements which were nonetheless unable to entirely extinguish it, had its inception in the first 300 years of Christian history. While Islam broke forth upon the world as a mighty spiritual, cultural, and military impulse, an impulse that spread through half of the known world in the space of a single generation, conquering the Persian Empire, filling the power vacuum left by the fall of the western Roman Empire and the waning strength of Byzantium, Christianity lay under oppression by Rome for a full three centuries—an oppression which, while certainly legal and political, was also cultural, theological, and spiritual. The early church had to contend not only with martyrdom in the arena but with the seemingly endless attempts to water down the person, nature, and mission of Jesus Christ, peace and blessings be upon him. Nonetheless the fact remains that virtually every religious cult in the entire compass of early Christianity—even the Greek Mystery cults and the Neo-Platonic revival—failed to measure up to the profundity, the spiritual and cultural power, the sheer mercy of the Divine Revelation that was Jesus Christ. And this state of affairs, in which Christianity in Western Europe and the Levant was, with entire legitimacy, lord of all it surveyed spiritually speaking, held good (leaving aside certain "esoteric" communications in the interfaith dimension) all the way into the nineteenth century. It was only then that such influences as colonialism and missionary activity finally brought Christendom face-to-face with other world-civilization-creating Divine revelations, both older and newer, that for the first time could fully match it both culturally and spiritually, these being Vedantic Hinduism, Buddhism, and at least the bare beginnings of a true understanding of Islam: its magnificent art and architecture, its pre-eminent mathematicians and scientists and astronomers and physicians, its profound philosophers and theologians, and—last but not least—its exquisite poets, master-singers like Rumi and Hafiz, who began to open the European soul not only to the beauties of Persian and Arabic verse but to the wonders and mysteries of Sufism. This was the first and most fruitful opening, though not without its tragedies (unless we count the Crusades, rich in tragedy as well) of the Christian West to the soul of Asia—an opening that neither the Catholic Church nor the Western World as a whole has yet fully learned to evaluate, assimilate, and effectively respond to.

CHAPTER TEN

To the Muslims, Jesus was and is a prophet ("is" because he is expected to return at the coming of the Hour, the end of time, to slay *al-Dajjal* the Antichrist)—a prophet who is, according to one perspective, pre-eminent over all others in the dimension of the *batin*, the Inner, thus—according to the doctrines of the greatest Sufi Shaykh, Ibn al-'Arabi—making him the "Seal of Sanctity," just as Muhammad, peace and blessings be upon him, is pre-eminent in his ability to encompass both *batin* and *zahir*, both the Inner and the Outer, by virtue of his unique synthesis of mystical teaching and social law-giving, a synthesis that earned him in Ibn al-'Arabi's system the title "Seal of Prophecy." To the non-Christian Jews, on the other hand, Jesus was a renegade, an apostate from Mosaic Judaism, while to the pagans he seemed to be little more than another rendition of one of their many gods, particularly dying-and-resurrected gods of fertility like Attis or Adonis or Osiris; or of Dionysus, who established wine as a sacrament and who, like Jesus, was also called "the Vine"; or of Orpheus, who descended into the underworld as Jesus did to rescue a lost soul; or of the Persian deity Mithras, who, also like Jesus, was named "The Good Shepherd." Why, the Roman authorities must have asked themselves, did these Christians so intransigently resist the syncretism that had made all the other gods, gods of Rome's conquered and colonized peoples, good citizens of the Empire, worthy of civic cults and statues in the Roman Pantheon? What could this kind of aloofness and zealotry portend but a subversive intention with regard to Rome, a seditious agenda to violate the *Pax Romana*? (There had even been talk of offering the Jews a statue of Yah-weh in the Pantheon, and some of them had apparently warmed to this proposition, until the Jewish Revolt put an end to that "hopeful" possibility.)

CHAPTER TEN

And now these Christians, founded by a Jew, show themselves to be even more aloof and clannish than the Jews themselves! Obviously they must be up to no good.

Jesus, however, was not Adonis, or Attis, or Osiris, or Dionysus, or Orpheus, or Mithras. The Christians called him the Only-Begotten Son of God, as later the Muslims, who accept the doctrine of the Virgin Birth, would call him (in the words of the Qur'an), not Allah, certainly, but nonetheless *His word which He conveyed unto Mary*, and *a spirit from Him* [Q. 4:171]. Nor was Jesus merely a myth, a symbolic idea—though he was certainly also that; he, like Moses and Muhammad, was born into history, and transformed history. But if, for the first oppressed and suffering 300 years of their own history, the Christians had submitted to imperial Rome and denied the uniqueness and transcendental supremacy of Jesus Christ, under both the cruel persecution and also undoubtedly the exasperated but friendly persuasion of the surrounding pagan world, there would have been no Catholic Church—no church which, until 1054, was one with what is now called Eastern Orthodox Christianity, which together constituted the One, Holy, Universal, and Apostolic Church of Christ—and consequently no fraternal embrace (wherever we may place it on the spectrum between sincerity and hypocrisy) between His Holiness Pope Francis and Ahmed el-Tayeb, Grand Imam of Al-Azhar.

So—is the aloofness of the Catholic Church now at an end? And if so, what will this mean for the flourishing, for the integrity, for the very survival of Roman Catholicism? Is this the Great Triumph of Universal Truth, or the Great Apostasy that at least the traditional Catholics have been living in fear of ever since

CHAPTER TEN

the Second Vatican Council, a seemingly well-founded fear that has brought the Roman Catholic Church nearer to a true schism than at any time since AD 1054?

As for the first possibility, perhaps identifiable in some ways with Joachim de Fiore's doctrine of the Age of the Holy Spirit, the final Age of the world that is destined to conclude the tripartite cycle that began with the Age of the Father (the Old Testament) and the Age of the Son (the New Testament), this possibility of an eschatological unveiling of the Transcendent Unity of Religions before the coming of the Hour is dealt with as follows by the Traditionalist/Perennialist author and Jewish convert to Islam, Leo Schaya, writing from the perspective of Jewish esoterism:

> According to Jewish tradition, the entire Torah of Moses amounts to no more than a single line of the **Sepher ha-Yasher** [the "Book of Justice" which Elias will bring with him, comparable in some ways to the **Umm al-Kitab** in Islam, "the Mother of the Book"], which means that this Book, by virtue of not being "scriptural" but "operative" in nature, will be the veritable final accomplishment of Scripture, the "realization" which by definition goes immeasurably beyond the "letter." At the same time, Judaism tacitly places the remaining "lines" of this "Book" at the disposal of all the Divine revelations, whatever they may be, each one formulating or announcing in its fashion the same Eternal Truth and the same Destiny of man and the world. The "Book" of Elias is the integral Wisdom of the unanimous Tradition and

CHAPTER TEN

the eschatological Manifestation of the one and only Principle. For the Jews, Elias represents the transition from traditional exclusiveness to the universality which they too possess, since they affirm that the Tishbite will raise his voice so loud to announce the spiritual peace that it will be heard from one end of the earth to the other; and the Doctors of the Law teach that "the righteous of all nations have a portion in the life to come" or, again, that "all men who are not idolaters can be considered Israelites." Elias must re-establish all things in the name of, and for the sake of, that spiritual "peace" which the Messiah will bring once and for all: it will be crystallized forever in the New Jerusalem "founded by—or for—peace," according to the etymology of Yerushalem or Yerushalaim. Elias came down, and has come down for centuries, to the world below to prepare, with the concurrence of those he inspires, this final state of humanity. He reveals, little by little and more intensively and generally toward the end, the spiritual and universal essence, the transcendent unity of all authentic religions. It is as if the radiant city were being patiently built by putting one luminous stone after another into place. The motivating power of this task can be called the "Eliatic flow," at least in the orbit of the Judeo-Christian tradition, whereas other traditions will each use their own terms to describe this same universal flow. According to the terminology of Jewish esotericism, this flow belongs to the "river of highest Eden," the "river of Yobel" or "great Jubilee" which is final

CHAPTER TEN

Deliverance. Revelations calls it "the river of the water of life, clear as crystal" (Rev. 22:1); it will be crystallized in the "precious stones," the unquenchable lights of the New Jerusalem. ["The Mission of Elias", *Studies in Comparative Religion*, vol. 14, Numbers 3 & 4, 165–66]

The doctrine of "the Book of Elias" is strictly paralleled by the Shi'ite Muslim doctrine that when al-Mahdi emerges from his occultation he will bring a new Book. That this Book represents the Primordial Tradition itself, which transcends the revealed traditions without negating them, is indicated by the tradition that the Mahdi will "rule the people of the Torah according to the Torah, and the people of the Gospel according to the Gospel, and the people of the Qur'an according to the Qur'an." [Nasir al-Din Tusi, ***Ghayba***]. We must never forget, however, that the Satanic counterfeit of the Great Jubilee is the Regime of Antichrist, whose "unity of religions," like the one nearly established by Nimrod before God decreed the failure of the Tower of Babel, will be a horizontal, worldly unity, not a vertical and transcendental one—not a unity of Truth but merely a unity of Power. Now that inexorable historical forces have broken all the religions out of their traditional matrices and forced them into confrontation, now that "pluralism" is not only an idealistic hope but also, for good or ill, an inescapable fate, the great question in the field of religion is: What kind of "unity" or "pluralism" will we end up with? Will it be a true spiritual unity based on a great Latter Day unveiling of the Primordial Tradition, or a cynical, corrupt, and ruthlessly enforced unification of the religions, accomplished by tempting them to embrace a worldly pseudo-spirituality, and

CHAPTER TEN

by backing up that temptation with the overt or implied threat of violent persecution if the temptation is rejected—a *Dajjalian* pseudo-unity established in the name of global hegemony and mass control of populations? Which way will it go?

One of the watchwords of Vatican II and the Post-Conciliar Church, now 60 years old, has been reconciliation with the world according to the principle of *aggiornamento*, "bringing up to date." What was once to be vigorously rejected—according to Catholic doctrine if not always Catholic practice—namely that regime which the Muslims call *al-Dunya* and the Christians "This World," is now to be embraced. "Worldliness" is no longer a vice but a virtue. "Modernism" is no longer, in the words of Pope Pius X, "the synthesis of all heresies," but the inescapable keynote of our time, not something to be fearfully rejected but rather to be courageously and creatively engaged with. Consequently, in light of this 180-degree turn of the Catholic Church, if not against its 2000-year history, at least against the triumphal and imperial Church of the Counter-Reformation, all vigilant Muslims must ask the following question: Has the Catholic Church under Francis embraced Islam by at long last recognizing it as a brother Revelation in the great prophetic family of the Abrahamic religions, sent in the form of the Holy Qur'an to the Prophet Muhammad by the same God who sent Jesus Christ into the womb of the Virgin Mary? Or has he reached out to Islam merely as another "demographic grouping" or "socio/political/cultural sector" of This World? Is his unprecedented gesture a sign of the event foreseen for these latter days by the prophet Joel in the Old Testament, when (and this is God Himself speaking), "I will pour out My Spirit on all flesh, and your sons and daughters shall prophesy, and your young men shall see visions, and your old men shall dream dreams"? [Joel 2:28] Or is it little more than a diplomatic coup, a gesture—though diplomatically clothed in religious language—that is limited to the world of politics, a word I like to define as "the art of the ephemeral"?

The profound significance of "Fraternity for Knowledge and Cooperation" lies precisely in the fact that, while celebrating—as all Christians and Muslims of good will must—the great potential good that may come out of this apparent détente between Islam and Roman Catholicism, as represented by "Document on Human Fraternity for World Peace and Living Together," it eloquently poses this very question:

> Beyond our generally positive reaction to the Document, it also seems necessary to make some cautious reflections, in the form of a warning with regards to a latent danger....that the values mentioned by the Document, and recalled in this comment, might be interpreted or practiced in a partial or excessive way, outside the field for which they were designed by the Creator....
>
> Fraternity in diversity is the cornerstone of the text, but there is a danger that this concept might be interpreted in too sociological or psychological a sense. In this case we would be left with a solely human, "too human" interpretation of religious fraternity, according to which man would be adored as he is, worshiped instead of God, despite the continued use of the word "God" as a mere formality, a word no longer referring to a

Reality that we aspire to know. A respect for differences should not become an excuse for the adoration of the particular and the phenomenal in and of itself, where contingency replaces the Eternal.

Remember when religion was spiritual? Remember when the basic idea of religious life was to avoid sin, cultivate virtue, and prepare one's soul for Paradise? The social interpretation of the nature and function of religion, which both Islam and Christianity have approached, and continue to approach, from their own characteristic starting-points, has always been part of the religious worldview, but it has never been the primary or central one—except in periods of turmoil and decadence. Jesus specifically enjoined "corporal work of mercy" for his followers, such as visiting the sick, feeding the hungry, and sheltering the homeless—and yet he made it very clear that "The poor you have always with you," [Mark 14:7] and "My Kingdom is not of this world." [John 18:36]. Likewise, Muhammad, through the institution of the *zakat*, the obligatory tithe for the maintenance of widows and orphans, the poor and the infirm, might be considered to have founded (all negative connotations of the term aside) the first "welfare state." Yet he and the Holy Qur'an repeatedly emphasize the brevity of life and the relative unreality of earthly existence, while orienting the entire aspiration of the Islamic *ummah* toward the attainment of Paradise in the *akhira*, the next world. (The Sufis, of course, interpret this aspiration in a radically *batini* sense by recognizing the next world as mysteriously present already within this present world, in the depths of the spiritual Heart.)

CHAPTER TEN

There is a strange and unrealistic prejudice afoot in our contemporary world which holds that "other-worldliness" implies a cold indifference toward, if not an active hatred of, the earth, the body and the human race. Nothing could be further from the truth. True other-worldliness is inseparable from a keen sense of the Mercy of God, a Mercy that can't help but overflow in works of Mercy, both corporal and spiritual. Those who consider this material world to be all there is are generally (though not always) avaricious, cynical, and grasping, conditions that are ultimately based on the despair of life and the fear of death that lie at the roots of the materialist worldview; their contracted affections and sensibilities usually allow them little scope for heartfelt compassion. On the other hand, those who place their hopes in Eternity rather than time, and who have consequently renounced the useless struggle to satisfy the inherently Divine aspirations of the human soul within a shrunken material world that can in no way correspond to them, are free to shower that world with the Divine Bounty they feel themselves to be in the presence of, and are unreservedly open to receiving. Far from believing that "there is only so much compassion to go around," they recognize that the generosity of God has no end; in Islamic terms they live and act according to *Bismillah al-Rahman al-Rahim*, performing everything "in the name of God, the all-Merciful, the all-Compassionate." Yet the direct love of God (*Mahabbah*) and knowledge of Him (*Ma'rifa*) are recognized, in both Islam and Christianity, as intrinsically higher and more central than "good works." St. Thomas Aquinas classed the contemplative life as a higher calling than the active life; and though he saw the "mixed" life in which contemplation and action are united as the highest station of all—a life quintessentially exemplified

CHAPTER TEN

by the Prophet Muhammad, peace and blessings be upon him—he nonetheless continued to place contemplation on a higher plane than action, since he considered the action of the activist/contemplative as being a direct overflow from the depth of his or her contemplation, not the other way around. Even the paradigmatic modern Christian "sister of mercy," Mother Theresa, immediately left the bedside of whatever ill or dying person she had been attending when the bell rang for prayer, because prayer and nothing else was the source of her ability to console the suffering.

The authors of "Fraternity for Knowledge and Cooperation" see interfaith dialogue as capable of taking place on three distinct levels:

> From our point of view there are three types of dialogue between faiths: one of convenience, one of reality, and one of principle. The dialogue of convenience aims to avoid all thorny issues, it is a false, vague, horizontal approach, one that abolishes traditional doctrines, sacred symbols and ways of grace; in order to reconcile two adversaries it suffocates them both; this is certainly the quickest way to achieve a false peace that has been substituted for truth. Inspired by a philosophical indifference, or by a relativist universalism, the characteristic of this dialogue is the dissolving of values. This is a false dialogue because instead of recognizing and supporting religions and their sacred foundations, it ends up providing a cheap conception of human rights, above all promoting, in the place of true spirituality, the "right to indifference".

CHAPTER TEN

A second type of dialogue we might call "de facto" or "reality based": this consists of an understanding of religious people and the institutions that represent them on the basis of their common acceptance of certain moral values and metaphysical concepts, and in the understanding that they are faced with the common threat of secularization. This is the type of interreligious dialogue upon which the Document mainly focuses: "Dialogue among believers means coming together in the vast space of spiritual, human and shared social values and, from here, transmitting the highest moral virtues that religions aim for." Justice, goodness, beauty, fraternity and peace on the social level are "anchors of salvation" for all, but they can certainly not be substituted for the salvation of the soul, just as the means are not a substitute for the end. It is a matter of creating conditions for a shared and necessary peace such as Dante strove for, so that it is possible for all to live a life oriented to the search for God, the highest and last objective that mankind can aspire to.

This type of dialogue constitutes a necessary step towards the third type of dialogue, which we see as the most desirable of all. This last type of dialogue can be called the one of "principle", or "dialogue at the summit": it consists in recognizing the mode of Knowledge that discovers the one Truth above the veil of multiple forms. Saint Basil, commenting on the beginning of the Gospel of Saint John, exclaimed,

CHAPTER TEN

"Don't forget 'In the Beginning'! The culmination of the Principle cannot be understood while that which is outside of the Principle cannot be found." To reach this objective, the one we consider to be of the greatest worth, there appears to be a long way to go.

These three levels of dialogue might be briefly summarized by naming them the Socio-Political, the Intellectual (in the sense of *ratio* or *'aql*, not that of *Intellectus* or *Ma'rifa*), and the Contemplative. The "Document on Human Fraternity for World Peace and Living Together" seems primarily oriented to the second form of dialogue, while in no way remaining immune to the danger of lapsing into the first, into the "dialogue of convenience." This is a negative potential that menaces all interfaith dialogue in our time, given the fear of inflaming interreligious conflict and the general inability of the human psyche to remain for long in a state of paradox or ambiguity without experiencing either a paralyzing existential anxiety or else capitulating, in order to allay this anxiety, to shallow, facile, or disingenuous solutions.

As for the third and highest form of dialogue, the Contemplative, I don't believe we should wait until a directive to pursue this course comes to us from this or that established religious authority, particularly in times like these. Such an engagement will most likely be initiated by the contemplatives themselves: for the Roman Catholics, the monks of the contemplative orders; for the Muslims, the Sufis. About the potential for this rarest kind of interfaith action—which, though necessarily employing forms, must be grounded in the Formless dimension of the Divine Unity—the "Fraternity for Knowledge and Cooperation" document has this to say:

CHAPTER TEN

For persons who are sensitive to spirituality and contemplation, to support one another in exclusively material or sentimental terms is neither true support nor true fraternity. We need to cultivate mutual respect between our different communities on the basis of our common proclamation that God as One, helping each other to remember that our central aim is to honor the name of the Lord, especially in the difficult times that our humanity is now passing through. It is for the attainment of this goal, as interreligious relations and Islamo-Christian dialogue continues, that we find it important and opportune to give wider expression to certain actors who could truly play a prominent role—namely, the contemplative orders, that is to say the Christian monastic orders and the Sufi orders of Islam, those who are custodians and cultivators, in different forms and at different levels, of the contemplation of God, since it is from this perspective that they call one another "brothers."

This dialogue between contemplatives in the spirit of a higher brotherhood is one that was both posited and actively engaged in by perhaps the most famous Roman Catholic contemplative of the twentieth century, Father Thomas Merton, who was in active correspondence and interaction with Qadiri *fuqara*, Eastern Orthodox hesychasts, and Tibetan Buddhists (among others), and whose Cistercian (Trappist) monastery, the Abbey of Gethsemani, is near enough to my home in central Kentucky to have become a congenial space for short meditative retreats by my wife and myself. Merton's example, however, stands not only as a model but also as a warning, since he was apparently unable to open to other religions without losing his hold on his Catholic faith. According to his *Asian Journals*, which record his first and last major trip beyond the bounds of his monastery, he felt that his visit to the great Buddhist statues at Polonnaruwa, India, had provided him with the major mystical experience he had long sought but been unable to access in a Roman Catholic context. Later on the same trip he delivered his final speech at a monastic interreligious conference in Bangkok. Ominously enough, the speech was on Marxism and monasticism—Marxism which had all but destroyed Christianity in Russia and Buddhism in Tibet. Immediately after delivering that speech—as if to provide a symbolic warning—Fr. Merton retired to his room, where he died suddenly in his bathtub by accidental electrocution.

Nor should we forget the highly significant "Paths to the Heart" conference which my wife and I attended at the University of South Carolina in 2001, shortly after 9/11, where Eastern Orthodox Christians and Muslim Sufis, including Bishop Kallistos Ware and Dr. Seyyed Hossein Nasr, met to discuss the meaning of the spiritual Heart in their respective traditions; the proceedings of this event should be studied by anyone involved with monastic or contemplative interfaith dialogue. The Schuonian Traditionalist perspective was provided by the convener of the conference, Dr. James Cutsinger, who took his listeners on a brilliant and illuminating ascent of the Great Chain of Being. Unfortunately, however, when we reached the apex of the ontological hierarchy we did not find ourselves in the Presence of God, but rather in the domain of Interfaith Amity, where the various faiths floated

CHAPTER TEN

together like magnificently-appointed yachts on the placid sea of the Transcendent Unity of Religions.

I believe that interfaith dialogue, especially on the level of contemplative theory and practice—while rich in spiritual potential—also presents certain dangers. Stepping beyond the boundaries of the Tradition that has formed us, or rescued us, initially places us in a no-man's-land where nothing short of a deeper sense of the Presence of God will protect us from the danger of falling into the "outer darkness" between the faiths where that Presence is deeply eclipsed and counterfeited. We are only justified in exposing ourselves to this danger by the need to avoid what may be an even greater danger: namely, that the God-given religions, each sealed in its own self-referential cocoon, might lose sight of the One Objective Referent that provides the *raison d'être* for all of them, and so go to war with each other according to the game plan of *al-Dajjal* and his globalist agents.

In view of the call to dialogue in "Fraternity for Knowledge and Cooperation", I suggest that all interested parties, while maintaining due vigilance in the face of the dangers of this approach, lose no time in reaching out to Roman Catholic, Sufi, Buddhist, and Eastern Orthodox contemplatives about the possibility of carrying on interfaith dialogue on the highest level. Time is short, yet Eternity surrounds us; it is this that makes it possible for us to avoid both haste and procrastination, but rather to act according to God's time—the sort of time we Sufis call the *waqt*—the *nunc stans* of Aquinas, the eternal Present Moment—the only point in the temporal dimension from which both God's subtle Guidance and His irresistible Will can be heard, understood, and obeyed.

CHAPTER TEN

A dialogue between contemplatives would necessarily involve words and concepts, but it would need to be founded on something deeper than an encounter of ideas—namely, an encounter of *presences*. It would therefore necessarily be based not on a brotherhood, or friendly rivalry, characterized by endless talking, but on a brotherhood of Silence. In was the Virgin Silence of the Prophet Muhammad, peace and blessings be upon him, that allowed the Holy Qur'an, the Word of Allah, to be heard and recited, in the clear Arabic tongue; it was the Virgin Silence of Mary that allowed Jesus, peace and blessings be upon him—the Word made flesh—to be born into this world. Perhaps a union of the Inner Silences of these two great Revelations will allow a true common word between them to be heard, and spoken, in the chaos and darkness of our times.

PART TWO

THE ANTINOMIANISM OF FRITHJOF SCHUON

INTRODUCTION TO PART TWO

It may feel strange and out-of-place to many readers that I have devoted over half of this book on Perennialism and its potential role in today's world to a consideration of the insights and manifestations of a single representative of that school, Frithjof Schuon—particularly since he has been dead for a quarter-century, and in view of the fact that his direct influence on the religious landscape seems to have been substantially less than that of figures like Julius Evola or René Guénon. Be that as it may, I believe that the doctrines articulated by Schuon and the highly significant events surrounding him present us with the widest possible spectrum of the potential benefits and pitfalls of the Perennialist perspective. These are the influences that anyone will have to contend with who wants to take Perennialism seriously, not simply as an area of academic study but as an approach to the spiritual life that is uniquely representative of the quality of our time, a time of unparalleled collective deception and unprecedented spiritual opportunity.

CHAPTER TEN

Antinomianism has always been a part, or shadow, of religion. When the law, the norm, the *nomos* becomes petrified, antinomianism duly arrives to crack it open again—open to Grace, or else open to lethal dissipation. The way of the orthodox Sufis has been to crack it open in the vertical direction only, leaving it intact in the horizontal one—as both a refuge and a crucible—where it must encounter not only the strictures of the law but the undeniable contradiction, and challenge, of other religious universes. Yet the true antinomians who can't abide such compromises are not content to remain within what, to them, must appear as a narrow monastic cell lit with a single skylight. They must break out—and when they do, chaos is unleashed. The *necessary* power of such chaos is not only to sweep away the darkness of all the formal limitations that constrict the spiritual vision, but equally to expose the hidden egotism of both the proud orthodox believer and the proud antinomian rebel to the ruthless power of dissolutionary Justice. Consequently the reign of *legitimate* antinomianism, the "one brief shining moment" when its annihilation of orthodox limitations is precisely in line with the Will of God, is always short. The explosion of light, light threaded through with unseen darkness, that was Frithjof Schuon might well have been just such a moment, one of those times when God does something truly unexpected, seemingly in contradiction to the norms that He Himself has established—as when he commanded His prophet Hosea to marry a prostitute. Is this a purification? A hard chastisement? An instant of pure unconditioned Mercy? A trap for the unwary? A Counter-Initiatory subversion? A rigorous test? In any case, whenever such a brief moment of the breakthrough of the Unconditioned into conditional existence comes to its end, a great separation of the Sheep from the Goats must take place, a meticulous and ruthless evaluation, according to the criterion not only of Knowledge but of Love, of all the many and varied consequences of that powerful explosion whose last echoes are just now fading away into the distance—seeing that, in the apocalyptic context of today's darkened and dissolving world, Love itself *is* the face of Rigor because we have betrayed Love; Mercy itself, because we have rejected it, *is* implacable Justice. And in view of the fact that Frithjof Schuon was called both to re-establish the universal norms of Tradition in all its guises, and simultaneously to break those norms, for good or ill, in the name of either pure unconditioned Truth or of the imperatives of his own individualistic genius, all the massive contradictions and illusions that have dogged his enterprise must have been inevitable from the beginning—just as inevitable as their necessary sequel is, namely the rigorous analysis and exposure of every one of them. And so all of this—his truths, his errors, his defiant individualism as well as his translucent intellectual purity—must be included, without mitigation or evasion, in the total didactic that his life and writings represent, since all this is in line with the precise quality of the times. The present section of this book was written to advance, in some small way, this lesson and this dialectic.

CHAPTER ELEVEN

The Pivotal Importance of Frithjof Schuon

Frithjof Schuon was in many ways the greatest of the Traditionalist/Perennialist writers, and certainly one of the pre-eminent spiritual authors of the modern age. The British Muslim and one-time Traditionalist writer Charles le Gai Eaton characterized him, even though Schuon was born in 1907, as "the last of the 19th Century geniuses"—one who, since he concluded that line of illustrious eccentrics, was necessarily a genius in the field of religion. And the fact that Schuon himself provided a perceptive critique of the "genius"-type as a secularized version, or inversion, of the medieval saint adds a keen note of irony to Eaton's evaluation. In him the archetype of the Traditional saint or sage and that of the individual genius who is a law unto himself collided, blended and polarized. This rare event, which was the actualization of an equally rare historical moment, helped to produce both the subtlest insights and the most maddening

CHAPTER ELEVEN

contradictions in his metaphysical philosophy. Consequently, before we address his errors, it is necessary to clearly establish his stature, particularly since he still languishes in relative obscurity when compared with René Guénon, though his behind-the-scenes influence on the more religiously-inclined of the international ruling class, particularly in the Muslim world, is apparently quite extensive. We must attempt this if only to prove that he is imminently worth criticizing, seeing that his errors are distortions of metaphysical truth on the highest possible level, blemishes on the surface of a peerless spiritual masterpiece.

Here below are what, in my view, are some of his most significant achievements in fields of comparative religion and traditional metaphysics:

1) His re-statement of the Hierarchy of Being, in generic terms in his ***Survey of Metaphysics and Esoterism***, in specifically Islamic terms in ***Dimensions of Islam***, where he draws upon the "Five Hadhrat" (Divine Presences) of Ibn al-'Arabi. This allowed him to make the important distinction between the Neo-Platonic "Beyond Being"—the Islamic *Al-Dhat* or Divine Essence, equivalent to the Godhead of Meister Eckhart, the *Ungrund* of Jakob Boehme, the Vedantic *Nirguna Brahman*—and the "Pure Being" of the Personal God—the Muslim *Allah*, the Vedantic *Ishvara* or *Saguna Brahman*—which ontologically transcends it, thereby also demonstrating the growing metaphysical unanimity of the world's religions as their mystical centers are approached, a perspective that powerfully supports the objective reality of spiritual Truth and one that allowed him to carry on his own brand of "esoteric ecumenism".

CHAPTER ELEVEN

2) His definition of the Supreme Principle in terms of the Absolute, the Infinite and the Perfect, with the Absolute subsisting as the archetype of the Divine Transcendence as expressed in the Christian conception of God the Father, the Infinite as the archetype of the Divine Immanence and of God the Holy Spirit, and the Perfect as the archetype of the Personhood of God manifest as God the Son, a doctrine that also includes the polarity between the Absolute and the Infinite as the essence of the hypostases of *Shiva* and *Shakti* in tantric Hinduism. This is undoubtedly one of the highest and most comprehensive views of the nature of God that has ever been articulated;

3) His re-enunciation of the epistemological principle, taught by Mulla Sadra and others, that Knowledge is based on an unveiling of the intrinsic union of the Knower with the Known, which includes the principle that the *Nous*, the Transcendent Intellect within the human form, is one in essence with its Divine Object;

4) His introduction of the poetic and aesthetic element in his exposition of metaphysical and esoteric spirituality that was largely missing in René Guénon;

5) His correction of Guénon's view of Christianity, emphasizing that it had not lost its esoteric dimension as Guénon believed but that Christian esoterism, in line with the teachings of Dionysius the Pseudo-Areopagite, is epitomized in the sacramental order, with Baptism corresponding to the mystical station of Purgation, Confirmation/Chrismation to the station of Illumination and the Eucharist to the station of Union, simultaneously explaining the lack of well-defined orthodox

esoteric schools within Christianity, corresponding to the Sufi *tariqas* within Islam, by the fact that Christianity is an "eso-exoteric revelation", an esoteric doctrine originally designed for initiates but now preached openly to the masses;

6) His establishment, following Guénon but surpassing him, of the "axial" nature of terrestrial humanity and the centrality of the Human Form as opposed to the more elevated but relatively peripheral status of the angels, thereby producing a profound esoteric *tafsir* of the Qur'anic *Amana* or Trust [cf. Q. 33:72], as well as of the account in Q. 2:30-34 that Allah told Adam the names of all things in the pre-terrestrial world, leading to the rebellion of Iblis (the Muslim Satan) based on his refusal to prostrate himself to Adam when Allah commanded him and all the angels to do so before the First Man was sent down to Earth as Allah's vicegerent—an esoteric anthropology that carries the essence of the Traditionalist critique of the modern and postmodern worlds, which critique is especially crucial today in the face of the present deconstruction of the human form by transgenderism, transhumanism, artificial intelligence etc.;

7) His clear distinction, also following and clarifying Guénon, between the Psychic and the Spiritual domains;

8) His universal eschatology, elucidating the many destinies of the human soul after death, especially as it appears in **Survey of Metaphysics and Esoterism**;

9) His "emanationist theodicy", which explains the necessity of evil as based on the increasing distance of manifest existence from its transcendent Source as that manifestation descends the ontological hierarchy, until (though this is a principle

CHAPTER ELEVEN

that Schuon failed to emphasize) a point is reached where it becomes possible for sentient beings possessing free will to consciously turn against God, a descent that is inseparable from the principle that if privation and the *potentiality* of evil—rather than the actualization of that potential based on the misuse of free will—were not woven into the fabric of the universe, that universe could not exist as a creation separate (in a certain sense) from God, because it would in fact *be* God;

10) His defense of the Traditional faiths in the face of the imposed religious pluralism of the modern world by his clear articulation, based on his doctrine of the "relative Absolute", of the Transcendent Unity of Religions, making clear that this Transcendent Unity is neither a syncretistic amalgam of the faiths nor a new revelation that supersedes them (though he sometimes appears to have wavered on this point), and emphasizing the truth that the formal diversity of the religions is every bit as providential and metaphysically necessary as is their Transcendent Unity;

11) Above all, his defense of *transcendental objectivity* against every form of subjectivism and psychologism, which forms the basis of his definition of the metaphysical order as a reality which transcends the entire Psychic or Imaginal realm, whether individual or collective, situating this realm on the Intermediary Plane that lies above the corporeal world as reported by the five senses but below the celestial world, the world of the Intelligibles that constitutes the metaphysical order per se. In doing so he defined God as the Absolute Object whose reality remains perfectly unaffected by whatever

experiences of Him we may undergo and whatever views of Him we may entertain, thereby annihilating at a single stroke the metaphysical pretensions not only of psychology but of postmodernism and "spiritualized" physics as well. But he didn't stop there. After firmly subordinating all possible subjective experiences of God, whether by human being, or by jinn, or by angel, to That One's transcendental objectivity, he crowned this essential restatement of traditional metaphysics by articulating the principle that when God as the Absolute Object fully annihilates all our subjective experiences of Him, He is transformed into the Absolute Subject that lies behind and within those experiences as their ultimate Experiencer, this being Schuon's rendition of the central Vedantic principle of the *Atman*, the Indwelling Divine Witness, the Absolute Self. If it hadn't been for Schuon's unparalleled achievement in this regard I would never have understood what Ramana Maharshi meant when he spoke of the Self that transcends the I-sense and remains unaffected by either its birth or its disappearance, just as it was the Maharshi who ultimately opened my eyes to what Schuon was alluding to when, in **Survey of Metaphysics and Esoterism**, he spoke of "the Absolute Subject of our contingent subjectivity." Without his distinction between limited, relative and contingent subjectivity as that which witnesses a contingent, relative, and thereby still subjectively-limited object, and an Absolute Subject which is at the same time the Absolute Object of its own consciousness—an absolute *Sat* (Being) which, in polarity with an absolute *Chit* (Consciousness), subsists as an absolute *Ananda* (Bliss)—and all this in a mode not only of Trinity but of seamless Unity—I would never have grasped

CHAPTER ELEVEN

the muddle-headedness of the various uses of the terms "subjective" and "objective" in virtually every contemporary field of philosophy, physics and psychology. If pure metaphysical intelligence operating alone, without regard for either the affections or the will, were capable of redeeming the human race, then Frithjof Schuon—except for his errors!—would have been the universal savior.

And beyond even these eleven monumental achievements, he solved so many other thorny problems in metaphysics and religion that when surveying spiritual doctrines from many different traditions I continually run up against dilemmas that he alone seems to have provided the solutions for, while remembering succinct phrases of his that express certain metaphysical principles more clearly and definitively than any other writer I have ever encountered.

CHAPTER TWELVE

How to Read Frithjof Schuon: The Importance of a Second Look

On my first reading of Schuon's books I was profoundly impressed by his *concision*. Two examples will suffice:

The first illuminates certain essential differences between Islam and Christianity, and is as follows: "In Islam there is no sanctity outside of esoterism; in Christianity there is no esoterism outside of sanctity" [from his essay "Modes of Prayer" that appears in **Stations of Wisdom**]. When I first encountered this formulation I said to myself: "This expresses so much in so brief and concentrated a form: the fact that most of those recognized as saints in Islam have emerged from the organized Sufi *tariqahs*, or at least from the general perspective of *tasawwuf*, plus the fact that no organized esoteric brotherhoods comparable in stature to those *tariqas* have arisen within Christianity; whatever quasi-esoteric organizations have appeared in the Christian world over the centuries, often in the form of various craft guilds who held esoteric interpretations of their technical secrets, are clearly secondary to the quintessential esoterism of Christianity, namely the sacramental order, the grace of which is most fully assimilable not through any explicit esoteric doctrine but through the purification of the soul that finds its model and reaches its pinnacle in a monastic context. How amazing that Schuon was able to say all that and more in a mere eighteen words."

The second example, having to do with the relationship between Revelation and Intellection, is as follows: "Revelation is an Intellection of the macrocosm; Intellection is a Revelation of the microcosm" [from ***Esoterism as Principle and as Way***]. "What a jewel of metaphysical expression!" (I said to myself)—"a concise verbal Yin/Yang sign that perfectly renders, in epistemological terms, the reality of a metaphysical Truth that transcends, and at the same time unites, the dimensions of Subject and Object."

The truths that came to me via my first impressions of formulations like these I continue to see as valid and useful—and yet a second, more critical reading has revealed various less helpful implications of them that were not initially apparent. QUESTION: Does "In Islam there is no sanctity outside of esoterism" literally mean that all Muslim saints have been Sufis, practitioners of *irfan*, esotericists of one kind or another? If so, that statement is obviously not true. The Prophet's companions, for example, were not esotericists per se, though the polarization between esoteric and exoteric perspectives was much less pronounced in the Prophet's time, while within the character of the Prophet himself these two were seamlessly united. Yet those companions remain paragons and exemplars of the essential Muslim character—more so than the "People of the Bench" who were in many ways the direct ancestors of the Sufis of later years; consequently they satisfy all the criteria of sanctity without being "esotericists" per se. (Why didn't I see this the first time around?) Likewise the formulation "In Christianity there is no esoterism outside of sanctity" ignores certain pivotal figures such as Dante Aligieri and Meister Eckhart—Dante whose knowledge, if we are to believe his **Divine Comedy**, though clearly esoteric in certain areas did not directly emerge as the fruit of realized sanctity but rather aided him in his struggle to attain such sanctity—and Eckhart whose esoteric *gnosis*, *Ma'rifa* or *jñana* is immediately recognizable as the central keynote of his character and expression. Though we are certainly not justified in imagining that this *gnosis* was in any way distinct from sanctity in his soul, neither does it appear—any more than in the case of Dante—as the final fruit of a tree of which sanctity was the seed; some people, in both Islam and Christianity, though sanctity could in no way be foreign to them, are destined from birth to be "knowers." So what on a first reading presented itself to me as the quintessential Truth of the distinction between Christianity and Islam, after a period of critical reflection revealed itself to only be "sort of" true; I had to overcome my initial near-hypnotic fascination with the apparently "magisterial" clarity and certainty of that formulation of Schuon's, and embark on a less intoxicating but more balanced and critical course of moderating its excesses, filling in its blanks, and slowly letting my eyes recover from the brilliant flash of light that had temporarily blinded them, until I could begin to see those less "absolutized" realities that had been hidden under the veil of that light. And this, I believe, is precisely how Schuon should be read. In order to fully receive his teachings—or, to speak more accurately, the teachings that came *through* him, some of which he might actually not been fully cognizant of—it is necessary to assimilate them in two distinct phases: the first, intellectually intoxicated and "devotional"; the second, sober and critical.

As for the second of his two formulations, "Revelation is the Intellection of the macrocosm; Intellection is the Revelation of the microcosm," the first thing I saw in it was the important distinction between a Divine Revelation directed to an entire human collective and a *gnostic* unveiling received by, or attained by, a single individual, these being two modes of the transmission and/or realization of metaphysical Truth that are polarized in one sense while being strictly analogous and consonant in another. "Wonderful!" I said. "This is a re-statement of doctrine that appears in the Qur'an as *I will show them My signs on the horizons* (the outer world) *and in their own souls until they are satisfied that this is the Truth. Is it not enough for you, that I am Witness over all things?* [Q. 41:53]."

But wait—what exactly does "an Intellection of the macrocosm" mean? The word "macrocosm" is usually not used to denote a human collective, but the totality of the created universe, of which we, the human microcosm, appear to be a part. Is Schuon actually saying that the sun, the stars, the galaxies are either the recipients or the promulgators of a Divine Revelation?

Obviously not—yet his use of the word "macrocosm," upon sober critical reflection, appears much less precise and quintessential than it did on a first reading. And what about "Intellection is a Revelation of the microcosm"? Is Schuon implying here that the person in whom the faculty of Intellection is fully developed has no need of any outer Revelation, and can therefore dispense with the norms and dictates of Tradition? If

CHAPTER TWELVE

so, then there is no necessary and intrinsic relationship between Revelation and Intellection, these being the names for two distinct and separate realms, the first fundamentally exoteric, directed to the masses, the second essentially esoteric, pertaining to the individual capable of *gnosis*. It remains unclear whether or not Schuon meant to imply this by the passage in question. But as we will see below, there is clear evidence that Schuon sometimes did believe precisely this. The actual state of affairs, however, is otherwise. The merciful, nourishing rain and the warming and illuminating sun of Revelation, emanating not from the sensual macrocosm we call the "universe" but from the subtle macrocosm of the objective metaphysical order, are precisely what cause the seed of Intellection to germinate and sprout within the spiritual Heart, thereby opening the Eye of it; likewise it is precisely the Heart's Intellection that unveils the quintessential truths of Revelation, cracking the shell of the letter to expose the kernel of the Spirit, and thereby allowing Revelation to penetrate the spiritual Heart ever more deeply. To deny this fundamental reciprocity between Revelation and Intellection is to render Revelation intellectually limited and Intellection Promethean, thereby deconstructing the whole notion of the primacy of Tradition, both historical and primordial.

Did Schuon actually teach such a profound and destructive error, inadvertently placing a worm at the root of the whole Traditionalist enterprise? Not always, certainly—only *sometimes*; the passage quoted below, in the chapter entitled "Two Esoterisms" from **Survey of Metaphysics and Esoterism**, includes one of those times:

CHAPTER TWELVE

The word "esoterism" suggests in the first place an idea of complementarity, of a "half" as it were: esoterism is the complement of exoterism, it is the "spirit" which completes the "letter." Where there is a truth of Revelation, hence of formal and theological truth, there must also be a truth of intellection, hence of non-formal and intellectual; not legalistic or obligatory truth, but truth that stems from the nature of things, which is also vocational since not every man grasps this nature.

But in fact this second truth exists independently of the first [!]; hence it is not, in its intrinsic reality, a complement or a half; it is so only extrinsically and as it were "accidentally." This means that the word "esoterism" designates not only the total truth inasmuch as it is "colored" by entering a system of partial truth, but also the total truth as such, which is colorless. This distinction is not a mere theoretical luxury; on the contrary, it implies extremely important consequences.

Thus esoterism as such is metaphysics, to which is necessarily joined an appropriate method of realization. But the esoterism of a particular religion—of a particular exoterism precisely—tends to adapt itself to this religion and thereby enter into theological, psychological and legalistic meanders, while preserving in its secret chamber its authentic and plenary nature, but for which it would not be what it is.

CHAPTER TWELVE

There is much truth in this passage, as well as much misdirection and illusion. Readers of Schuon should be alert at the outset for one of his most characteristic passions, namely the passion (possibly Geminid in origin?) to wield what he often referred to as "the sword of discrimination," and consequently to *split things in two*. This passion was the origin of his obsession with spiritual typology—the *jñani* or "intellectual man" vs. the *bhakta* or "emotional man", as if these two spiritual tendencies were mutually exclusive in the human character, as well as his emphasis on the distinction between esoteric and exoteric spirituality, on "God become man" vs. "God as such", etc. etc.; the list is quite extensive. All of these distinctions are illuminating, up to a point, and often truly necessary—but if they are never united again on a higher level, the result is in some cases disastrous. At times Schuon does reunite them, triumphantly; at other times, however, he simply leaves in a state of divorce and alienation what should properly be unified by a deeper realization—a realization that never quite supervenes.

To begin with, I must question whether the "colorless esoterism of total truth" and the "intrinsically colorless esoterism colored by partial truth" actually constitute a real and necessary division. Certainly "esoterism" colored by the historical, ethnic and psychological contingencies of a particular religion must begin as a partial, limited truth—and once the impulse appears to express the nature and implications of the total truth that is realized at the apex of such an esoterism, given that even an esoteric perspective conditioned by "theological, psychological and legalistic meanders" must harbor within it "its authentic and plenary nature," it must again assume its theological, psychic and legalistic trappings in order to make itself intelligible to the human collective to which it is addressed. But if this is the case, then what is the true nature and definition of a "colorless" esoterism that lies entirely outside such limitations, outside any Traditional religion based on a Divine Revelation? What makes it any different from the esoterism of a given historical religion, as far as the *esoteric essence* of the realization it provides is concerned? As I see it, the only thing that makes it any different at all, since the realizations attained by each of the "two esoterisms" are identical—given that the Truth is One—is its *individualistic* nature. So what Schuon is really saying here is that there is no essential difference between the realization attained by the traditional religious mystic and that arrived at by the non-traditional freelance—which inevitably leads us to suspect that he might have included himself in the second category. If so, then Tradition—and, by extension, Revelation—are essentially unnecessary, at least in certain individual instances, thus calling into question Schuon's usual identification as a "Traditionalist". But if Intellection is independent of Revelation instead of Revelation being its necessary polar complement, then the individualistic mysticism of the spiritual freelance, operating through personal Intellection alone, is open to the danger of Prometheanism, to the belief that the spiritually gifted individual might pull himself up by his (or her) own bootstraps, that such an individual is free to take Heaven by storm, in the absence of Heaven's permission and without Heaven's help. How unexpectedly different this is from Titus Burckhardt's position—though that position is clearly based on Schuon's teachings—as he expresses it in "A Letter on Spiritual Method" from his book ***Mirror of the Intellect***:

CHAPTER TWELVE

There is no spiritual method without these two basic elements: discernment between the real and the unreal, and concentration on the real [these being the last two of Schuon's Six Stations of Wisdom]. The first of these two elements, discernment or discrimination (*vijñana* in Sanskrit), does not depend on any special religious form; it only presupposes metaphysical understanding. The second element, however, requires a support of a sacred character, and this means that it can only be achieved within the framework of a normal tradition. The aim of method is perpetual concentration upon the Real, and this cannot be achieved by purely human means on the basis of individual initiative; it presupposes a regular transmission such as exists only within a normal tradition.... To be precise, there is no spiritual path outside the following traditions or religions: Judaism, Christianity, Islam, Buddhism, Hinduism and Taoism; but Hinduism is closed for those who have not been born into a Hindu caste, and Taoism is inaccessible.

My suspicion of a certain Prometheanism on Schuon's part is further reinforced by his definition, in "Two Esoterisms," of Revelation as not only "formal and theological" but also as "legalistic and obligatory" in the passage quoted, and of Intellection, on the contrary, as "non-formal and metaphysical" as well as "vocational"—in other words, as both non-Traditional and essentially individualistic. Here Revelation is defined entirely as *exoterism* and is consequently seen as devoid of Intellection, while Intellection itself, since it is vocational, is taken to be an *esoteric* function and power of the enlightened *individual*, not in any way a gift of Revelation or an ability that can only develop, or is most likely to develop, within the embrace of a revealed traditional faith in response to traditionally established channels of grace and guidance. Such an esoterism has no need of Revelation since it blooms and comes to flower within the isolated individual according to that individual's unique spiritual destiny.

How far this is from anything deserving the name of Traditionalism! Nonetheless we must accept the undeniable fact that there have always been individualistic mystics and metaphysicians who have come to their realizations outside the context of any formal Revelation. They are rare, they are subject to unique spiritual dangers since they live beyond the morally and intellectually protective bounds of any traditional faith, but they have always existed and will undoubtedly continue to appear. But even such freelance sages never come to their higher realizations without the intrinsic help of Revelation—Revelation in the sense of the grace and guidance of the Deity as directed to them personally, outside the mediation of a particular religious collective. They have never simply bloomed spontaneously from within—unless we consider the revelatory Word of God that awakens Intellection to be a function of that very "within," seeing that "the Kingdom of Heaven is within you."

And as for the great collective Revelations being essentially unrelated to Intellection, since this is considered to be a "vocational" and individual affair—as the section quoted above certainly implies—this notion stands in stark contradiction to so many of Schuon's other teachings, most particularly his definition of the Qur'an as "God made book," just as Christ is

CHAPTER TWELVE

"God made man." Apparently he had temporarily forgotten in this case that the great Revelations, though they are destined for entire human collectives, have most often to come only to individuals—those individuals we call "prophets"—and that no human individual whose spiritual faculties are inoperative, who remains closed to Intellection, has ever received such a Revelation. And does he actually mean to imply that the Qur'an is strictly "legalistic", limited to establishing human "obligations," but in no way *gnostic* or esoteric, never addressing itself to the human potential for the intellective understanding of spiritual Truth? (Or, for that matter, that Jesus was some sort of exoteric lawgiver, but certainly not the Way the Truth and the Life?) If so, then he has much in common with today's Wahhabi/Salafis, the most exoteric and anti-Intellectual manifestation of the religion of Islam—ironically so, since in general he was more opposed in outlook to the Wahabi/Salafi perspective than almost anyone else I could name. At the very least such a radical separation between Revelation and Intellection as Schuon seems to make in the above passage apparently indicates—if we ignore, that is, his many other statements to the contrary—that his understanding of Islam as a plenary religion revealed by God, one that addresses itself to all the human faculties as any true religion must, was woefully deficient. A more likely explanation for lapses such as this may be that Schuon often tended to forget some of his most characteristic doctrines in his eagerness to elucidate some particular insight that impressed itself upon him in the heat of the moment; it was as if he wrote by something akin to poetic inspiration rather than soberly considering how a particular doctrine fit within his larger metaphysical scheme. In some cases this mode of expression shows itself to be ultimately based upon his intuition of a metaphysical paradox that he understands progressively and dialectically rather than comprehending it as a whole in a single moment; in other cases, however, what he comes up with must be seen as a direct contradiction to many of the other things he taught. And in the case of the radical separation between Revelation and Intellection that is implied in the passage above, I hope I may be forgiven for wondering whether his motivation for over-emphasizing this distinction might be based on his desire to free himself from whatever "legalistic obligations" his acceptance of Islam as a Divine Revelation might place upon him; when referring to Frithjof Schuon's "antinomianism," this is exactly what I'm talking about. And though I feel compelled to ask this question, I do not feel competent to answer it with any degree of certainty. We must accept the fact that the motives of others are a closed book, especially in view of the fact that even our own motives are often enigmatic to us.

Be that as it may, whoever is capable of reading Frithjof Schuon critically, while still remaining open to his many illuminating insights, has begun to learn how to assimilate the doctrines of one of the most pivotal spiritual teachers of modern and/or postmodern times, as well as training him- or herself in how to discern and expose many of the errors and inversions that beset the metaphysical enterprise in these last days of the Kali-yuga.

CHAPTER THIRTEEN

Metaphysical Errors in the Writings of Frithjof Schuon: Their Role in Discernment

Once the Sufi master Ala al-Dawla al-Simnani saw the Prophet in a dream, and asked him:

"What do you say on the subject of Ibn Sina (Avicenna)?" The Prophet replied, "He is a man whom God caused to lose his way in knowledge."

Introduction

I have been studying the writings of Frithjof Schuon for a full 35 years, and since it has now been 26 years since his death, in this chapter I hope to clarify my emerging sense of the significance of his life's work, its strengths and weaknesses, and the best use to which it might be put at this time. That Schuon was one of the greatest metaphysicians to appear in the last several centuries, at least in the West, is beyond doubt. He has had a greater influence on my worldview and intellectual development than any other writer—but that does not mean that I agree with everything he said. His presentation of the Traditional religions in terms of their eternal essences—certain personal prejudices apart—is in many cases without peer, and his "pure metaphysics" is undeniably profound in many ways. However, if his metaphysical perceptions are deep, his errors and delusions are equally deep, making him far and away the most equivocal and self-contradictory spiritual teacher I have ever encountered.

Though Schuon has been critiqued from the sociological and the moral standpoints, the tendency has been either to accept his metaphysical writings as holy writ or else reject them wholesale, whether from the viewpoint of the orthodox theology of one particular religion or according to the general postmodern obsession to deconstruct all "overarching paradigms," including that of traditional metaphysics. The aim of this chapter is to confront his metaphysical ideas directly, seeking to determine how valid they are in terms of traditional metaphysics itself. In the various attempts to evaluate Frithjof Schuon that I am aware of there has been far too much demonization and hagiography, in my opinion. What is needed now is for a sober assessment of the strengths and weaknesses of his doctrines, on the level of discourse where he himself placed them, to become acceptable, even welcome, in the greater Perennialist world. Schuon was neither God nor the Devil; he was a hugely inspired but flawed human being operating under unprecedented historical conditions. Once we accept this premise, his writings may yet yield treasures in response to informed exegesis that were effectively hidden under the veil of uncritical devotion.

In view of the often hidden contradictions in Frithjof Schuon's writings, my own study of his ideas has come in two phases: the first, an assimilation of his doctrines; the second, an analysis of his errors. Both of these phases have been immensely rewarding. To take only one example of the positive aspects of his teaching, which I've detailed above, when he speaks of the Absolute and Infinite as Beyond Being, from which Pure Being or the Personal God emerges, his teaching is truly and legitimately universal. His Platonic or Neo-Platonic categories of Being and Beyond Being are strictly equivalent to the Allah/*Al-Dhat* of Islam, the God/Godhead of Christianity, and the *Saguna Brahman/Nirguna Brahman* of Hinduism. On the other hand, I am not sure he always saw the difference between presenting metaphysical doctrines that are truly universal, and judging one discrete Tradition in light of another when it suited him, which is a much more dubious practice. In this chapter we will consider various points at which Frithjof Schuon departs from the Traditional orthodoxies, criticizing these departures, in some cases, according to criteria established by Schuon himself. To reiterate a case-in-point I have already dealt with above, I accept the value and usefulness of Schuon's formulation, "Revelation is an Intellection of the macrocosm; Intellection is a Revelation of the microcosm." But does he mean that the presence of individual "microcosmic" Intellection can make adherence to Revealed religious forms unnecessary, or that the Revelations given by God to humanity will have no necessary effect on the individual Intellection of the gnostic or *arif*, either to inspire it or to defend it from error?

CHAPTER THIRTEEN

Schuon's answer remains uncertain, though in his definition of "orthodoxy" in the following passage, he certainly seems to accept Revelation as binding even upon the intellectually enlightened individual:

> Orthodoxy is the principle of formal homogeneity proper to any authentically spiritual perspective; it is therefore an indispensable aspect of all genuine spirituality. To be orthodox is to participate by way of a doctrine that can properly be called "traditional" in the immutability of the principles which govern the Universe and fashion our intelligence. [From "Orthodoxy and Intellectuality," appearing in **Stations of Wisdom**.]

The question is, did Schuon himself always follow this principle? Seeing that he radically abridged the Muslim *shari'ah*, rarely mentioned the Holy Qur'an or the Prophet Muhammad (peace and blessings be upon him), and seemingly placed the Vedanta and Kashmiri Shaivism above Islam in several instances, we are compelled to answer in the negative and to conclude that although Frithjof Schuon was certainly a Perennialist, he was by and large not a consistent Traditionalist, at least as defined by René Guénon in his chapter "The Necessity for a Traditional Exoterism" from **Initiation and Spiritual Realization**. And once we understand that in some cases he did not practice what he preached, the entirety of his written corpus suddenly appears in a radically different light.

The paragraph quoted above does indeed present a concise, accurate, sagacious and highly useful definition of the "orthodoxy"

CHAPTER THIRTEEN

he often extolled but nonetheless did not always strictly adhere to. And such "magisterial" passages as this one can be found throughout his many works. Nonetheless, those of us who accept the reality of Tradition in René Guénon's sense, who have both an understanding of the true nature of orthodoxy and an active intuition of the sacred, will be unwilling to easily accept Schuon's apparently heterodox "cross-traditional" doctrines, some of which would only be justifiable in the case of a new Divine Revelation, which Schuon explicitly denied that he had brought. In **Understanding Islam** he declares that "It is essential to understand that after a certain cyclical period and the hardening of the terrestrial ambience which it comprises, God no longer speaks, at least not as Revealer. In other words, after a certain period, whatever is put forward as a new religion is inevitably false; the Middle Ages mark *grosso modo* the final limit". Here we see a paramount example of the radical contradictions that plagued Schuon's enterprise, contradictions that were perhaps inevitable due to the fact that—as our times clearly demand—he was called upon both to expound a universal metaphysics and to revive and speak in the name of the Traditional orthodoxies. At the very least we would certainly be hard pressed to characterize the Maryamiyya Tariqa he founded as traditionally Islamic. I will grant that orthodox Sufism itself has often been accused by the exoteric *ulama* of just this sort of heterodoxy, but that is largely due to their inability to recognize the intrinsically Islamic nature of *tasawwuf*—something that was incontrovertibly demonstrated by Abu Hamid al-Ghazali, among others.

Schuon's initial goal was clearly to unveil the esoteric dimensions of the world's religions, a goal that he triumphantly achieved in many ways. But as soon as the esoteric is *exoterized* as a new religious or quasi-religious form—a tendency that, whatever the founder's conscious intent might have been, will prove very difficult to resist in practice—given the grim quality and formidable pressures of the times—the transformation of even the most enlightened belief-system into a self-enclosed cult becomes one possible outcome. This kind of exoterization of the esoteric can only be considered heterodox in Traditional terms, and will thus fall under Guénon's definitions of either Pseudo-Tradition or Counter-Tradition, consequently I believe that the task before us is to clearly distinguish Schuon's magisterial presentation of the *sophia perennis* from whatever heterodox, quasi-exoteric religious forms might have grown up around it, either deliberately or inadvertently, as well as to thresh and winnow his written works themselves to isolate the precious gems of truth that he culled from all the major religions of the earth, and from the brilliance of his own inspiration, so as to liberate them from the false and destructive contexts in which he sometimes placed them. There is no question that many of the writings of Frithjof Schuon are almost incomparably exalted, at least in comparison to the darkness of the times, but they are not perfect, even when considered apart from the false context that imprisons them. There are holes in them. If there were no holes in them, imbalances to be righted, over-emphases to be moderated, errors to be put right, deficiencies to be made good, they would not be fertile. Like the household of a Babylonian king, they would have followed their sire to the tomb to be buried alongside him; they would have died with their progenitor. But their survival is in fact guaranteed by the fact that, when his doctrines are studied alongside of the scriptures, theologians, saints and sages of the Wisdom Traditions they are largely based upon, such that they work to illuminate those Traditions and at the same time make themselves available to be corrected by them, they retain the power—at least when coupled with a commitment to a Traditional spiritual Path—to establish their pupils in a principal Truth that transcends even its own highest mode of expression. It is from this higher vantage point that the deficiencies of both teacher and teaching—God willing—might be seen and rectified. After taking in all I was likely to assimilate from Schuon's positive teachings, some years ago I began the "postgraduate course" whose curriculum was made up not of his truths but of his errors, the discernment and correction of which—made possible in large part by the valid elements in Schuon's own doctrines—have taught me that there are more things in heaven and earth than I dreamt of during the time I was reading the works of Frithjof Schuon purely as a devoted pupil. Speaking for myself, I can honestly say of my relationship to the Schuon's *opus* what William Blake said of the human eye: "I look through it, not with it." By means of his imperfections and contradictions—which reflect many of the spiritual deceptions we all must contend with in these times, most but not all of which he was ultimately able to triumphantly dispel—he has provided us with a way to continue to develop our discernment and deepen the enlightenment we drew from him, now that he is no longer with us. I only hope we will not be prevented from availing ourselves of this rare opportunity by a misplaced devotion to the person of the man himself, and to the mere abstract *idea* of the Truth he was sent to teach, rather than to the concrete Truth itself.

CHAPTER THIRTEEN

Schuon on the Creation and the Fall

In *Survey of Metaphysics and Esoterism*, Frithjof Schuon says:

> It is in the nature of the Good to wish to communicate itself: to say Good is to say radiation, projection, unfolding, gift of self. But at the same time, to say radiation is to say distance, hence alienation or impoverishment; the solar rays dim and become lost in the night of space. From this arises, at the end of the trajectory, the paradoxical phenomenon of evil, which nonetheless has the positive function of highlighting the good *a contrario*, and of contributing in its fashion to the equilibrium of the phenomenal order.

In Schuon's metaphysics and cosmology (at least as I understand them), the Formless Absolute (*Nirguna Brahman*; Godhead; Beyond Being) "emanates" the Personal God (*Saguna Brahman*; Pure Being; the Creator), Who in turn brings into outward manifestation certain of the possibilities latent in the Divine All-Possibility or *maya-in-divinis*, thereby creating the celestial, psychic, and material universes. God does not positively will evil, and He possesses the power to abolish any particular evil; however, in the nature of things He could not negate the existence of evil as such without annihilating creation itself, which only exists by virtue of the ontological level it occupies, where evil is an inescapable possibility, woven as it were into the fabric of things. If the universe did not contain the possibility of evil and privation, it would not be the universe, but God Himself; consequently it would be unable to exist "apart" from Him. The Absolute, being intrinsically Infinite, must overflow into manifestation by virtue

CHAPTER THIRTEEN

of All-Possibility since there is nothing in its nature to prevent it from doing so; this overflow results in the progressive attenuation of Being in its outer manifestation until the point is reached where the advent of evil, as "the possibility of impossibility," becomes possible. This doctrine of manifestation is profound, presents us with perhaps the most convincing theodicy that has ever been articulated, and is entirely compatible in my opinion with both the Primordial Tradition and the Abrahamic faiths, as well as with Neo-Platonism—as long as we allow a place for the deliberate fashioning of the world by a Divine Creator, and consequently for the drama of fall, salvation, judgment and final restoration, while understanding that this drama is a subset of, not a contrary to, the emanation and return-to-Principle of universal manifestation; Beyond Being emanates Pure Being, the Personal God, Who in turn creates, maintains, and judges the universe. As I see it, this schema is entirely in line with Schuon's metaphysics, at least in their most common rendition. Thus Schuon does not actually deny free will, but rather places it in a larger metaphysical context, thereby freeing it from the sense of arbitrariness that has led some to question the validity of it.

So universal Emanation necessarily contains within it the possibility of particular Creation, which in turn introduces the possibility of a Fall. Neither Emanation nor Creation, however, *are* the Fall. Creation sets the stage for a Fall, but does not actualize it; only rebellious free will can do that. One might argue that it is inevitable—in more or less "actuarial" terms—that some among an indefinite multitude of beings endowed with free will would choose rebellion, but this does not negate the reality of freedom in each individual case, nor the justice of the grim consequences earned by those who misuse it. Unfortunately, Frithjof Schuon did not fully elucidate the relationship between the personal God who creates and judges, and the Formless Absolute out of which He "emerges"; consequently his theodicy, undeniably profound on its own level, often seems to take the place of the orthodox Christian and Islamic doctrines of creation *ex nihilo* and the personal and general judgment, appearing to refute them rather than placing them in a wider and more enlightening context.

According to Schuon, the Real, the Sovereign Good, must communicate itself to (and as) celestial and cosmic manifestation, by virtue of the fact that what is Absolute is also necessarily Infinite, and no bound can be set to the Infinite. And it is certainly true that celestial and cosmic manifestation arise from the necessary and Infinite overflow of the superabundant Reality of the Absolute. But insofar as this manifestation is also a veil, the possibility of Satanic subversion is latent within it. For God to communicate Himself to cosmic existence is only good, but it is a limited good, not the unlimited reality of the Sovereign Good; the Supraformal necessarily manifests Itself in terms of form, and every form, as Schuon points out, is a limitation. Insofar as existence is good in itself, such limitations are neither evil nor subversive. And yet they harbor the possibility of evil and subversion by the very fact that limited forms are always paired with imperfect knowers, sentient beings who are limited in perspective just as the forms they perceive are limited in scope. And as soon as limited forms as perceived by limited knowers make their appearance, the possibility of idolatry arises, which I will define here as the tendency to "willfully mistake" a limited form for the reality of the Absolute which has manifested it, and which subsists within it as its essential Reality. There can be no evil in the Divine realm; the seeds of evil do exist in the celestial realm, but they remain latent since they have no context for deployment; it is only in the psychic realm that evil actually constellates as a subversive force. Schuon is right that evil only makes its appearance at the end of the trajectory of cosmic manifestation—not at the ultimate end, however, which is matter, but rather on the psychic plane, where "worlds" constructed with the ego, not God, as their proximate cause first become possible. Nonetheless, the existence of Lucifer testifies to the fact that the subversive privation which is, or will become, evil, has its beginnings at the apex of the celestial order; otherwise he could not have fallen "from heaven."

Schuon, however, teaches an entirely different doctrine of Creation (or Emanation) and Fall in his earlier book *The Transcendent Unity of Religions*, a doctrine I believe to be erroneous in many ways, and one which he later redressed by the doctrine of "necessary emanation" presented above. He says:

> What the exoteric perspective represents as evil or the Devil only corresponds ... to a partial view and is in no way the equivalent of the negative cosmic tendency that is envisaged by the metaphysical doctrines, and which the Hindu doctrine designates by the name tamas; but if tamas is not the Devil, and more correctly corresponds to the Demiurge, insofar as it represents the cosmic tendency that "solidifies" manifestation, drawing it downward and away from its Principle and Origin, it is nonetheless true that the Devil is a form of tamas, the latter being considered in this case solely in its relations with the human soul. Man being a conscious individual, the cosmic tendency in question, when it comes into contact with him,

necessarily takes on an individual and conscious aspect, a "personal" aspect according to the current expression. Outside the human world this tendency may assume entirely impersonal and neutral aspects, as, for example, when it is manifested as physical weight or material density, or in the guise of a hideous beast or of a common and heavy metal such as lead ... and if it were to disappear—an absurd proposition—all bodies or physical and psychic compositions would instantaneously volatilize. Even the most sacred object therefore has need of this tendency in order to be able to exist materially, and no one would be so rash as to assert that the physical law that condenses the material mass of, say, the Sacred Host is a diabolical force or in any sense an evil.

Here Schuon sees the Divine manifestation not as a necessary overflow of superabundant Being, but as the action of an outside force that somehow "drags Being down" into outward manifestation, a force he identifies with the Demiurge—though it is nonetheless possible to take the materializing *tamasic* Demiurge as the creative overflow of superabundant Being as seen from "below"—and yet, until that overflow has supervened to cosmically actualize a given Divine Possibility, there is no "below" from which this overflow could be seen as a *tamasic* materialization; consequently the perspective of creation as a Divine overflow must always take precedence over that of creation as a densification and materialization. There is certainly a legitimate place for the Hindu concept of *tamas*, the cosmic solidifying force which, when it predominates over *sattwa* (purity) and *rajas* (action) in a

CHAPTER THIRTEEN

given soul, leads it to perdition, but its place is not as the primal Agent of creation, as Schuon seems to be saying; to assert that this Agent is a *tamasic* Demiurge who, in relation to humanity though not in itself, is precisely the Devil, rather than a positive manifestation based on the necessary overflow of superabundant Being—identified by him with the Personal God—is to flirt with the error of the sectarian Gnostics, who saw cosmic manifestation as a veil over the Divine (which it certainly is) but not also as a manifestation of the Divine (which it also most certainly is), who asserted the Transcendence of God but not His Immanence, thus departing from both Christian orthodoxy and the Primordial Tradition. Schuon immediately mitigates this error by denying that material solidification is evil in itself, something that the Gnostics most often asserted, but when he places the *tamasic* tendency at the point of the primal manifestation of the Divine as the initial impulse for this manifestation, he is clearly in error.

Schuon's affinity for heretical Gnosticism also appears in the following passage from ***The Transcendent Unity of Religions***, quoted appreciatively by Patrick Laude in ***Keys to the Beyond: Frithjof Schuon's Cross-Traditional Language of Transcendence***:

> In order to save one of the "sick" parts of humanity, or rather "a humanity," God consents to be profaned; but on the other hand—and this is a manifestation of His Impersonality, which by definition lies beyond the exoteric point of view [the French original is "*point de vue religieux*" or "religious point of view"], he makes use of this profanation ... in order to bring about the final decadence of the present cycle of humanity, this decadence being necessary for the exhausting of all the possibilities included in this cycle....

CHAPTER THIRTEEN

"What is most striking in this passage," Laude comments, "is the characterization of religion as a kind of profanation of the Divine." Apart from the rather odd suggestion (to say the least!) that humanity is saved by *decadence*, given that religion is decadent in essence, the notion that God's Self-revelation in terms of a given religious form is a "profanation" (rather than, speaking in Christian terms, a *kenosis*, a Divine self-emptying, or in Kabbalistic terminology a *tsim-tsum*, a Divine withdrawal) is part-and-parcel of the false Gnostic characterization of the creation itself as a fall. This is nothing less than an overtly Luciferian inversion of the Primordial Tradition. And I must emphasize once again that it is in no way true to say that a *tamasic* Demiurge, who in relation to us is precisely the Devil, creates the universe by drawing existence downward and away from its Principle and Origin—since he would already need to be situated within a primordial creation that clearly did not exist yet in order to accomplish this—rather than (as Schuon asserts in his later books) that the Original Principle, by its intrinsic Infinity, necessarily overflows into celestial and cosmic manifestation. And this overflow, by its necessary attenuation as it progressively departs from its Principle into dimensional existence, casts as its inevitable shadow the negative possibilities of *tamas*, since *tamas* is relatively privative. Given that we find ourselves inhabiting a material world that is secretly host, as our own soul is, to higher worlds of form as well as to the Divine Essence that transcends all forms, the *tamasic* solidifying tendency is necessary to our earthly existence without thereby acting as an absolutely impenetrable veil over the higher realms we bear within us, since without it those higher realms would immediately subsume us. To take only one example, if we never developed a sense of separate individual identity (an ego, in other words) we would never be able to transcend this ego in the course of the Spiritual Path; transcendence of form, whether by sacrifice or by Intellection, first requires the attainment of form. But the *tamasic* tendency and the Demiurge who personifies it must never be taken as the first agent of creation, by action, by subversion or by anything else. Nor can the Demiurge simply be identified as the "negative" aspect of creation, or the personification of creation itself as negative in the sectarian Gnostic manner, since as Schuon himself maintains, *tamas*, which in universal terms is a neutral reality, only becomes subversive and actively evil in relation to man. And to maintain this definition of it without qualification is in itself unwarranted, given that *tamas*, while constituting a burden and a veil for us, the burden of material existence, is not actively subversive or devilish, even when viewed strictly in relation to our humanity. *Tamas* is one thing, neutral and even necessary for cosmic manifestation, but the Devil is something else. And if *tamas* only becomes devilish in relation to the human soul and world, then what can we make of the Christian doctrine of the rebellion of the angels, and the fall of Lucifer, prior (ontologically speaking) to humanity's creation? Nor is it correct to present the Devil as possessing only a heavy, opaque, *tamasic* quality, which we may refer to as *satanic*; he also exhibits a swift, lightning-like and ingeniously delusive *luciferian* quality. He is not only perverted *tamas* (barren ignorance) but also perverted *rajas* (self-will) and perverted *sattva* (corrupted intelligence). Lucifer represents, not the descent of the Principle into increasingly outward manifestation, but the potential on every level of the ontological hierarchy for delusion, privation, and subversion, the concrete manifestation of which however is only made possible by that very descent. As the "light bearer" he is symbolic—in his unfallen mode—of the *Nous*, the Primal Intellect, the first eternal motion of God's knowledge of Himself as distinct from His Essence, whereas—in his fallen mode—he symbolizes the possibility of spiritual subversion and metaphysical error on the highest possible level, and, in terms of the human microcosm, the subversion the uncreated Intellect in man, the *Nous* itself, which appears in the Qur'an as the refusal of Iblis to bow down to Adam [Q. 2:34; 7:11; 15: 31-34; 17:61; 18:50; 20:116; 38:75]. As Frithjof Schuon taught, the Uncreated Intellect within the human form cannot be subverted in its ultimate essence, but it most certainly can be counterfeited and veiled. According to Schuon in **Language of the Self**:

> For the "volitional" or "affective" man [the *bhakta*], God is "He" and the ego is "I," whereas for the "gnostic" or "intellective" man [the *jñani*], God is "I"—or "Self"—and the ego is "he" or "other."

Applying this distinction to Lucifer, we can imagine his fall as made possible by a descent from the intellective or *jñanic* station to the volitional-affective station, coupled with a refusal to accept the necessity of this creative descent—the later consequences of which God, in the first chapter of Genesis, looked upon and called "good." If he had accepted the necessity of the descending radiation of the Absolute in the direction of manifestation, Lucifer would have been able (in his own case) to redress its potential deficiencies through submission to God's creative will. Instead, he opposed it. In holding on to the memory of a "higher" conception of God as the Formless Absolute, he failed to understand that God's celestial and cosmic manifestation is in no way a departure

CHAPTER THIRTEEN

from His Essence, but rather a veiling of that Essence for the very purpose of revealing It on more outward levels. In other words—like the sectarian Gnostics—he looked upon God's creative act not as a positive Self-manifestation but strictly as a Fall. And by this very rejection of cosmic existence, which was both an intellectual error and a willful rebellion based upon that error, he transformed it into a Fall: this is the "primordial irony." Lucifer failed to understand that "If I ascend up to heaven, Thou art there; if I make my bed in hell, behold, Thou art there" [Psalm 139:8]. The ambiguity of existence, which is the ambiguity of *Maya*, is: that while manifestation must depart from the Essence, the Essence can never depart from Itself—and what is manifestation, on every level, but the revelation of that very Essence?

Lucifer looked within himself and saw the image of the *Atman*, the Absolute Divine Witness, but he saw it as an object of his knowledge, not himself as an object of Its knowledge. This primal limitation placed upon Intellection (or rather, this primal appearance of Intellection apart from the Absolute One, that is, an Intellection capable for the first time of knowing the One as an "external" object) can still be defined as a stage of the descent of the Absolute into manifestation, not as a subversion of that manifestation, not as a Fall. Lucifer's intellectual error—which in terms of his free will was also an act of rebellion—was to identify his now limited selfhood with the Absolute Reality he saw within himself, rather than submitting to that Reality and worshipping It, which was now required of him given the present stage-of-descent of Divine manifestation. As soon as manifestation descends from the purely intellective station to the volitional-affective one—in other words, as soon as free will is born—the will is required to submit, and the affections to love. This act of immediate submission to the new and more limited condition—not the will to reject it by holding on to the memory of the former and higher one—is the only way back to that higher one.

If Lucifer had retained the higher level of consciousness represented by the *Atman*, he would have remained rooted in the Absolute Witness which witnesses only Itself, and would consequently have been able to witness the cosmic unfolding, by virtue of the Eye of God within him, as a positive Divine manifestation, not a Fall. As soon as he saw the *Atman* as an "object," however, no longer as the Witness by which he witnessed and which also witnessed him, the Fall became possible. This was the primal intellectual limitation, a limitation which, because it posited God as an object, equally posited Lucifer as an independent entity. As an apparently independent entity he found himself possessed of an independent will, which could either submit to and adore this newly-arisen objective God or else deny Him and worship itself instead. Unwilling to redress the consequences of his intellectual limitation through submission and adoration, which—in his case—would have once more immediately unveiled the *Atman* as the Universal Witness, and effected the reintegration of the Personal God into the Formless Absolute, God into Godhead, Lucifer held on to the memory of that higher state in which himself as subject, and God as Object, had not yet polarized—a state which at this stage of the cosmic unfolding he could now identify only with himself, not with God. He saw the objective Personal God as a veil covering the Essence, but not as a theophany of that very Essence—the precise metaphysical error of the sectarian Gnostics. Thus, in the name of the "preservation" of the level of consciousness of the *Atman*, he barred the only effective road of return to that *Atman*; he rejected God, entered into a state of self-worship, and fell: and the etiology of the fall of Lucifer is, precisely, the etiology of the ego. We can understand by this that the possibility of self-idolatry, of the egoistic denial of God, was present from the first moment of the unfolding of universal manifestation. But it was present only as one possibility within the embrace of All-Possibility ("the possibility of impossibility" as Schuon has called it), not as a necessity on the level of free will, since if it were present as such a necessity the will would not be free. As soon as form is born, both potential obedience, resulting in a vision of the metaphysical transparency of all forms, and potential rebellion, based upon the idolatry of these forms, are born along with it.

Universal manifestation can also be viewed in terms of the Hindu doctrine of *Maya*, which is substantially identical with Schuon's "emanationism" (and in many ways with Neoplatonic emanationism as well), with the notion that Reality must, by Its nature, communicate Itself in a descending order of celestial and cosmic manifestations, each lower ontological plane being both more attenuated and more opaque and solidified than its higher predecessors. [NOTE: The Vedanta employs the concept of *Maya* to assert that all that is apparently other than Brahman is illusory; but this concept is also capable of functioning in a more positive mode as a way of explaining both the necessity of apparent manifestation, and its fundamental nature as real in one sense and unreal in another—according to the traditional simile, "like a rope mistaken for a snake."] But this truth does not license us to ignore the ontological level upon which, and subsequent to which, evil must progressively be defined in terms of the abuse of

CHAPTER THIRTEEN

free will by angelic, Jinnish, and human beings. When the Noble Qur'an says *I seek refuge in the Lord of Daybreak from the evil of that which He created* [Q. 133-1-2], it is not saying that God deliberately created evil, or (as Carl Jung main-tained in ***Answer to Job***) that God is somehow half evil Himself; if this were true, there would be no refuge in Him. As Schuon repeatedly points out in his writings, God is the Sovereign Good, and as such He cannot positively will evil, seeing that evil is not a positive reality on any level, but, precisely, a privation.

As Schuon teaches in ***Gnosis: Divine Wisdom*** and elsewhere, *Mahamaya*, as the "magical" manifestation of the Absolute, presents us with a universe that is neither real nor unreal, a world that is not strictly non-existent, but nonetheless not what it seems. Insofar as it manifests a cosmos apparently composed of limited forms arranged in various relations to one another, and subject to natural law, it is *Avidya-maya*, or "ignorance-appearance"; insofar as it presents us with forms which by their very existence testify to the Real, and which by their essential qualities exist as reflections of the Names or Qualities of God, it is *Vidya-maya* or "wisdom-appearance." Thus *Maya* cannot be strictly identified with the evil Demiurge of the sectarian Gnostics, who recognized cosmic manifestation in its aspect of *Avidya-maya* but not in its aspect of *Vidya-maya*. To them, the crystalline spheres of the circling heavens were an ingeniously-contrived cosmic prison ruled by oppressive spiritual powers; in no way could they "declare the glory of God" [Psalm 19:1]. A more useful and esoteric understanding of the Demiurge, in my opinion, would make him an allegory of the ego—as I believe that the Zoroastrian Angra Mainyu was also originally conceived to be, judging from his appearance in the ***Gathas***. To take the ego as the virtual "creator" of a universe considered as a privative illusion has certain affinities with Buddhist doctrine, but only in light of the fact that Buddhism, unlike the Abrahamic faiths, does not ask the question "how and why did the universe come to be?" but rather "by what misperception, based on craving, did the suffering of fundamentally illusory sentient beings come to be?" But to take the negative action of a privative *tamasic* Demiurge as positively creative in ontological terms, as Schuon seems to have done in *The Transcendent Unity of Religions*, is to concoct a heterogeneous doctrine that works in neither Hindu nor Buddhist nor Abrahamic terms, and one which—if taken as an independent doctrine (independent of Revelation, that is)—has little to recommend it.

The Devil is not evil because, like the Gnostic Demiurge, he creates this cosmos of heaviness and material limitation, but rather because he subverts it. The goal of all cosmic manifestation, the "lowest" point where God can be reflected as integral Being, is the terrestrial human form. And as every religious Tradition teaches, either openly or esoterically, the centrality of the human form, despite the heaviness and opacity of its material manifestation (whether or not this be considered the product of a "Fall"), gives it a potential spiritual precedence over even the highest angels, since it is the central, though distant, reflection of God in the material cosmos, whereas the angels are the higher, but relatively peripheral, reflections of the various Names or Qualities of God. Man alone exists as a synthesis of all the Names: a "stewardship" or "Trust" he is free either to realize or betray.

So the Absolute, by virtue of Its Infinity, radiates Itself through the descending echelons of celestial and cosmic manifestation until it reaches the human form, which, by virtue of the possibility

CHAPTER THIRTEEN

of spiritual realization and Liberation, is the point where the return of universal manifestation to its Origin begins. This entire cycle of radiation and return is encapsulated in the *Basmallah* that begins every *surah* but one of the Noble Qur'an: *Bismillah al-Rahman al-Rahim*, "In the Name of God, the Merciful, the Compassionate." *Al-Rahman* is the "universal Mercy" that allows all beings to come into separate existence: the Mercy of Creation; *Al-Rahim* is the "particular Mercy" that establishes the criteria and provides the spiritual Path by which each being, insofar as it chooses to avail itself of them, may return to Allah.[2] However, owing to the freedom of the human will, without which God's own freedom could not be mirrored in humanity, the expansion and attenuation of the Absolute's cosmic manifestation does not necessarily end at the human level but may also sink below it. In Hindu terms this "sinking" may be seen as the result of the action of *tamas*, which according to its positive function materially stabilizes the cosmic environment in which earthly, incarnate man must exist, but which also, in terms of its negative

---

2 Man at the limit of cosmic manifestation, imprisoned in a material existence transformed from a theophany into a veil, is well symbolized by Prometheus bound to the rock, his liver being eaten by the eagle of Zeus. The liver—related to the *manipura-chakra* of the Hindu Tantra—when alienated from man's higher faculties becomes the seat of a "Promethean" self-will, a reckless willfulness that steals the fire of Zeus—the Intellect, the *Nous*—and transforms it into blind impulse. Man in the state of self-will represents the lowest point of cosmic manifestation (matter itself being incapable of rebellion, and thus fundamentally innocent), at which point cosmic existence must either begin its return to God, via the sacrifice of self-will, or else fall into an infernal or *titanic* state, which is no longer a veiling of God with a view toward His outward manifestation, but a plunge into chaos and non-entity. And the sole path of this return is the path of Intellection, either actual or virtual: the eagle of Zeus is a symbol of the *Nous* in the process of devouring the fallen self-will and transmuting it into Intellection again; thus the "punishment" of Prometheus, being precisely purgatorial, is the beginning of his salvation.

and potentially subversive function, veils the face of God, thus introducing "materialism" in all the senses of that word. That man has a body is not evil, though that body is subject to many evils. That he lives in a material world is not evil, though matter and material concerns are a heavy veil. The nature and activity of the Devil must not be sought in these mere facts of earthly man's existence but in the satanic subversion of their true significance. In one sense they are the product of a fall, of the loss of Eden that made it necessary for humanity to don these "garments of skin" [Genesis 3:21]; in another sense this very fall, according to St. Augustine, was a *felix culpa*, a "fortunate fault" destined not to confirm and solidify Satan's kingdom but to overturn it definitively. In light of this we can understand our present physical forms not as a punishment for Adam's sin, but as a product of God's mercy, Who willed a partial redress of the effects of that sin on a lower ontological level, thus opening humanity to the possibility of Redemption.

When, in its expansion and attenuation, cosmic manifestation falls below the human form because the human being, due to his betrayal of his delegated function of God's *khalifa* in the terrestrial world, has failed to recognize God in the totality of that manifestation, and thus by this act of discernment to return cosmic manifestation to its Origin, it enters the realm of what René Guénon calls the "infra-psychic," which is, precisely, the kingdom of Satan. Ontologically lower, but also subtler, than gross matter, the infra-psychic possesses all the darkness and opacity of matter without its nobility and stability, as well as the all swiftness, penetration, and ingeniousness of pure Intellection without its orientation to Divine Truth: the "possibility of impossibility" with a vengeance! (As we have already seen, the tendency toward heaviness and opacity can be termed "satanic" and the quality of ingeniousness and lightning-swiftness "luciferian.") It is here, not in the bare facts of material existence, either within humanity or outside it, that the nature and "function" of the Devil are to be found.

Though evil is certainly a *privatio boni*—a depletion of or limited access to the Good on a particular level of being—it is not a "mere" insufficiency. Certainly evil is a privation and nothing else, a privation of access to both Divine Reality (in ontological terms) and the Sovereign Good (in "moral" terms)—as well as, in terms both of the possibility of Intellection and an understanding of the doctrines derived from Revelation, a privation of the Truth, a veil over pure Intelligence. But what is often poorly understood by many who espouse a more-or-less emanationist view of Divine manifestation is that evil, privative though it be, does not manifest simply as a kind of weakness or lack but also as attack, subversion, and counterfeit. Where sound doctrine is wise, evil (as error) is not simply stupid, but infernally ingenious; where love is strong, evil (as hatred) is not only weak, but demonically cruel; where universal manifestation constitutes a Cosmos, an Order composed of a descending hierarchy of orders within orders, the kingdom of Satan also has its infernal modes of organization, its "lowerarchies" (to use the humorous term coined by C.S. Lewis), its dark *agendas*. Hell is not a neutral chaos but an inverted order; not a loveless indifference but an active attack upon Love; not a stupid impermeability to metaphysical Truth but a swift, ingenious, and infernally "intelligent" war upon that Truth. As a parasite on order, evil forms its own counterfeit order,

CHAPTER THIRTEEN

chaotic in essence but nonetheless marshaled into a semblance of order through naked power. As a parasite on love, it tempts us to give our love to that which is in the process of destroying us, even as the drunkard loves his bottle or the addict his drug. As a parasite on Truth, evil forms its own inverted metaphysics, and inverted morality as well; it forges its own Counter-Tradition and Counter-Initiation with scraps and fragments of doctrines purloined from the Primordial Tradition, and from the various Divine Revelations that are its branches. It prepares, is presently preparing, and is at this very moment acting to subvert, attack, destroy, counterfeit, and supplant whatever remains of this Tradition—whether doctrine, institution, moral standard, faithful believer, or metaphysical sage—in this earthly world. Only when it has succeeded in destroying the last vestiges of the Primordial Tradition, thus bringing this cycle of manifestation to a close, will it itself die, and die by starvation, because it has no principle of life within itself but can exist only as a parasite on the Real.

And so evil is not a "mere" privation of the good, any more than starvation is a "mere" lack of food. It is all too easy, however, for those who hold to the true doctrine that evil as a privation, not a positive force, to see it as a "mere nothing" that can be safely ignored—particularly by those who in their spiritual life overly concentrate on the intellective pole (the realm of metaphysics) to the detriment of the existential pole (the realm of sanctity). Such people may foolishly believe it is relatively easy, at least for those with a degree of metaphysical discernment, to "rise above" evil, that there is really no such thing as "spiritual wickedness in high places." Such complacency is not derived from true metaphysical insight, however—which includes the gift known as "discernment

CHAPTER THIRTEEN

of spirits"—but from that state of spiritual delusion which the Buddhists name *deva-loka* in reference to the *samsaric* world where ignorance is bliss, the realm of the long-lived gods in which the realities of impermanence and karmic rigor are hidden under a veil of aesthetic refinement and false spiritual elevation—until it is too late.

In order to understand the doctrine of evil-as-privation in any effective way and to avoid its potential pitfalls we will need to hold to a metaphysic (as well as to the intrinsic moral standards which exist as reflections of it) that both grants evil its true place in the universal order—so as to free God from the twin slanders that He is either good but too weak to prevent evil, or all-powerful but too evil, or too nihilistically indifferent, to will the good—and that also grants evil its full gravity, while providing access to the complete panoply of traditional powers and skills by which it may be combated: doctrinally, ascetically, and theurgically. To settle for anything less is to reduce metaphysics to an abstract academic exercise, a parlor game for people who want to entertain themselves with truth instead of saving their souls by means of it.

This world, filled with suffering though it may be, is a creation of Divine mercy, not a product of infernal subversion. In human terms, the possibility of the subversion of a merciful creation (at least in the present Kali-yuga) arises first from our misperception of that creation as material only, opaque to the light of God, and secondarily from the many ill-conceived actions that flow from this primal error. Subversion is based *in potentia* on the necessary "departure" of creation from God, via emanation, so that it may exist in its own right, but it is only realized in act by the misuse of free will, which—again in human terms, and ignoring the angelic rebellion that preceded us and still affects us—begins when we succumb to the temptation of ignorance and ends when we express this ignorance concretely through transgression and sin, further reinforcing it by means of them.

Jesus encapsulates in a single line [Luke 17:1] both the necessity of the *possibility* of evil in terms of emanation and the actualization of evil in terms of the misuse of free will: "It is impossible but that offenses shall come, but woe to him through whom they come!" A truly plenary esoterism, in view of the metaphysical truth that limitation is necessary for Divine manifestation, does not ignore or denigrate perspectives more limited than itself, but rather embraces them as providential and grants them their precise position and function in the universal order. And although Schuon's doctrine of the necessity of God's manifestation by virtue of the fact that the Absolute is also necessarily the Infinite, and his corresponding doctrine that the manifestation of evil as "the possibility of impossibility" is also necessary once a certain level of attenuation-of-manifestation is reached (because Infinity is also All-Possibility), are metaphysically profound, we nonetheless need to leave room in them for more circumscribed orders of reality where sin, salvation, and judgment hold sway. If we fail to do this, we place the great truths Frithjof Schuon uttered beyond effective assimilation by the human soul, thereby separating knowledge from salvation, and the elucidation of metaphysical truth from the operative realities of the spiritual Path. Schuon himself recognized this distinction of levels and the necessity of both of them in **The Transcendent Unity of Religions**:

> The difference between the religious and metaphysical conceptions of evil does not mean . . . that one is

CHAPTER THIRTEEN

false and the other true, but simply that the former is incomplete and individual whereas the other is integral and universal....

The reader may remember at this point that Schuon made nearly the opposite attributions to religion vs. metaphysics in ***Survey of Metaphysics and Esoterism*** above, calling metaphysical intellection "vocational"—that is, individual—and characterizing the function of Revelation, which is the source of all the religious dispensations, as "formal," "theological," "obligatory" and "legalistic"—which is to say, collective.

The universal metaphysical view does not negate the more individual religious one—if it did it could only represent a false and Luciferian metaphysic—but rather places the religious conception of evil within a wider context that allows us both to understand its limitations and to recognize its essential value and use. The true doctrine of the Absolute and its inseparability from the Infinite recognizes the providential necessity of the relative. Unfortunately, in his own case, Schuon often seems to have placed himself "above" the religious viewpoint, recognizing no authority higher than his own discernment. He was most certainly a metaphysical genius, but it seems that he may to some extent have lost control of that very genius, as so many geniuses have. When he maintains that many things that seem like contradictions from the exoteric point of view are, from the esoteric standpoint, no more than differing metaphysical perspectives on the same reality, perspectives that are entirely acceptable if not providential given that metaphysical truth transcends explicit dogmatism, he is entirely right: many of his own apparent disagreements with himself can be legitimately explained in just this way. Some of

CHAPTER THIRTEEN

these disagreements, however, are contradictions, pure and simple, expressions in the face of which we are required to declare: "you can't have it both ways." Gnosis cannot support contradictions that are obvious and undeniable, seeing that dishonesty, even if it is unconscious, necessarily veils Intellection.

Intellect and Will

Schuon placed the Intellect on a higher ontological plane than the will and he was entirely justified in doing so, since the Intellect contemplates What Is while the will considers only what might be if it possessed sufficient *might* to actualize the possibility in question; this is the Traditional distinction, enunciated by Ibn Sina and Thomas Aquinas among others, between God as Necessary Being, that which "cannot not be," and manifest existence as Possible Being—all of the possibilities of which, and many that have never descended into manifestation, are nonetheless eternally actualized within God, according to what Schuon called *maya-in-divinis*. It is from this Necessity/Possibility distinction that Schuon's exaltation of intellective or *jñanic* spirituality over volitional-and-affective or *bhaktic* spirituality arose—a distinction that is valid and useful as long as we don't push it too far by using the primacy of the Intellect to deny the pivotal nature of the will, or by forgetting that the *bhaktic* path, if carried far enough into what is called *parabhakti*—a degree of devotion that transcends the subject/object dichotomy—can attain *gnosis* or *jñana* in and of itself. It is nonetheless true that the sort of pseudo-*bhakti* that is based on a reluctance to embrace *jñana* once one is called to actualize it, due to a fear of the rigors this ultimate transformation will entail, which requires nothing less than a "dying before you are made to die" (in the words of the Prophet Muhammad). A false *devotion* to *jñana* that remains content to stay on the level of a mere emotional identification with the *idea* of knowledge, is on a far lower level than either realized *jñana* or true *bhakti*.

It was undoubtedly in line with the true hierarchy of the human faculties that places the Intellect higher than the will that Schuon conceived of God more as the One Who enlightens human intelligence than as the One Who commands and guides human volition. Unfortunately, he appears to have misinterpreted or mis-applied this true hierarchization to the point where he believed that an intellective intuition of metaphysical Truth is sufficient in and of itself to conform the entirety of the soul to that Truth, without the strengthening, purification and dedication of the will; it may in fact have been this error that lay behind his antinomian tendencies. Nor must we ever forget that God's Eternal Will is inseparable from His intrinsic Nature, since He is not Who He Is passively, like the cosmic elements that must obey natural law in spite of themselves, but is so actively and intentionally; this is one of the meanings of Aquinas' definition of God as "Pure Act." Likewise the human individual whose will is fully subordinated to his or her God-enlightened Intellect is necessarily also submitted to the Will of God. If the individual will follows What Is, it will recognize the Divine Intellect as its Lord; consequently the intellectual perspective of that individual will be purified and enlightened. If, on the other hand, it follows its own whims and passions, the various possibilities it hankers to actualize, then it will press that individual's intellect into its own service, either to rationalize its actions or to devise strategies to help it get what it wants. This is how the individual will is transformed into self-will, with the result that the Divine Will is contradicted and the Divine Intellect veiled. Schuon, on the other hand, may have sometimes believed—at least in his own case, in line with his assertion of the "ultimate authority" of his own discernment—that if the Intellect is recognized as higher than the will, which describes the station of the "intellective man" in Schuon's terminology, then the will is free to do whatever it wants, since the intellective man is not bound by the laws necessary to control the passional behavior of the "volitional man," who occupies a lower spiritual caste. Here we can see the problematic nature of Schuon's over-emphasis on spiritual typology, as if the "intellective man" were entirely beyond any need for obedience, just as the "volitional man" is supposedly closed to any higher degree of spiritual understanding—a conception that is certainly highly convenient for the "intellective man" who wishes to indulge his antinomian tendencies, even though it has no basis in reality. To make the will-based soul and the intellect-based soul mutually exclusive to the degree sometimes suggested by Schuon's definitions is in no way warranted, seeing that *bhaktic* tendencies are discernible even in Ramana Maharshi, while moments of true *gnosis* can be found even in St. John Climacus. Schuon saw *bhaktic* or devotional spirituality as based on the subject/Object duality in which the human devotee is "I" and God is "He," a duality that is transcended, in *jñanic* or intellective spirituality, by the perspective according to which God is "I" and the human *jñani* is "he." This is both true and profound; it was this teaching that finally let me understand the *jñanic* spirituality of Sri Ramana Maharshi. However, when Schuon strictly identified the perception of God as Object with Love and the non-dual realization of God as the Universal Subject (the *Atman*) with Knowledge—which he sometimes did—he was far wide of the mark. Mental knowledge, even if it contains an element of metaphysical intuition, also sees God as "Object"—an Object of study, research, and contemplation. Likewise, non-dual Knowledge most certainly does not leave Love behind, but is in fact the highest realization of Love, in which lover and Beloved are One; as Ramana Maharshi put it, "imperfect *jñana* and imperfect *bhakti* are different; perfect *jñana* and perfect *bhakti* are the same." And Schuon sometimes knew this. At other times, however, he was capable of seeing Love Itself as "secondary" or "preliminary." The shaykhs of the *silsila* of Shaykh Ahmed al-'Alawi, who initiated Frithjof Schuon into the Sufi way, also teach that Knowledge, *Ma'rifa*, grows out of Love, *Mahabbah*—but it never leaves Love behind, since *Ma'rifa* is in fact the perfection of *Mahabbah*.

The Devil, who is no mean metaphysician himself, has often recognized, in this entirely justified act of placing the Intellect hierarchically above the will, the perfect opportunity to twist this essential teaching by appealing to the intellectual pride that is the besetting temptation of the gnostic, the *arif*, thereby setting up a disastrous conflict between Love and Knowledge. And it is precisely the mystical philosopher whose heart has become cold because he or she has cultivated Intellection while neglecting to dedicate the will to obedience and to purify the affections from concupiscence who is most easily tempted by the Devil to seek a compensatory "warmth" in an aesthetic eros that, while still capable of damning Love with faint praise from the supposed higher viewpoint of Knowledge, attempts to take refuge from the pain of its lovelessness in the Divine Beauty and its multiple and delightful earthly manifestations. To exalt Beauty while denigrating

Love is, however, the perfect recipe for invoking *Avidya-maya*, along with all the catastrophes she brings in her train.

To believe that the problems of "voluntarism" and spiritual self-will can be solved simply by "rising above" the will entirely into the realm of the Intellect is profoundly misdirected. These difficulties are solved only by consciously submitting the will to the Truths that the Intellect, as well as Divine Revelation, have unveiled; to simply "dismiss" the will in the face of the Intellect rather than submitting it to that Intellect as its proper Lord is a sure recipe for an unholy mixture of spiritual obsession and spiritual paralysis. And if this paralysis ever succeeds, with the Devil's help, in masquerading as contemplative impassivity in the face of the Absolute, then it will have become a disease that is virtually incurable for those who have contracted it.

On First Positing, Then Collapsing, Hierarchy-*in*-*Divinis*

Schuon and his fellow Traditionalists have labored long to re-establish the Traditional sense of ontological hierarchy, the Great Chain of Being, in face of the leveling tendencies of the modern and postmodern world. Nonetheless, hierarchy cannot be ultimately predicated of God Himself, though whether Schuon was clear on this point remains open to question. In ontological and cosmological terms, to collapse hierarchy in most cases simply brings everything to a lowest common denominator, which usually turns out to be materialism. Theoretically, such collapse may be taken as positing the universal Immanence of God; but without having first realized the Divine Transcendence, which cannot be done without resort to a sense of ontological hierarchy, this Immanence cannot be realized in any effective way, since it is precisely God's Transcendence of all things that is immanent in all things. However, when speaking of the Divine Nature itself, we must collapse the hierarchy. Frithjof Schuon presents us with a scheme where Beyond Being is placed hierarchically above Pure Being, Pure Being hierarchically above the Logos or Demiurge, etc. This is a necessary step for us to begin to grasp the true nature of the Godhead, both within Itself and in Its relationship with the cosmos. But if we leave it at that—which Schuon sometimes appears to do—it begins to seem as if there is a primary God Who is Beyond Being, a secondary God Who is Pure Being, a tertiary God who acts as the Demiurge, etc., and this (speaking in Christian terms) sets in motion the unconscious slide toward Arianism and a number of other heresies. In other words, when speaking of the nature of God, if we begin by positing hierarchy, we must end by collapsing it; otherwise we will arrive, at the end of our speculative road, at one God who is Not, another God who Is, and a third God who Acts, thereby denying the Divine Unity. But the truth is that God Is Who He Is both essentially and intentionally. God is not God passively, as creatures must be creatures simply because they can't help it, but actively, seeing that He is Pure Act. And between the bare fact that He is God and His eternal *intention* to be God—His intrinsic Will, that is, the Will that is indistinguishable from His Being, not His Will in relation to the possibilities of manifestation—there is not a shadow of a hair's-breadth of a distinction. Logos and Godhead are One; the God Who acts, the God Who is, and the God Who is beyond even Being are one and the same. But insofar that we attempt to "define" (a word which means "set a limit to") God in terms of this Unity, we must also posit Him as lying infinitely beyond this and all other definitions; He is Beyond Action and Beyond Being precisely because He is beyond definition.

Beyond Being is not a "higher God," but simply the fact that God is Infinite and Absolute and thus transcends all attributions; that God is Pure Being is not a "slightly lower" God, but simply the fact that in relation to us and all manifestation He is the One Who Is, while we—except for His free gift to us out of the infinite store of His Being—are those who are not. And to say that God is an acting, creating, and governing Will is not to posit a still lower God, a cosmic Demiurge, but only to say that, insofar as the sentient beings of the manifest world may be said to will and to act, His Will and His Action infinitely transcend and dominate the will and actions of creatures; precisely because we are merely virtual and relative doers, God must appear to us as the True and Absolute Doer. So in order to understand God properly from a Schuonian metaphysical perspective, one must first posit Beyond Being, Pure Being, and Active Logos, and then immediately collapse that hierarchy by an understanding that this distinction arises from an attempt on our part to understand God in three different ways according to three different points-of-departure. These points-of-departure are objective and necessary; they are not simply subjective phantoms. And yet the Reality of the Absolute and Infinite God infinitely and absolutely transcends them. We often resist collapsing the hierarchical conception of the Divine Nature like this because in order to do so we must sacrifice our highest metaphysical conceptions of the Divine and submit to the annihilation of the limited subject who likes to speculate on the nature of God, and may feel that it has become rather proficient at this art. But we must collapse it—hopefully with every breath, with every invocation of the Name—or else intellectual pride, whose final outcome is ignorance and stupidity, will eat us alive. There are states, times and levels in which piety is wiser, closer to *gnosis*, than even the subtlest metaphysical discrimination.

Schuon on the Eucharist

On page 95 of ***Logic and Transcendence***, Schuon says:

> If in truth the Eucharistic species have literally become the flesh and blood of Jesus, how much better off are we for this so to say "magical" operation, given that the value of this flesh and this blood lies in its Divine content, and that this same content can itself penetrate the bread and the wine without any "transubstantiation"? For we can neither desire nor obtain anything greater than the Divine Presence; if that Presence were in a tree, the tree would then be equivalent to the body of Christ, and there would be no need to ask oneself whether the wood was something other than wood, or to conclude that it was a tree without being one or that it was a "form" that contradicted its substance, and so forth. It is not the body of Jesus that sanctifies God, it is God who sanctifies it.

Schuon, in this passage, seems to be denying the necessity and validity of the eucharistic Consecration, since "transubstantiation" is essentially synonymous with "Consecration" in Roman

CHAPTER THIRTEEN

Catholicism. And insofar as he speaks of the Divine Presence "penetrating" the bread and wine without transforming them, which transformation he compares to an act of magic, he would appear to see Christ not as "the Word made flesh" but as the Word "occupying" the flesh of Christ, a conception departs significantly from the traditional dogma of the Incarnation. And exactly what does he mean when he insists that "it is not the body of Jesus that sanctifies God, it is God who sanctifies it", when the transubstantiation of the bread and wine in the Eucharist, which he denies, is the very sign and the substance of that sanctification-by-God? We may speculate that Schuon accepts the Eucharist as a kind of "primordial" sacrament due to the fact that it is host to the Divine Presence by virtue of God's Immanence, though not in any special, sacramental sense, since elsewhere he maintains, correctly I believe, that created things testify to the God who creates them first by their bare existence, since (as the first chapter of Genesis teaches) Being in itself is good, and secondly by the symbolism of their forms, which reflect the Divine Attributes, just as existence itself reflects the Divine Essence. If indeed, in denying the transubstantiation which he terms a "magical operation" ("theurgic" would be a more accurate term) could add any new dimension to this state of affairs he denies that the Eucharist represents a special mode of the Presence beyond the symbolism, and the bare existence, of the bread and wine, he also implicitly denies, as the Lutherans and other Protestants do, the necessity for a validly ordained Roman Catholic or Eastern Orthodox priesthood, though elsewhere he apparently accepts the reality of the Consecration as understood by Orthodox Christians. In any case, his denial of the transubstantiation of the Eucharist works to obscure, or ignore, the truth that God's Presence occupies a hierarchy of degrees in relation to manifest existence, which is itself a hierarchy; if this were not so, the degrees of spiritual realization, the rungs of the Ladder of Divine Ascent, would be entirely subjective, corresponding to no objective ontological order, and thus spiritually barren. If God may be present to humanity not only by the simple fact of our existence and by the intrinsic symbolism of the human form, but also by sacramental grace, by sanctification, by Intellection, then He can and must be present in the species of the Eucharist not only by their bare existence and their formal symbolism, by which they are host to the Immanence of God, but by the special grace of the Sacrament itself, instituted by Christ at the Last Supper. And this last mode of the Divine Presence, though not the others, requires that an ordained priest, with the correct intention, pronounce the correct words of Consecration above the species.

When Schuon says "We can neither desire nor obtain anything greater than the Divine Presence; if that Presence were a tree, that tree would be equivalent to the Body of Christ," is he implying both that this Presence does not manifest as a hierarchy of degrees in relation to us, and that God either is incapable of instituting a Sacrament as a special channel of Grace, or that He did not in fact do so in the case of the Eucharist? This remains uncertain. To say this would be equivalent to saying "if God is present in the name Allah, He is equally present in the name Pickle"; if special channels of Grace—Sacraments, Holy Names—are unnecessary and thus do not effectively exist, then Pickle will do just as well as Allah, allowing us to employ *La ilaha illa Pickle* as a spiritually effective invocation—though except for such distorted passages Schuon in no way accepted such a notion, given that he established the invocation of the Name of God, in Sufic mode, as the central "sacrament" of his *tariqah*. Yet a certain ambiguity remains when it comes to the validity of the Catholic sacraments, since his objections to transubstantiation in the passage are little different from those of any worldly cynic who proudly declares that "I don't believe in all that hocus pocus" ("hocus pocus" being a parody of the words of consecration, *Hoc est Corpus Meum*). Furthermore, if we accept his argument that the Consecration is unnecessary because God is already present intrinsically in the bread and wine without it, then by the same token He is intrinsically present in the tree; therefore to say "*if* that Presence were a tree" is out of place: that Presence *is* a tree, and is bread and wine, and is the human body, and is the body of a dog, and is anything else at all, all with equal justification—if, that is, the only mode of Presence we accept is the intrinsic one based on the bare existence of the object in question. The whole *raison d'être* of the Eucharist, however, is that God chose to manifest His special sacramental Presence exclusively within the species of bread and wine—certainly according their formal symbolism, seeing that a Sacrament could not employ inappropriate symbolism any more than Pickle could be a Name of God, but not exclusively so. And if "we can neither desire nor obtain anything greater than the Divine Presence"—if, as is apparently being implied here, there are no more universal and more circumscribed, more general and more quintessential degrees of this Presence—then what becomes of the spiritual Path? What becomes of growth in "wisdom and age and grace" such as the Gospels attribute to Christ Himself? How can Christ say to us "I come that ye should have Life and have it more abundantly" if the Divine Life is exclusively Absolute, if it possesses no relative degrees by which we may, through

CHAPTER THIRTEEN

God's Grace and Mercy, draw nearer to Him? If life is only Life Absolute, in which there is neither growth nor diminution, then how can we increase it, cultivate it, embrace it? And how can we pray with the Prophet Muhammad, peace and blessings be upon him, "O God, increase me in Knowledge" if Knowledge, like Life, is exclusively Absolute? If the Truth is only Absolute Truth, if it does not also manifest itself, through Divine Mercy, as relative and partial so as to meet our own relativity and partiality and gather it back to the Absolute Reality, then how can we travel the Path? We are denied Union with God by our very nearness to Him. The first words of Schuon's book ***Understanding Islam*** are: "Islam is the encounter between man as such and God as such." True! But this encounter is not unmediated; it does not take place without the *salat*, the Ramadan fast, the pilgrimage to Mecca, the veneration of the Prophet and his family, and the invocation of the Name, just as our relationship with God in traditional Christianity doesn't happen without the grace of the sacraments. To treat the Divine Presence as exclusively Absolute rather than as the Absolute manifesting in a hierarchy of degrees (as Schuon makes clear in many other places, even though he seems to have forgotten it here)—though it is certainly the Presence *of* the Absolute, and nothing else—is to affirm His Transcendence but deny His Immanence, to assert His incomparability but not His comparability, and to deny the reality of *maya-in-divinis* as well; it is to place Him at an absolute Distance which is also an implacable and unmediated Presence; it is to call for God to annihilate us without first allowing Him to *create* us. The sectarian Gnostics did something similar when they posited God as the Absolutely Transcendent, the Alien, and defined manifest existence as a veil over the Divine but not a manifestation of It.

CHAPTER THIRTEEN

Elsewhere Schuon, by way of compensation, speaks of sacred art, and virgin nature, and the human body as manifestations of the Divine; these, along with the Holy Name, are his sacraments, and they are worthy to be characterized as such. And by his doctrine of *maya-in-divinis*, the eternal subsistence of All-Possibility in the Necessary Being of God, he mitigates many of his own errors and imbalances. But in the passage above he has the temerity to reject the central mystery of the Christian tradition, and in so doing denies the Incarnation as well, from which the Eucharist is inseparable.

Lastly, how can the Consecration of the Eucharist be invalidated by construing it as "the body of Jesus sanctifying God rather than God sanctifying it"? The Consecration is not by any bodily power to forcibly invoke and incarnate God, but by the power of God through the priest to transform the species into the Holy Eucharist. Nowhere is the body of Jesus said to "sanctify God," nor is this ever implied; the Body is the manifestation and theophany of God, "of one Substance with the Father." It almost seems as if Schuon somehow considered the Consecration to be a Promethean attempt by terrestrial man to make God Divine through human power alone, as his use of the word "magical" would suggest. If, however, he had simply considered and accepted the orthodox doctrines of the Incarnation and the Eucharist, as any real Traditionalist would have done, he would never have had to "refute" such an absurd notion; it would never have entered his head.

Furthermore, one is led to ask: did Schuon deny the sacramental necessity of the Consecration as an esoterist, or (in effect) as a "cultural" Lutheran? Lutheran spirituality, which embraces the esoterism of sages such as Jacob Boehme, does not require a sacerdotally consecrated Eucharist, but Catholic and Eastern Orthodox spirituality certainly do. Schuon himself defended the validity of Baptism, Confirmation/ Chrismation and the Eucharist against René Guénon, who believed Christianity had lost its esoteric dimension, by recognizing these three sacraments as in essence esoteric initiations, with which I fully agree; Dionysius the Areopagite said substantially the same thing in *The Ecclesiastical Hierarchy*. Here, however, Schuon appears to deny an orthodox conception of the same sacraments he defended against René Guénon's incomprehension. One would have thought that Schuon's "plenary esoterism" would have allowed him to see the particularities of the Lutheran way, the Catholic way, and the Eastern Orthodox way from a higher standpoint, accepting the foundational doctrines of each without feeling he had to evaluate one in terms of another, thereby precipitating various anti-Traditional "bleed-throughs." But this does not seem to have been the case, at least in *Logic and Transcendence*. In *In the Face of the Absolute*, Schuon is more explicit about his acceptance of the Eucharistic consecration than he had been in the earlier book, yet he still thinks it appropriate to judge Catholic theology according to Eastern Orthodox theology, in "horizontal" terms, rather than accepting each church, in "vertical" terms, as a unique and providential rendering of the Christic revelation, which the Transcendent Unity of Religions ought to have allowed and required him to do:

> For the Catholics, the Eucharistic presence of Christ is produced, not by "implantation" or "consubstantiation," but by "transubstantiation," meaning that "the substance

of the bread no longer remains," which they justify—abusively in our view—with the consecrating words of Christ; according to this theory the "substantial form of the species no longer remains," not even their "raw material." The Orthodox, for their part, either do not admit transubstantiation, or they do not admit that it implies "a substance that changes and accidents that do not change"; their intention is to remain faithful—quite wisely—to the Eucharistic teaching of St. John Damascene, according to whom "The Holy Ghost intervenes and does what transcends all word and thought. And if you enquire as to how this happens, let it suffice you to know that it happens through the Holy Ghost .... that the Word of God is true, effective, and all-powerful, the manner of it remaining unfathomable."

The fact remains, however, that in practical Catholic terms, though certainly not in Lutheran or Orthodox ones, an acceptance of the Real Presence and the validity of the Consecration cannot be maintained if the doctrine of transubstantiation is denied.

In *In The Face of the Absolute*, Schuon says: "Heaven could will a phenomenon such as the Lutheran communion; but it is impossible that it will the Lutheranization of the Catholic Mass [as was the result of the Second Vatican Council], for God cannot contradict Himself on one and the same plane," thus partly redressing—or else simply contradicting—his own *de facto* Lutheranization of the Mass in *Logic and Transcendence*, when he defines as "abusive" the Catholic doctrine that the words of the Consecration indicate transubstantiation. And if He could not allow a Lutheranization of the Catholic Mass, how could He will an Eastern Orthodoxization of the Latin theology of the Mass, given that the two churches are now in many ways distinct both liturgically and theologically, just as both are distinct from Lutheranism—especially since most present-day attempts to reconcile Catholicism and Eastern Orthodoxy are largely in the spirit of Vatican II, and thus partake of its tendency to grant theological and liturgical questions second place in favor of certain political considerations, including the sort of external "unification" of the Christian churches that could only be a Satanic counterfeit of the intrinsic Unity of the Church founded by Christ? The Catholics and the Orthodox are one in retaining the consecrating function of the priest, and all three churches (as Schuon points out) accept the Real Presence, though the Eastern Orthodox and the traditional Catholics deny that the Lutheran communion is host to that Presence. Nevertheless, there can be no orthodox Roman Catholic doctrine of the Eucharist without the transubstantiation, which the Eastern Orthodox deny, nor can there be an Eastern Orthodox doctrine of the Sacrament that does not accept the need for the consecrating priest, which the Lutherans deny. All three Christian churches might have provided Frithjof Schuon with stable doctrinal foundations for an esoteric exegesis capable of overcoming their limitations vertically without his having to "adjust" one to the other horizontally. But since he apparently refused to accept certain foundational doctrines of these traditions, at least on occasion (particularly those of Roman Catholicism), the opportunity to carry on such an exegesis in depth—an operation that Schuon would seem to have been eminently capable of—was lost in certain areas. Of course we must always draw the line between a limited though providential doctrinal perspective and an outright abuse that denies a central doctrine of the tradition in question, though it is not always clear exactly where to draw this line; a sect that rejects either the humanity or the Divinity of Christ, for example, can in no way be called Traditionally Christian. But to reject or "adjust" a limited though spiritually operative perspective because it seems weak in certain areas to a certain metaphysician where another perspective appears strong, to invoke that second perspective so as to compensate for the supposed deficiencies in the first, is not the *orthodox* esoteric way, since it rejects legitimate doctrinal authority by attempting to make an amalgam of two properly distinct orthodox viewpoints, often based largely on personal preference; this approach ultimately posits a purely horizontal unity of religions, not a vertical and Transcendent one. The true Traditionalist method, as I see it, is to accept a particular traditional, orthodox formulation precisely as transmitted, free of any "improvements" or "adjustments", and only then submit it to an exhaustive esoteric exegesis.

Schuon on the Trinity

In *Logic and Transcendence*, (Perennial Books edition, 1975) Schuon explains the development of the Christian doctrine of the Trinity in the following terms:

> The theology of the Trinity does not constitute an explicit and homogeneous revelation; it results on the one hand, like the concept of transubstantiation, from a literalistic and quasi-mathematical interpretation of certain words in the Scriptures, and on the other

hand from a summation of different points of view, deriving from different dimensions of the Real.

Here Schuon implicitly denies the possibility that the dogma of the Trinity, clearly an intrinsically esoteric doctrine, could have been transmitted in integral form by Tradition rather than Scripture; furthermore, the significance of the obvious theophany of the Trinity at the Baptism of Christ, where the Son appears in the figure of Jesus, the Holy Spirit as the Dove, and the Father as the disembodied Voice declaring "this is My beloved Son in Whom I am well pleased" [Matthew 3:17], seems to have escaped him entirely. He also ignores the possibility that the Trinitarian doctrine might have derived in part from the esoteric doctrines of the Jews, specifically from the first three *sefiroth* of the Kabbalistic Tree of Life, Kether being roughly analogous to the Father, Hokmah to the Son, and Binah to the Holy Spirit. It is true that the renditions of the *sefiroth* we possess appeared centuries after Christ, but the origins of the Kabbalistic doctrines, undoubtedly transmitted by word of mouth (the word Kabbalah itself means "transmission" or "Tradition"), certainly predated Christianity. And as the Eastern Orthodox Christians recognize, the Trinity was prefigured in Genesis by the three angels who visited the patriarch Abraham; the traditional Orthodox icon of the Trinity is a portrayal of this episode. The Threeness of the One God represents a unique and self-consistent perspective that could never have resulted from a mere "literalistic and quasi-mathematical interpretation of certain words in the Scripture"; nor is Schuon justified, in my opinion, in seeing the Trinity as a heterogeneous, and by implication inopportune, amalgam of differing points of view. Like every traditional metaphysical doctrine, it is integral

CHAPTER THIRTEEN

and unified in its own terms, and therefore spiritually potent and effective; in short, insofar as Schuon asserts the heterogeneous nature of the doctrine of the Trinity, he can no longer be called a Traditionalist.

Frithjof Schuon then goes on to present four objections to the doctrine of the Trinity, largely in its Thomistic rendition. First, he says that it is not possible to assert that the Threeness of God is identical to His Essence, since that Essence is necessarily One alone, Trinity representing a motion away from the Essence toward manifestation and multiplicity. Secondly, he asserts the logical impossibility of the notion that the Persons are distinct from one another while each being equal to the Essence, since such a view necessitates the assertion that the Persons are equal in one sense and subordinate in another, which (he erroneously claims) no theologian can maintain. Thirdly, he complains of the doctrine that the *Persons* are also *relations* within the Godhead, since they would logically have to be either one or the other. Fourthly, he objects to the supposedly arbitrary nature of the number Three, since in terms of the various levels of God's Self-manifestation other numbers are also valid, as different Traditions attest. Let us deal with these four objections one by one.

As for Schuon's first objection, the doctrine of the identity of the Threeness and the Oneness of God need not satisfy logic since it was not derived from logic, but rather from direct metaphysical intuition; it is based on an intellective understanding that the Transcendence and Immanence of God are in no way opposed, but that His Immanence directly manifests His Transcendence while His Transcendence prevents the vision of His Immanence from degenerating into a literalistic pantheism, with the Father (at least according to my own perhaps-not-entirely-orthodox perspective) standing as the archetype of God's Transcendence, the Son of His Immanence, and the Holy Spirit of the fundamental identity between His Transcendence and His Immanence. His second objection, that the Persons could not be distinct without occupying different hierarchical ranks, is no more difficult to entertain than Schuon's own doctrine of *maya-in-divinis*, though these two doctrines are by no means identical. If (according to Schuon) the Absolute God is necessarily also Infinite, and if Infinity allows for an infinite multiplicity of "versions" of the Absolute, which are nonetheless that very Absolute and nothing else—and I believe this to be one of the implications or possible renderings of his *maya-in-divinis* doctrine—then why cannot the Three Persons of the Trinity, though differentiated, all be equally Divine, equally Absolute, seeing that differentiation does not always imply rank? The doctrine of procession indicates an "eternal sequence" in the deployment of the Divine Nature, but not a difference in rank between the "simultaneous phases" of that deployment. Schuon's own metaphysics might have allowed him to clearly understand and accept this—if, that is, he had not temporarily forgotten it in his apparent flurry of "irritation" with the orthodox Christian formulation.

The Son and the Holy Spirit proceed from the Divine Essence, which the Eastern Orthodox identify with the Father (though Catholic theology adds that the Spirit proceeds from both the Father and the Son), although from the perspective of their common Essence—which according to Aquinas all Three equally partake of—each possesses the fullness of the Godhead, both in themselves and by the principle that each Person in some sense includes the other two. A distinction may nonetheless be made between the Essence in Itself, which is beyond all relations—a Reality rendered, alongside the Trinity, by Dionysius the Areopagite in his ***Mystical Theology***—and the Father, who is that same Essence considered in relation to the other Persons, as well as to the totality of manifestation. Dionysius says: "Trinity! Higher than any being, any divinity, any goodness," but also speaks of the Essence as "the Cause of all things" while declaring that It is "[not] a spirit in the sense in which we understand the term. It is not sonship or fatherhood and it is nothing known to us or to any other being." But the perspective of the procession of the Persons and the perspective of their common Essence are never presented separately by either the Greek Fathers or Aquinas; orthodox Christian doctrine insists upon subsuming the Trinity into the Essence immediately and at every point, on pain of positing a quasi-polytheistic or "demiurgic" Trinity that is not fully Divine: the One God is Three, and the Three Persons are the One God. The Hebrew Kabbalah, if it had been taught openly as exoteric "theology," would likely have been forced to maintain something similar in terms of the *sefiroth*, to repeatedly emphasize the *Shema* so as to guard against polytheism, to constantly remind us that "all the *sefiroth* are Kether and Kether is Ein Sof," or something of that nature. Here certain implications of Schuon's profound and accurate characterization of Christianity as an "eso-exoteric" revelation, an esoterism taught openly to all believers—which he does not seem to have grasped the implications of in this case—might have clarified things by asserting that the eso-exoteric nature of Christianity makes it necessary to "literalize" an esoteric mystery so as to turn it into an object of belief instead of an object of *gnosis*, by means of an explicit theological formulation in which "illogicality," far from being simply the product of muddled thinking, functions operatively as "mystical paradox," suggesting and directing the attention of the believer to realities that lie beyond expression by the verbal mind, seeing that "faith is virtual gnosis." And the difficulties Schuon discerns in the Thomistic formulation are avoided in any case by Eastern Orthodox trinitarianism, which identifies the Father with the Essence per se, and sees the other two Persons as deployments of this in-itself-unknowable Essence of Whom no icon can be made ("none has seen the Father at any time" [John 6:24]) in the direction of manifestation ("who has seen Me has seen the Father" [John 14:9]), subordinate to the Father in terms of Procession but not in terms of Essence—the Son, according to the Nicene Creed, being *homoousios*, "of One Substance [or Essence]" with the Father.

Immediately after his "deconstruction" of the Trinity, Schuon "restores" the doctrine in terms that are in many ways orthodox. Viewed "horizontally," he says, the Persons are equal; seen in "vertical" terms, they form a hierarchy, a perspective that is certainly allowed, for example, by Christ's declaration that "the Father is greater than I." And although he presents this schema more or less as his own, it is really little more than a gloss upon various essentially orthodox doctrines—specifically, the dogma that each Person embraces the fullness of the Godhead, and the complementary dogma that (in Eastern Orthodox terms) the Son and the Holy Spirit proceed from the Father, or (in Roman Catholic terms) that the Son proceeds from the Father, and the

CHAPTER THIRTEEN

Spirit from the Father and the Son.[3] This version of Schuon's rendering of the Trinity possesses the virtue of being more explicit than most, and consequently possesses a greater capacity to throw light on certain aspects of the trinitarian mystery, while at the same time remaining, by its very explicitness, more vulnerable than the orthodox formulations to various heterodox misunderstandings. Furthermore, in the above formulation, which is substantially in line with the orthodox trinitarian theology of both the Eastern and the Western churches, he clearly presents the Persons as equal in one sense and subordinate in another, which he has just asserted to be impossible for theology—though apparently not for metaphysics, at least his own metaphysics. At this point, Schuon's tendency to make a quasi-absolute distinction between "esoteric" metaphysics and "exoteric" theology trips him up, causing him to forget that Jesus Himself, on the authority of scripture, asserts both his identity with the Father [John 10:30] and his subordination to Him [John 14:28].

In terms of the objection that the Persons cannot equally and at the same time be both Persons and relations, it is true that, when

---

3   The Eastern Orthodox see the Transcendent Father as the Source, in terms of procession, of the Son—who (in my view) is the synthetic Immanence of God in and as the human form, both celestial and terrestrial, the archetype of which is the trans-cosmic Christ considered as the Father's eternal Self-knowledge. They also understand the Father as the Source of the Holy Spirit, the Person that I (at least) take to represent the Immanence of God that creates and underlies universal manifestation, and this version of procession is undeniably true and opportune. The Catholics, on the other hand, say that the Holy Spirit proceeds from both the Father and the Son—the famous, thorny *filioque*. However (as I see it), the Catholic formulation does not really deny the Father as the sole Source of the Spirit, but simply posits the Son, considered to be the synthesis of universal manifestation *in divinis*, as the goal and end-point of the Holy Spirit's trajectory, thus making the Spirit the medium whereby the Son stands in relationship to the Father, the Manifest to the Unmanifest, Immanence to Transcendence, as in the act of prayer.

CHAPTER THIRTEEN

Aquinas defines the Trinity as "composed" of Persons who are also relations, this results in some rather awkward formulations—though if Schuon, in deference to Aquinas, had been interested in plumbing the truth of the notion of Persons who are at the same time relations, he might have brought in the Buddhist doctrine of "Indra's Net," which holds that all entities, being void of separate self-nature, are precisely relations and nothing else, though they must appear and act as real persons, and do in fact possess the full integrity of real persons. Even though this Buddhist formulation is certainly not compatible with the obvious sense of Thomism as it stands, nor in fact with any version of orthodox Christian trinitarianism, it might have opened the door for Frithjof Schuon to an understanding that personhood is relational in essence by virtue of the Immanence of God's Transcendence in all things, as when Jesus told his disciples, in John 14:20, that after his death, resurrection and ascension, when he no longer appeared visibly in this world, "On that day you will know that I am in my Father, and you in me, and I in you"—but he failed to avail himself of this opportunity.

Before going any further, however, it must be understood in this context that the function of Christian theology is largely to guard against error, as we can see from the fact that most dogmatic formulations accepted by the Church councils arose in answer to heresies. If Aquinas had denied that the Persons were also relations, he would have fallen into a literalistic tri-theism; if he had said that they were fundamentally relations rather than distinct Persons, he would have fallen into the heresy of modalism. As it is, he attempted to render a mystery in the most accurate and explicit language possible in order to safeguard orthodoxy,

CHAPTER THIRTEEN

but he could not avoid the fact that every metaphysical principle has a mysterious aspect that transcends any language by which we might attempt to render it. And it is also true that, in asserting that the Persons share a single Essence, he has seemed to some almost to be posting this Essence as a kind of fourth "Person," thus firmly demoting the Trinity to a lower level; this, however, is no more than a phantom of language, based on our inevitable tendency to conceive of words as always referring to concrete objects. In Eastern Orthodox trinitarianism, as we have seen, the Father, considered as "God per se," is the equivalent of the Essence, from which the other two Persons proceed—yet the Son and the Spirit are no less God in essence than the Father is. However "illogical" this may seem to those seeking to catch transcendent mystery of God in a diagram satisfying to human rationality, it is entirely in line with the Transcendent/Immanent nature of the Deity, and effectively renders the fullness of the Divine Presence in a mystical and spiritually operative manner.

Lastly, Schuon asks why God must arbitrarily be conceived of in terms of Three rather Two, as with the Hindu *Saguna Brahman/Nirguna Brahman* or the duality-in-Unity that manifests as Shiva/*Shakti*, or Four, as with the Medicine Wheel of the Native Americans, based on the four cardinal points; or some other number. The answer is simple: it is because the Christian Revelation is specifically based upon the Threeness of God; and each Divine Revelation, as Schuon himself asserts in **Christianity/Islam: Essays on Esoteric Ecumenism**, must comprise an element of uniqueness, otherwise it could not exist as a distinct and integral tradition. Nor do we hear Schuon asking impatiently why the Native Americans must arbitrarily conceive of the Divinity as manifesting in terms of a Quaternity, not a Trinity; his problem seems to be with Christian doctrine alone. Furthermore, the number Three is almost universally associated with the celestial realm and the number Four with the terrestrial, as for example in the symbolism of the ***I Ching***. This fact, especially in light of the obvious parallels between the Christian Trinity and the Vedantic Sat-Chit-Ananda ("Being-Consciousness-Bliss"), puts the Trinity in "good company" from a universalist perspective as well. We must always remember, however, that such similarities do not imply identity; the Christian Trinity, despite all its parallels with other traditional doctrines, remains unique.

Later on in the same chapter of ***Logic and Transcendence*** where he dismisses the Trinity as a "mathematical summation," Schuon partly redresses his earlier errors by presenting a view of the Trinity that is much more useful, satisfying, and enlightening, as well as more compatible, for all its imperious condescension, with Christian orthodoxy—though not entirely so, since Schuon still does not seem to understand either the mystically operative nature nor the metaphysically justifiable status of the formulation "the Persons are the Essence" according to principle of the essential non-differentiation between the Divine Transcendence and the Divine Immanence. He says:

> The Trinity affirms itself on three planes which exoterism confuses, and cannot do otherwise than confuse in view of its concern for a simplifying synthesis and for what is psychologically opportune with reference to certain human tendencies or weaknesses. The first plane, as we have seen, is that of the Essence itself, where the Trinity is real, because the

CHAPTER THIRTEEN

> Essence admits of no privation, but undifferentiated, because the Essence admits of no diversity; from this standpoint one may say that each Person or each Quality-Principle is the other, which is just what one cannot say from the standpoint of diversifying relativity. The second plane is that of the Divine Relativity, of the creative Being, of the personal God: here the three Quality-Principles are differentiated into Persons; one is not the other, and to affirm that they are the Essence is to pass without transition, either by virtue of a purely dialectical ellipsis or through lack of discernment and out of mystical emotion, on to the plane of absoluteness and non-differentiation. One may envisage also a third plane, already cosmic but nevertheless still Divine from the human point of view, which is the point of view that determines theology, and this is the luminous Center of the cosmos, the "Triple manifestation" (Trimurti) of the Hindu doctrine and the "Spirit" (*Ruh*) of the Islamic doctrine; here also the Trinity is present, radiating, and acting.

This passage has much to recommend it, since it includes metaphysical doctrines which, while not acceptable to the common theological mind, are true, profound, and in no way heterodox, doctrines that are properly analogous to and (up to a point) compatible with—though certainly not identical to—orthodox Christian trinitarianism. And this begs the question: If the Trinity derives from "a literalistic and quasi-mathematical interpretation of certain words in the Scriptures" and represents merely "a summation of different points of view," how could it be susceptible to the kind of esoteric metaphysical exegesis Schuon provides here? First he denies that the Trinity is an integral doctrine carrying the force and authority of Revelation, and then proceeds to treat it as precisely that—and you can't have it both ways.

This passage is not without its problems, however. For example, Schuon neglects to inform us that the doctrine that each Person contains or embraces the other two is not his own formulation but is derived from the theological principle the Latins call *circumincession*, and the Greeks, *perichoresis*. Furthermore, to identify the Hindu Trimurti with the Christian Trinity as it appears at the apex of the cosmic order is not justified. The Trimurti—from one point of view—occupies the same ontological level as Schuon's concept of the Trinity in its cosmic reflection, but Brahma the Creator, Vishnu the Preserver, and Shiva the Destroyer cannot in any manner be identified with the Father, the Son and the Holy Spirit of Christianity, though it is uncertain whether Schuon means to so identify them; and certainly these Divine hypostases of Hinduism also possess a transcendent aspect that places them on a much higher plane than that of their roles as Creator, Preserver and Destroyer in cosmic terms. Likewise the Christian Trinity operates in all cosmic phases and functions while absolutely transcending them; nonetheless the Trinity and the Trimurti can in no way be identified (though certain analogies exist) since they spring from two unique and separate Divine Revelations. Here Schuon descends from a valid "esoteric ecumenism" to a facile comparison of elements from different traditions that are properly distinct, and should be allowed to remain so. And when Schuon complains that the differentiated

CHAPTER THIRTEEN

Trinity can only be identified with the Essence "either by virtue of a purely dialectical ellipsis or through lack of discernment and out of mystical emotion," he forgets that every tradition always both renders the doctrine of the Divine and its cosmic manifestation in terms of a hierarchy of levels, and also collapses this hierarchy; if it did not do so, the hierarchical presentation of metaphysical reality and cosmic existence would quickly become not a hierophany but an idol. The Buddhists (in Theravadin terms) first make a strict differentiation between Nirvana (the Absolute and Real) and *sangsara* (the relative and illusory)—and then (in Mahayana terms) they collapse this two-term hierarchy by asserting, in the **Lankavatara Sutra**, that "samsara is Nirvana." When the Buddhists declare that *tathata* or "suchness"—a given entity precisely as it appears—is one with *shunyat*a—"emptiness" in the sense of freedom from all limiting determinations, which is none other than the characteristic immanent/apophatic Buddhist approach to the Absolute—they are in essence presenting their own rendition of what Christians call the Immanence of God. Likewise the **Tao Te Ching** says: "The Tao is the source of the ten-thousand things ... this is the greatest treasure of the universe," while Chuang Tzu, in the same spirit, says that the Tao subsists even in excrement. Likewise Ibn al-'Arabi teaches that all things have two natures: in terms of their formal creaturehood they are nothing; in terms of their Essence they are God. All traditions collapse the hierarchies they establish; why should Christianity alone be faulted for doing so? It is true that, in reaction against the pantheistic tendencies abroad in late antiquity, Christianity was reluctant to assert that all "natural" things were Divine in Essence. Yet Christ said both "the Father is greater than I" [John 14:28]—thus asserting the perspective of Transcendence—and "before Abraham came to be, I Am" [John 8:58]; "who has seen Me has seen the Father" [John 14:9]; "I am in the Father and the Father in Me" [John 14:11]; "I and the Father are one" [John 10:30]—thus establishing the perspective of Immanence, at least in terms of his own person. And He went beyond even this: in saying "abide in Me and I in you" [John 15:4], He extended the Immanence of the Divine to all who accepted Him. Furthermore, Eastern Orthodox theology asserts that Christ, by his death and resurrection, sanctified and transfigured the entire cosmos, thereby gathering all things back, virtually at least, into the Immanence of God. Certainly this Immanence is presented in terms of a spiritual power specially conferred by God rather than being recognized as an intrinsic aspect of reality—but what good is it to assert intrinsic truths in the absence of the Grace and Power to realize them? The philosophers might expound in the abstract on the intrinsic Immanence of the Absolute until they were blue in the face, and never transmit to their pupils the power to realize this truth in the concrete; this is precisely why the Divine Economy required the Incarnation of Christ. And Schuon also forgets that the relative is subsumed into the Absolute not merely by "a purely dialectical ellipsis or through lack of discernment and out of mystical emotion," but precisely by *gnosis* itself; it is completely so subsumed *only* by *gnosis*. Schuon's inability to recognize this fact belies his exaltation of pure Intellection over "mystical emotion"; if his intellectual discernment had been operating in the present instance, he would not have attributed to mystical emotion, or a lack of discernment, or a cheap dialectical trick, what Intellection alone can accomplish. He presents a profound and illuminating hierarchy of levels on which the Trinity subsists, but then faults the Christians, and the Christ of Scripture as well, for collapsing it; in so doing he asserts the valid perspective of Transcendence while denying the equally valid perspective of Immanence, once again manifesting a certain bias reminiscent of the sectarian Gnostics. In many other instances he presents an entirely acceptable doctrine of Transcendence and Immanence, but here he appears to forget it.

Furthermore, when Schuon faults "exoterism" (by which he may or may not mean orthodox Christian doctrine) for "confusing" the three levels of the Trinity—the undifferentiated and transpersonal level, the differentiated or personal level, and the cosmic level—he forgets that he himself subsumes the cosmic and the personal into the transpersonal. But the "confusion" of these levels by exoterism does not give esoterism the right to concretize the distinction between them to the point where they become mutually exclusive. True esoterism understands the provisional nature of all formulations of metaphysical Truth—that is, their role as *upayas*—and thereby avoids setting up its own formulations as, in effect, alternative theological dogmas. In **Esoterism as Principle and as Way**, Schuon makes a distinction between the higher metaphysical or "horizontal" Trinity in which the Persons are not as yet differentiated, and the lower "vertical" Trinity where they are differentiated by virtue of ontological gradation. Both of these perspectives are totally justified, and Schuon is possibly without peer in his exposition of the first; this is one of the high points of his "pure metaphysics." The higher "horizontal" perspective is entirely orthodox in Christian terms according to the dogma that each of the Persons embraces the fullness of the Godhead, while the lower "vertical" one is susceptible of an orthodox interpretation according the dogma of the procession

CHAPTER THIRTEEN

of the Persons, though not if this procession is interpreted in literally subordinist terms, thus making one Person "inferior" to the others, since—as should be obvious—God cannot be "inferior to Himself." Schuon, however, doesn't stop there—would that he had!—but goes on to fault orthodox Christian theology for maintaining that "the Trinity is the Essence," because to say this is not logical, seeing that "to affirm that they are the Essence is to pass without transition, either by virtue of a purely dialectical ellipsis or through lack of discernment and out of mystical emotion, on to the plane of absoluteness and non-differentiation." But one *must* pass from the plane of the differentiated Persons to that of the non-differentiated Absolute by one means or another, on pain of denying the Unity of God, the *Credo in Unum Deum* of the Nicene Creed, which Schuon himself affirms in so many other places and in so many different ways. He stands, as it were, outside the orthodox understanding of the Trinity, considering it as if it were intended as a strictly logical doctrine, and then calls it illogical, thus falling into the delusion that, since he is viewing it from the outside the Christian tradition, as a non-participant, he is necessarily viewing it from a higher standpoint; a similar delusion has affected countless orientalists and academic students of religion. Furthermore, he fails to note the fact that he himself passes from the plane of the differentiated Persons to the plane of the non-differentiated Absolute in his doctrine of the vertical vs. the horizontal Trinity, the Trinity in its metaphysical and undifferentiated mode; why is this exposition not equally illogical, not also an unwarranted "passage without transition" from one plane to another? He obviously doesn't believe that the "horizontal" and "vertical" Trinities are two different metaphysical realities, simply that they are two different perspectives that are already intrinsically united on a higher level. Certainly he uses more words to effect the "transition" from one to the other than the bare dogmatic assertion that "the Persons are the Essence," which is necessarily simplified because its entirely legitimate (though not unproblematic) purpose is to reformulate a product of gnostic Intellection as an article of collective belief. Nor is the passage from the plane of belief to the plane of Intellection affected by "mystical emotion"; it is affected, precisely, by Intellection itself. If Schuon had been capable of accepting the Christian dogma of the Trinity, precisely as it stands, as an effective support for the direct Intellection of the principle it represents, if he had been willing to respect Christian orthodoxy because he knew how to see its dogmas in their metaphysical transparency, he would not have needed to take the heterodox path of denying certain elements of them, but could have kept to the *gnostic* path of providing the kind of brilliant metaphysical exegesis of them that he was eminently, almost uniquely capable of, and that he actually accomplished (up to a point) in his profound meditations on the "horizontal, metaphysical" Trinity. If he had not harbored a deep-seated prejudice against the authority of Christian dogma, which I can only see as based on a personal need to assert his personal "esoteric" superiority over all the Revealed religions, he could have remained entirely faithful to orthodoxy, and thus to Tradition. As it is, however, he rejected essential elements of them, thereby illustrating exactly how what might be called a luciferian pride (but God knows best) can distort even the highest metaphysical perceptions and principles. It is one thing to disagree with a particular theological formulation—but to challenge the central principles and mysteries of a religion that is admitted to be based on a Divine Revelation, and even to do so in the name of Tradition, is suggestive of some very grim possibilities. In any case, Frithjof Schuon, in terms of his Trinitarian doctrines, cannot really be called a Traditionalist.

If we are in any sense Traditionalists we must admit that Christian Trinitarianism represents a valid perspective on the Divine Nature—a perspective that, in concrete terms, possesses the full authority of that Revelation (which, either for the reason I fear or for some reason, Schuon sometimes denies), and is therefore charged with an undeniable spiritual efficacy. If this were not the case, Christianity could never have produced its great saints and sages. In contemplative, experiential terms, to encounter God as transcending all sense experience, mental concepts, and intellective realizations—God the Father—is to encounter the fullness of the Godhead; likewise to encounter Him as the Essence of all manifest forms, emanating the Energies that create those forms, and to encounter Him as the Perfection of the human Person Who is at the same time the Source and Epitome of all manifest forms—God the Holy Spirit and God the Son—is likewise to encounter the Godhead in Its fullness; none of these encounters need be supplemented by the others in order to make a complete theophany, because each of the Persons contains the other two and consequently represents the Divine Essence without division or privation. As Schuon correctly maintains in *Logic and Transcendence* and elsewhere, the Christian Revelation is founded upon a unique theophany, the Incarnation of Christ; consequently God is most centrally conceived of in terms of His manifestation to man, and as man; this is why the doctrines of the Trinity and the Incarnation are mutually-supporting and inseparable. Yet God-as-Man in no way veils or subordinates

CHAPTER THIRTEEN

God-as-Universal-Life and God-as-Unknowable-Essence, since the entirety of the Godhead subsists in each. If Schuon could not accept this, then he did not understand Christianity.

It is true that Muslims must approach God strictly through His unmediated Unity, through Allah as *Al-Ahad*, just as Christians—though the Nicene Creed proclaims *Credo in Unum Deum*, "I believe in One God"—must approach Him through His Unity-in-Trinity. Nonetheless, certain denials of trinitarianism in the Qur'an, as we have already seen above, are actually closer to orthodox Christian doctrine than one might suspect. When Q. 5:73 rejects the notion that Allah is "the third of three," this is much closer to a denial of the Arian heresy than of orthodox trinitarianism, which in no way asserts that God is "the third of three," but rather that the One God subsists in all three Persons, not just one of them. Ibn al-'Arabi too expresses a trinitarian conception of Allah in his "Salih" chapter from the **Fusus al-Hikam**: Allah is Lord in relation to the servant—or in relation to the cosmos—but the Essence of the servant and the cosmos, though not of their limited forms, is equally Allah and nothing else, because there is nothing else; Allah is the Only Being, the only One who, according to His name *Al-Samad, is* in His own right. Likewise the polarities Lord/Servant and Lord/Cosmos are resolved for Ibn al-'Arabi in a third term, the Reality, Whose Essence is also Allah and nothing else—consequently the Threeness of Allah does not deny or compromise His Unity, but rather testifies to it. Ibn al-'Arabi's doctrine can in no way be identified with Christian trinitarianism; nonetheless, on an esoteric level, it is not incompatible with it. Likewise, though the Christian doctrine of the Incarnation is necessarily denied by

Islam as the heresy of *hulul*, orthodox Christology nonetheless maintains that even by virtue of the Hypostatic Union of the two natures of Christ, the Divine and the human, Christ's human nature never actually becomes Divine. So what then is the Incarnation, exactly? Through subtleties like these the doctrinal gap between Islam and Christianity can be narrowed, to a degree—yet if the two can never finally be made one on the plane of form, what good is this "narrowing" in the final analysis, except perhaps—perhaps—to lessen the rancor between the religions? The Muslims have their way, the Christians theirs. We know that the Prophet Muhammad, peace and blessings be upon him, referred to the Christians, in his Covenants with them, as *mu'minin*, "believers," and the Qur'an expresses great respect for Christian monks, whom Muhammad certainly knew professed the trinitarian doctrine. Yet the Prophet also made it clear that there was to be "no monasticism in Islam," just as the Qur'an declares that there is to be no trinitarian dogma as an article of faith. Therefore we are left with the truth expressed in Q. 5:48:

> *Had Allah willed He could have made you one community. But that He may try you by that which He hath given you (He hath made you as ye are). So vie one with another in good works. Unto Allah ye will all return, and He will then inform you of that wherein ye differ.*

Schuon and Christian Orthodoxy

So Schuon—in line with the spirit of the modern world—had definite problems with certain orthodox doctrinal formulations, particularly Christian ones. For example, he apparently had great

CHAPTER THIRTEEN

difficulty in accepting the Hypostatic Union, the central Christian dogma relating to the Incarnation, and in this he is certainly not alone; the union of the Divine and human natures in Christ has presented more problems, and thus spawned more heresies, than any other dogma in the Christian world. How could that single human body actually be, or have been, the flesh of God, either in terms of Christ's human flesh or as the Holy Eucharist? All I can say is, to accept this dogma as orthodox and therefore true is to open the way for the most profound metaphysical speculations; to deny or downgrade it is to lose that opportunity. The Arians and the Docetists, however—whatever valid insights their doctrines might have embraced or suggested—ultimately took the easy way out by maintaining that Christ was a created being like an Archangel, or a theophanic apparition, rather than an incarnation[4];

---

4 Given that Schuon tended to see a certain truth in Docetism, one wonders if the fact that, in Islamic terms, the Holy Qur'an—which he compares to the Incarnation of Christ, maintaining that the Qur'an is "God-become-book" just as Christ is "God-become-man"—is a theophany but certainly not an incarnation, unduly influenced him to give more than he should have to the Docetist perspective (see for example the chapter "Some Difficulties Found in Sacred Scriptures", footnote 32, in ***Form and Substance in the Religions***), which can only be a heresy in Christian terms. One of the dangers of comparative religion is that it may sometimes produce "bleed-throughs" like this. If the incommensurability of the Revelations in certain areas of doctrine is not respected, if it is forgotten or denied that the full "reconciliation" of such divergences is possible only in the Transcendent or Formless dimension—by virtue of *gnosis*, that is, not by any degree of mental intelligence—then heterodoxy and syncretism are the inevitable result. As for the apparent heterodoxy of the Monophysites according to consiliar standards, as I see it they do not literally deny the humanity of Jesus like the Arians or the Docetists did; after all, the Coptic Christians preserve ancient traditions relating to the exact route taken by the Holy Family in their flight into Egypt. It's simply that the Divinity of Christ, which all orthodox Christians accept, overwhelms in its tremendous reality all other considerations for them, making the consiliar formulations relating to the Hypostatic Union seem carping, petty and impious; at least that's my own impression. Someone better informed on Monophysite theology than I am might be able to set me straight on this point.

the same skirting-of-the-issue can be seen in the Apollonians, who agreed that Jesus Christ had a human body but could not accept that He also possessed a human soul.

But if Jesus Christ was God in human soul and human flesh, what can this mean? It is apparently in line with the Sufic/Akbarian doctrine that God is the Essence of all forms, thus making every manifest form the product of what might seem to be a sort of Hypostatic Union—were it not for the fact that, according to Ibn al-'Arabi, God is, while other-than-God is not, except as a reflection of Him and by virtue of the gift of His Being, and consequently that the union of two real principles—which would constitute the heresy of *hulul*, "incarnationism"—cannot be accepted in Islamic terms. Jesus Himself, according to St. Paul, came to give His followers the power to become Sons of God as He was [Galatians 3:26]; and he told the Pharisees, "ye are all gods and sons of the Most High" [John 10:34, quoting Psalm 82:6]. So it would seem that He posited a kind of universal Divine-human incarnationism, at least *in potentia*. But it is impossible to ignore the pre-eminence and uniqueness of the Person of Christ in the Christian universe, particularly in view of such statements as "before Abraham came to be, I Am" [John 8:58]. In Traditionalist/Perennialist/Vedantic terminology He is precisely an Avatar, an embodied expression of one of the veridical Self-Revelations sent by God to man. Furthermore, a Christian does not become a Son of God simply by realizing, through Intellection, his or her virtual Divinity as an intrinsic aspect of the nature of things; he or she does so by virtue of a power that is given to him through Christ's Atonement, a power that must be accepted but may also be rejected, as is proved by

CHAPTER THIRTEEN

the example of Judas Iscariot. It is possible to see this power as effecting an unveiling, via "infused Intellection," of truths previously hidden; but as Schuon himself points out in **Stations of Wisdom**, "Intellection outside Tradition"—that is, outside the Grace that Tradition provides—"will have neither authority nor efficacy," though apparently he did not feel bound by this principle in his own case. If he had been more willing to accept certain orthodox dogmas before he fully understood them—on faith, that is, faith being virtual Intellection—then, given the power of his metaphysical discernment, he might have been able to expound them on a deeper level than any of his contemporaries. Unfortunately, he did not always accept this challenge. Since Schuon apparently took his own "discernment" as the highest criterion and source of Truth, he sometimes gave the impression that *he believed whatever he thought*, that he took God's Self-revelations to humanity not as criteria for metaphysical Truth so much as material to be elucidated and evaluated by the "greater" criterion of his own admittedly formidable intellective abilities. This seems to have led him, at least on some occasions, to see the Revelations as relatively "exoteric" limitations placed upon the more "esoteric" insights provided by the Intellective faculty, since it is clear that he did not consider himself particularly bound by them, even when explicating them. I believe that this intermittent tendency to give Intellection greater authority than Revelation prevented him from plumbing the quintessential esoteric depths of the Revelations he examined, even as it sometimes allowed him to see more deeply into these Revelations than almost anyone else; consequently he was actually less of a Traditionalist than he appeared to be. In light of this it will be helpful to remember what

CHAPTER THIRTEEN

Ananda K. Coomaraswamy said about his own approach to the Traditional spiritualities: "I had to learn not to think for myself."

One of the temptations inevitably faced by anyone who is knowledgeable about many different religious Traditions is the belief, sometimes not entirely conscious, that he or she is superior to all of them while being bound by none. The only way beyond this impasse, which will effectively neutralize the victim's spiritual life if it is not transcended, is to learn how to see the Traditions in question in their "metaphysical transparency"—not as limited "confessional" belief-systems but as a spectrum of operative spiritual Path, each one of which is capable of taking those qualified to walk it beyond the realm of belief entirely to the realm of objective Knowledge. And part of this vision of "the metaphysical transparency of the Traditions" is expressed in Schuon's principle that "all religion is to be found in a given religion"—a principle that he clearly articulated but was apparently unable to actualize, as witness the syncretism he ultimately fell into (see below). Because: if all religion is to be found in a given religion, then it is not only possible but necessary to remain faithful to one particular spiritual Path, and walk that Path to the end. To make a full and conscious commitment to a single religion after accepting that God has sent more than one valid Revelation, and that more than one of these Revelations can be spiritually operative at the same time, might be called the "post-Schuonian challenge." As I see it, to understand the nature of this challenge, and then to fully meet it, is the only way forward for Perennialism beyond the profound insights and the dangerous mis-directions of Frithjof Schuon.

CHAPTER THIRTEEN

Primordialism vs. Tradition

Schuon gave a great impetus to two divergent tendencies. The first, Traditionalism, holds that, while metaphysical depth and the possibility of salvation exist in more than one religious Tradition, they rarely manifest apart from these Traditions—except in cases which are neither normative nor transmissible. Truth is One, and the various valid Traditions all point, especially in their esoteric depths, to this One Truth; nonetheless, that Truth never effectively manifests, in this world, apart from the particularity of the various Traditions—which, on the plane of the individual, means the particularity of one of them. This is the perspective that I myself hold to. The second tendency is Primordialism, which is based on the notion that all the Revealed religions are, as it were, various branches of the Tree of the Primordial Tradition, which was nothing less than God's original and world-creating Self-Revelation to, and as, the human form. I accept the reality of this Primordial Self-Revelation, and the Tradition that sprang from it. Contemporary "Primordialism," however, maintains that this Tradition can be found and followed in its original form even now, at the tail-end of the Kali-yuga—and this I certainly do not accept. We are no longer in the Golden Age; the nourishing fruit of the Tree of Religion now grows on the branches, not the trunk. According to Primordialist belief, the metaphysical commonality discernible in the various traditions actually supersedes those traditions, and is capable of existing apart from them as a "generic" metaphysics that is not merely true in the abstract, but spiritually operative and effective. From the standpoint of this generic meta-doctrine one is free to mix the forms of various religions—Native American rituals, Sufi practices, and Shaivite Hinduism, for example—in a kind of "esoteric syncretism," a practice that is justified by the belief that the religious traditions, by and large, are petrified exoteric shells that one need not take too seriously. In the 1990s I wrote to Schuon on the occasion of an appearance of an interview with him in *The Quest*, a Theosophical Society magazine, inquiring as to the nature of his practice in Bloomington, Indiana. The reply I received appeared not to be in his own hand; undoubtedly it was dictated to a secretary. One line from that reply stands out in my mind: "What we are doing is syncretism of a kind, but *not* the syncretism of the Theosophical Society." This response begs the question: If, according to Frithjof Schuon himself in **From the Divine to the Human**, "A given religion in reality sums up all religions . . . all religion is to be found in a given religion, because Truth is one," then how could syncretism of any kind have a legitimate place? Schuon often spoke of "the metaphysical transparency of phenomena," the intellective vision of all sense-objects as both symbols and instances of eternal truths. But what about "the metaphysical transparency of dogmas"? If the exoteric believer sees dogma in strictly "confessional" terms as indicating the exclusive validity of his or her own religion, wouldn't the esoteric sage, the gnostic, be able to see "through dogmas, not with them," all the way to the level of a "quintessential esoterism," without having to depart from the orthodox forms of the religion in question? If this is the case, then wouldn't Schuon's obvious attraction to his own brand of syncretism indicate a relatively exoteric and literalistic understanding of doctrinal truth—one that, because it did not possess the capacity to transcend (without rejecting) the limitations of formal Islam vertically, through esoterism, was induced to do so horizontally, through heterodoxy?

CHAPTER THIRTEEN

The big question is, was Schuon himself a Traditionalist or a Primordialist? The answer seems to be that in his writings he was in many ways a Traditionalist, though not strictly so given his universalism, while in his practice he was apparently in some ways a Primordialist—and now that the living man has passed on, we no longer have a good reason, or a plausible excuse, for glossing over the contradictory aspects of his legacy, which were all but inevitable given that he was called both to renew the several major world religions on an esoteric level and to articulate a universal metaphysics, both of which are undeniably called for by the quality and needs of our time. Nor can we ignore the possibility that Schuon's quasi-Gnostic bias toward the perspective of Transcendence might also, as his writings sometimes seem to suggest, have cast its all-but-inevitable shadow in terms of a compensatory emphasis on the Divine Immanence, which sometimes took the form of an attempt to "redeem the passions by spiritualizing them," in more-or-less tantric mode, as manifest in his appreciation for sacred nudity and his emphasis on "sacred aesthetics" (see his book **Images of Primordial and Mystic Beauty**), his desire to revel in the beauty of the manifest world, of nature, and the human body, in an attempt to realize "the metaphysical transparency of phenomena" so as to regain the immanentalist perspective that he had partially lost through his highly intellectualized transcendentalist bias. Such an approach however, as even authorities from spiritual traditions that recognize this possibility will admit, is fraught with pitfalls, and truly successful only in the rarest instances.

"Primordialist" tendencies, including the all-too-common temptation to denigrate traditional Christianity that for some reason seems inseparable from them, are discernible among some of Schuon's close followers as well. Whitall Perry, for example, would seem to have been a pure Traditionalist. Yet in *The Widening Breach* (1995), in the chapter entitled "Contours of the Primordial Tradition," he exhibits certain anti-Christian tendencies and Neo-Pagan leanings which, in my opinion, show evidence of a non-Traditional and potentially Counter-Traditional Primordialism. It will be helpful, I think, to look at Mr. Perry's "revised" Traditionalism, or Primordialism, in greater detail.

In rightly lamenting that the Christian world of the Middle Ages has now shrunk to a Christian religion "relegated to monasteries and churches as being, precisely, otherworldly," Perry crosses the line between a decorous mourning for medieval Christendom and a kind of gleeful dance on the grave of Christianity itself, especially when he asserts that "the Christian religion has finally become . . . the sordid secularization of faith." Christianity, in other words, is spiritually dead. Interestingly enough, my wife on one occasion heard New Age teacher Deepak Chopra say exactly the same thing in a radio interview: the Christian churches are all dead. What both Perry and Chopra seem to forget is that "I shall be with you always, even to the consummation of the age" [Matthew 28:20], that "the gates of hell shall not prevail" [Matthew 17:18] against the church of Christ, and that it was Jesus himself who first declared that "my kingdom is not of this world" [John 18:36]. The flowering of medieval Christendom had behind it the experience of the catacombs—and however degenerate many aspects of the Christian tradition may have become in our times, those catacombs still exist; they are in the process of being reinhabited by a "faithful remnant." And Eastern

CHAPTER THIRTEEN

Orthodoxy is without doubt a still living spiritual tradition, though certainly not immune to the degenerative influences of the latter days.

Perry quotes an Iroquois, Johnny Two Rivers, as follows: "Religion—it's a crutch for people who need it. A crutch is better than nothing, but people who can walk on their two feet spiritually don't need a crutch. If you see the Great Spirit in everything . . . you don't need this crutch." Perry comments that "obviously the Iroquois have their religion; but this was an elliptical way—somewhat in the manner of a Zen koan—of stressing the primordial and cosmic or 'shamanic' vision essential to the Indian perspective." We should remember, however, that Guénon, in ***The Reign of Quantity and the Signs of the Times***, said that shamanism, though it has elements in common with the highest spiritual traditions, must in many cases be suspected of serious degeneration—a degeneration which, of course, has affected the revealed religions as well.

One form taken by this degeneration of shamanism is the separation of the shaman from his full role vis-a-vis his tribe. Since Johnny Two Rivers was taking part in a Swiss/Canadian cultural exchange program in Lausanne, exhibiting Iroquois crafts and dances to the Whites, he might well have said what he said partly out of wounded pride. Shamanism is based on the individual spiritual exploit, within the context of a traditional tribal life and worldview. This is why it often tends to move in the direction of individualistic sorcery when taken out of that context, which is precisely what makes it, or a degenerate form of it, so attractive to many in the post-modern West who have lost, or discarded, their own spiritual traditions.

CHAPTER THIRTEEN

The idea that a spiritual or aesthetic appreciation of the natural world, unmediated by any religious tradition, can be an effective spiritual path was common to both the hippies and the New Age, though we can probably trace its roots at least as far back as Rousseau. Perry is most likely right about what Johnny Two Rivers meant by what he said, but the identical words spoken by a White westerner will likely mean something entirely different. Schuon himself said, in a video-taped interview, which included footage of him and his followers practicing their own version of Native American rites, "I'm not interested in religion." Did he mean that he had reached the "other shore" and could now leave the "raft" behind, or that an attachment to religious orthodoxy (Muslim in his case), including its exoteric and legalistic elements, which is presented as a *sine qua non* in many of the writings of the Traditionalists, as well as among all orthodox Sufis, could now only get in the way of his Primordialist rituals? And if he had no interest in religion, then why did he publish a highly significant journal named *Studies in Comparative Religion*?

"A Balinese priest once assured me," Perry writes, "that Jesus Christ would be welcome to a shrine here [in Bali], although the Christian Deity should not supersede the other gods, who own the island, having been the first to arrive. He also said, 'our land belongs to the gods, who have simply put us here as caretakers'—a perspective which ties in with the Qur'anic concept of vicegerent." How it ties in with the Qur'anic denunciation of polytheism, however, is less clear. To place Jesus Christ in a pantheon of other gods would be as destructive to the Christian religion as the work of Christian missionaries in Bali, which Perry rightly criticizes, was to the Balinese tradition. (By this I certainly do not mean to deny the right of Christianity or any religion to proselytize, which Christ commands His followers to do in any case by what has been called the Great Commission, but only to point out that a missionary activity that takes place in the context of a political or economic colonialism is compromised from the outset.) If Christianity had not resisted the identical temptation to relativize Christ through a rapprochement with late classical Paganism, it would not have survived. As for the spiritual validity of Balinese polytheism, if the Shaivite Brahmanism Perry names as playing the "predominant role" in Balinese religion actually provides an effective doorway leading out of the psychic multiplicity of the many gods—valid on their own level in the context of a traditional society that knows how to deal with them—to the Transcendent Unity of the Spirit, as the Advaita Vedanta as a whole does for Hinduism (and this is something I have no way of knowing), then I have no quarrel with the Balinese religion. But it is precisely this Transcendent aspect which so many postmodern westerners are in flight from, a flight that is at the basis of their attraction to "primitive" polytheisms of all kinds, including Voodoo and Santería. How, then, can the post-Schuonian Primordialists be strictly and in all cases differentiated from the hippies and their New Age successors—whose attraction to anything primitive and magical is well known, who had a great though often shallow and poorly-informed appreciation for Native American spirituality (which partly explains their long hair and head-bands), and who also had plenty of trouble with "exoteric, organized religion"—except by their rejection of drugs and rock-and-roll, and their more intellectually rigorous and aesthetically elevated treatment of many of the same themes? At the very least we can say that Schuon presented his Primordialism in terms of the highest

CHAPTER THIRTEEN

traditional metaphysics, while the hippies, the New Agers, and the Neo-Pagans were ultimately drawn in the direction of magical nature-worship and a glamorized "psychic" materialism. Schuon was in no way a polytheist, being a unitarian in Muslim terms and an *advaitin* in Vedantic terms, while the Neo-Pagans—and the New Agers to a degree—generally are polytheists, sharing with postmodernism the fear of anything remotely resembling Unity, and interpreting monotheism as no more than a form of imperialism in the religious field. But although Mark Perry (Whitall's son) once characterized the hippies, in a letter to my wife and myself, as "human weeds"—to which I jokingly replied that this could be construed as giving them a "primordial" pre-eminence over more cultivated human beings—the Indian Days and Primordial Gatherings of Schuon's circle appear to have many elements in common with the practices their hippy counterparts, at least to the outside observer. Certainly they were sometimes conducted by traditional Native American medicine men, but the hippies too had their traditional or semi-traditional medicine men, as did the later New Age. The Schuonian Primordialists, however, seem strangely ignorant of these affinities. Their seclusion from the world has apparently blinded them to the fact that the "Primordialist elite" they apparently believe they represent was in some ways pursuing a parallel course to that of the North American/Western European counter-culture—though on a much less populist level, to say the least—from the mid-60s to at least the 90s, thus making Frithjof Schuon, in some ways, "the last of the hippies." The interest in Eastern religions, the attraction to primitivism, the exaltation of the Divine Feminine, the spiritual appreciation of the beauty of the natural world—as well as the mixing of properly discrete spiritual traditions, the belief that the

CHAPTER THIRTEEN

esoteric or mystical core of those traditions could be separated from their exoteric foundations (that Sufism, for example, can exist apart from the Islamic *shari'ah*, as Idries Shah, for one, maintained)—all have been part-and-parcel of counterculture spirituality for the past sixty years; they are basically "Sixties" phenomena. (This is not to say that their roots do not reach further back. Two books by Richard Noll, **The Jung Cult** and **The Aryan Christ**, reveal that the early Carl Jung—whose quasi-spiritual psychology was well-critiqued by Titus Burckhardt in the chapter "Traditional Cosmology and Modern Science," subsection *Modern Psychology*, appearing in **Mirror of the Intellect**—to have been the practitioner of an overtly anti-Christian form of Neo-Paganism, complete with nudism, the attraction to the primordial, the appreciation of virgin nature, and the worship of the Divine Feminine, interests he held in common not only with the hippy counterculture but with many others in the Romantic culture of his time in greater Germany and Switzerland.) Nor have these "Primordialist" interests always been limited to the Bohemian counterculture in the United States; as my wife Jenny points out, at the very same time Schuon was conducting his "Indian Days" in Bloomington, Indiana, Hollywood was producing motion pictures like *Dances with Wolves*, starring Kevin Costner, for a mainstream American audience.

One thing among many that the New Age lacked was a serious intellectual elite (Ken Wilber and a few of his colleagues possibly excepted); have they finally inherited one in the post-Schuonian Primordialists? Probably not. Yet insofar as the emerging globalist elites, some of whom have a counterculture background (Bill Gates for example), are buying into "the wisdom of the ages," as

CHAPTER THIRTEEN

well as adopting various quasi-New Age ideologies that are less interesting to the masses today than they were thirty years ago, but apparently highly interesting to the ruling class, the Schuonian Primordialists may ultimately have found a market for their ideas. At the very least, Patrick Laude appears to have offered Schuon's Primordialism to the intellectuals of the globalist elites in his book ***Keys to the Beyond: Frithjof Schuon's Cross-Traditional Language of Transcendence*** (SUNY, 2021; see *Chapter Fifteen* for my review). I don't mean to imply that an interest in Eastern religions, primal spiritualities, and an appreciation for the Divine Feminine and the natural world such as Schuon, the Neo-Pagans, and the New Age hold in common are in any sense negative; an understanding of them is necessary today, in many ways, to any comprehensive spiritual worldview. But they need to be placed in the right relationship to one another, which is something that only an understanding of, and faithfulness to, the norms of the Traditional orthodoxies can do. Various non-Traditional quasi-esoteric "paradigms" of a generally New Age nature have long been used in the business world for the purpose of management training at least, and there are signs that similar ideas are also being employed by the globalist elites in order to influence mass belief, unhampered by the "backwardness" and "divisiveness" of the traditional faiths. (For a valuable introduction to the extensive but often overlooked influence of New Age ideologies, plus various governmental agencies of the superpowers, the United Nations, and a number of globalist foundations and think tanks, both on certain "esoteric" organizations and on the interfaith movement, as well as on the world religions themselves, see ***False Dawn: The United Religions Initiative, Globalism and the Quest for a One-World Religion*** by Lee Penn, which I was privileged to edit.)

CHAPTER THIRTEEN

In light of the growing influence of secular globalist organizations on the Traditional faiths—a trend that was highlighted for me when, in a phone conversation with a receptionist at the Council on Foreign Relations, she referred to the world religions as "constituencies"—I entered a high state of vigilance when I opened Patrick Laude's ***Keys to the Beyond***, particularly when he said that "the very notions of *sophia* perennis and *religio perennis* could not but be reformulated in the context of an increasingly globalized world," and spoke of the philosophia perennis as "a philosophical and theological lingua franca" one that "takes the fact of intellectual globalization as a starting-point and a motivating factor for the elaboration of a philosophical metalanguage." The contrast between this approach and the earlier prevailing doctrine that Schuonian Traditionalism is diametrically opposed to the root assumptions of the modern and postmodern world was stunning to say the least, since it represents a radical, though unacknowledged, about-face from earlier attitudes. It would seem that ***Keys to the Beyond*** represents the progressive triumph of Primordialism over Traditionalism in the continuing stream of spiritual intellectuality defined and "convened" by Frithjof Schuon—a triumph that could certainly make Neo-Schuonian Perennialism more attractive, and more useful, to those globalist elites who are working to extend their hegemony over the Traditional religions of the earth from a supposedly "higher" and more universal standpoint.

The influx of "alternative" (i.e., non-Judeo-Christian) religions which the West has experienced over the last sixty years, if not longer, represents both a true "eleventh hour" epiphany of universal spiritual wisdom for the latter days, and a subversive, syncretistic undermining of both Judeo-Christianity and the religions that have "invaded" its Traditional heartland (while abandoning their own), even on the esoteric plane: in Guénon's terms, both Tradition and Counter-Tradition. The esoteric doctrines that could only be assimilated on a mass level, though in a distorted form that was more psychic than spiritual, with the help of psychedelic drugs and various meditative practices taken out of their proper Traditional frameworks, appeared in the context of the Traditionalist School in their metaphysical and esoteric quintessence, as if reserved for a spiritual elite. Yet insofar as Traditionalism itself has failed in some cases to adhere to Traditional norms, it exhibits many of the same problems as its more chaotic counterculture relatives. In both cases, Tradition and Counter-Tradition—the wheat and the tares, the Truth and its Shadow—grew up simultaneously; nothing else was, and is, possible in the concluding phase of the cycle. In the words of a North African marabout, often quoted by the Traditionalists: "The doors to heaven and hell are open, from now to the end of the age." The normal channels of Truth were closing down: nevertheless the Truth had to come—even, perhaps, through LSD!—and certainly through Frithjof Schuon, his predecessors, his colleagues, and his followers. But when the Truth breaks in through unauthorized and unorthodox channels, it arrives in distorted and damaged form, and so must function as Judgment: this is the inescapable quality of our time.

As I have already made clear, I subscribe to Schuon's Traditionalism but reject his Primordialism, though in doing so I do not mean to denigrate Native American or other primal spiritualities, or to deny that all valid religious traditions ultimately stem from a single Primordial Spirituality of the Golden Age. It's

CHAPTER THIRTEEN

simply that we are no longer in that Golden Age; we are in the Kali-yuga. If there is one central belief of the New Age religions, it is the erroneous notion that the human race, or a remnant of it, could enter the Golden Age of the next cycle through spiritual growth and transformation, without the inconvenience of either apocalyptic judgment or personal death. This, however, is not the case: we cannot ignore the Revealed Traditions, or invent *ad hoc*, semi-traditional forms to "sacramentally" express our religious universalism, without falling into deep delusion. Such attempts are based on the error that universalism could have its own form, which is metaphysically impossible: forms are particular in essence.

Beyond this, it is necessary to admit that Schuon's Primordialism, as well as his intermittent demotion of devotional Love in the spiritual life to a second-class status with respect to Knowledge, ultimately bore at least one truly bitter fruit. Though the chapter "On Sacrifice" from his book ***The Eye of the Heart*** is filled with rare insights regarding the subject, with regard both to ascetical or spiritual sacrifice, including the "unbloody sacrifice" of the Eucharist, and to bloody sacrifice, whether animal or human, his treatment of this last form, that of human sacrifice, contains (not surprisingly) certain "Satanic verses" which, even though Schuon makes it perfectly clear that the religious dispensations that hold sway under present cosmological conditions rightly disallow the practice, obscure the essence of his argument. He says:

> As regards human sacrifice, one might ask the following question: by what "right" may a sacrificer immolate a victim against his will? To this it must be answered that the sacrificer does not act as an individual, but as an instrument of the collectivity which, being a

totality, obviously has certain rights over part of itself, namely the individual, on condition of course that this totality be unified by a spiritual bond and as a result constitute a real spiritual unity, a "mystical body" so to speak, and that in addition the sacrifice be approved, and therefore required, by God.

A plausible justification! Nonetheless, to grant a spiritual collectivity this sort of precedence over the *spotless* victim that any theurgically effective sacrifice requires is to forget the principle that the human form is the concentrated epitome of cosmic manifestation—just as the sacred collective is the relatively dispersed and not-fully-integrated epitome. The spiritually worthy human individual, as the bearer of what the Qur'an calls the *Amana*, the Trust, "synthesizes in himself through his [indwelling] divinity the totality of beings," these being Schuon's own words from the same chapter which he applies to Christ, but which are equally applicable, in my opinion, to anyone who has attained the status of *al-Insan al-Kamil*, the Complete Man, by realizing his primordial or "Adamic" human nature, his *fitra*, and is therefore worthy to be considered *spotless* in the eyes of God. This is why it is only the individual, never the collective, who can become a saint.

The "pure victim" is always the *sine qua non* for any spiritually effective sacrifice, animal or human. In the case of animal sacrifice, the victim must be without physical blemish so as to conform to its species-archetype—but in the case of human sacrifice, the only "pure" victim is necessarily the one who allows himself to be sacrificed, or who sacrifices himself, *voluntarily*, given that human beings are not animals: because what greater blemish could there be in the sight of God than the fear, despair and hatred of an unwilling victim—though in this case the blemish reflects upon the Satanic "religious" collective based on unwilling human sacrifice rather than upon the sacrificed victim himself? The victim sacrificed against his will curses the sacrificing priest and the whole regime he represents with his dying breath; consequently, as the practice of involuntary human sacrifice (such as that of the Aztecs, which Schuon rightly condemns) continues through the generations, these curses mount up, until finally their collective moral weight and accumulated psychic poison destroy the religious dispensation in question, and the society that has based itself upon it.

In order to believe that involuntary human sacrifice could in any way confer a spiritual blessing on the society that practices it, the collective conception of such sacrifice must already have degenerated into something on the order of "The gods live on blood, therefore we must continue to feed them all the blood they crave or they will wither away, and finally take us with them." This form of human sacrifice is, by and large, a kind of degenerate literalization of the first and essential sacrifice, which is that of the *ego*. The true and original conception is that the ego must be sacrificed in order to "feed" the Presence of God in the spiritual Heart; the Aztec notion that the hearts of innumerable victims must be torn from their chests in order the feed the Sun and save it from extinction is obviously a superstitious and literalistic exteriorization of the primordial truth of the matter. But if this is the case, then why did Christ need to enact—voluntarily, it must always be remembered—a bloody sacrifice, albeit the last fully effective bloody sacrifice of the Abrahamic line? The answer is, first, that he elected to both sum up and end in his own person the whole regime of blood sacrifice operative Jewish and Pagan worlds; second, that he needed to establish a form and degree of ego-sacrifice, albeit to be recapitulated only in an unbloody form, that would be intelligible and convincing not only to the Jews but to the whole world of late Pagan antiquity to which the Christian message was destined to be preached, as well as to all the spiritual ranks of faithful believers including the most earth-bound, not simply to a *gnostic* elite; third, that he needed to make it crystal clear that the sacrifice-of-self required by God must be radical and total, a sacrifice of heart, soul, mind and strength; if the willing victim were to sacrifice all *except* the body when that too was required of him, in the mitigated form of asceticism if not the total form of martyrdom, then his sacrifice would fall shy of the mark, since he would have balked at Christ's commandment to "take up your cross and follow me."

In Islam too this ultimate sacrifice is often required, in the form of death in war for the cause of religion, the supreme examples of this voluntary self-sacrifice being 'Ali and Hussein, whose deaths are recapitulated in mitigated though bloody form by the Shi'a in their practice of extreme physical mortification while mourning the two martyred Imams. Likewise the plains Indians, by the voluntary suffering they undergo in the bloody ritual of the Sun Dance—performed in the same spirit that animated the fierce asceticism enacted by the Toltec king Ce Acatl Quetzalcoatl in his attempt to dissolve the cult and sublimate the practice of human sacrifice in his own society—as well as in the *ethos* of the Lakota and other tribes who understood that death in war is a form of sacred martyrdom, as expressed by their saying "it

CHAPTER THIRTEEN

is a good day to die," were entirely in line—at least on an ideal level—with Christ's saying "greater love hath no man, than that he lay down his life for his friends" [John 15:13]. In such spiritual heroism, ultimately animated by Love and nothing else, what place is there for the degenerate and heartless practice of involuntary human sacrifice? And a thorough understanding of this principle is perhaps more necessary today than ever before, now that a massive revival of Paganism, or at least a degenerate shadow of it, threatens to re-introduce the regime of literal human sacrifice, as in the case of the mad dogs of ISIL or the drug gangs of Mexico. The subhuman violence of such groups has taken such a mythic turn that one wonders if they do not in fact represent an attempt, conscious or otherwise, to revive (in the case of Da'esh) the human sacrifices of the pre-Islamic Time of Ignorance, or (in the case of the drug gangs) the bloody religion of the Aztecs. All this is bad enough, even if we don't mention the apparent mass depopulation plans of the global elites. In any case, the time for a glib exposition of spiritual truth, no matter how profound it may be on the *intellective* level while being deficient on the *existential* level, is now unquestionably over.

In conclusion, I must make clear that I do not deny that Schuon's Primordialism is based on a valid and perennial symbolism; what it lacks is any explicit "apostolic succession" or *silsila* (the Sufi term for "chain-of-transmission"), which is why it can in no way be called Traditional in Guénon's sense. Nor do I deny that it has its place (like everything else) in the Divine economy. Its function in our own times, however, is essentially eschatological. As I see it, the Schuonian influence was eschatological by nature from the beginning, and as such acted to separate the "Sheep" from the "Goats." If Christians pray "lead us not into temptation," it is partly to acknowledge that, as is implied by certain passages of the Qur'an, as well as in the doctrine of *Maya*, God Himself can tempt; those who will not heed His guidance will be subjected to His deception, by which He will "give them enough rope to hang themselves." The doctrine of the Transcendent Unity of Religions, which stems from a level of metaphysical reality transcending all form, cannot be enunciated in times like ours without having a dissolutionary influence upon the forms of the Traditional religions. For some it has providentially provided perhaps the only way for them to adopt and remain faithful to a single religious tradition after realizing that God has sent more than one valid revelation, but for others it has simply relativized the faiths and thus drawn them ever nearer to the sort of religious syncretism, inseparable from a "generic" metaphysics that pretends to transcend the norms of the revealed religions, that will form an integral part of the regime of Antichrist. In earlier times the idea of a Primordial Tradition and a Transcendent Unity of Religions was understood and enunciated—sometimes openly, sometimes in secret—by major religious figures whose spirituality was strictly orthodox. These included St. Augustine within Christianity, Ibn al-'Arabi within Islam, and perhaps (as Guénon believed) the Knights Templars, at least in their early days before they became a spiritually subversive force in Christendom and an ancestor to today's financial and religious globalism. The Qur'an, with its doctrine of the Peoples of the Book and its designation of Adam as the First Prophet, and the Hindu *sanatana dharma* also posit a primordial Transcendent Unity of Religions. In earlier days, religious orthodoxy was strongly enough established in the collective to be able to withstand the

CHAPTER THIRTEEN

brief appearances of a Truth transcending religious exclusivism, which worked to prevent the dogmatic and cultural petrification of the Traditions. Today, however, such unveilings do not act so much to overcome the danger of the idolatry that always menaces exclusivism, the tendency to worship one's religion instead of God, as they work either to inflame such idolatry in reaction against them or to undermine the orthodox Revelations in the name of a Counter-Traditional universalism. The doctrine of Transcendent Unity of Religions is undeniably true, but it is a truth that this world, at the tail end of the Kali-yuga, cannot accept or assimilate. Consequently, when the level of Truth it emanates from, by the will of God, is unveiled to the world at large, when the esoteric core of the Revealed religions appears naked and unashamed, when "what was told in secret is cried from the rooftops," then the present cycle of manifestation will come to a close. In light of this, we may see Frithjof Schuon as a kind of ambiguous herald of the eschatological Christ of the Christians, of the Buddha Maitreya, of the return of the Prophet Jesus expected by the Muslims, and of the Kalki Avatara of the Hindus—who, like Christ as he appears in the Book of Revelations, is also "the Rider on the White Horse"—as well as, by virtue of the false and negative aspects of his teaching, of *al-Dajjal* or Antichrist, whose advent is inseparable from that of the Christ of the *parousia*. Consequently, when we encounter the unveilings of metaphysical Truth brought by Frithjof Schuon, we will often find ourselves in the presence of either the Truth told in the service of illusion (*Avidya-maya*), or of illusion manifested in the service of Truth (*Vidya-maya*); which one of these absolute alternatives will be effective in our lives depends entirely upon our own spiritual destiny and state-of-soul. When listening to

CHAPTER THIRTEEN

the truths brought by Frithjof Schuon, the Sheep will hear one thing and the Goats another—both versions of his message clearly willed by God, Who *guides aright whom he will and leads astray whom he will* [Q. 35:8]. God grant that we be among the Sheep!

Schuon's Appreciation for "Sacred Nudity": An Error in Perspective

The concept of sacred nudity occupied such a place in Schuon's doctrines that he was led to represent the Virgin Mary herself in the nude; the paintings in question appear in *Images of Primordial and Mystic Beauty* Abodes: Bloomington, 1992]. Michael Pollock comments in his introduction:

> A Catholic correspondent writes, "Schuon's representations of the Holy Virgin are an abyss of vertigo: a source of initiatic disillusion....The Virgin's Nudity, her naked immaculate earth, her transparent body of Glory, her flower of Virginity scorches the lids of our hearts. An epiphany of light, a garden of resurrected suns is food for the inner eye." As Schuon says in "The Mystery of the Veil": "By drawing back the veils, which are accidents and darkness, she reveals her Nudity, which is substance and light...." Needless to stress, these considerations apply essentially to every inspired image of the "Eternal Feminine," or let us say of Divine Femininity, as it appears especially in Hindu and Buddhist art. This they apply also to the apparitions of the White-Buffalo-Cow-Woman, which has been described to James Walker by a Sioux

CHAPTER THIRTEEN

informant: "The woman was very beautiful, it is said. She was completely naked, it is said. Her hair was very long, it is said." In a sacred context, nudity means not only primordiality, but also ipso facto archetypal Reality, and hence Divinity, or let us say the mystery of pure Being, beyond the countless masks and veils of relative existence.

It is my belief that Frithjof Schuon's Primordialism was an attempt to express certain truths within a context that ultimately could not receive them, that context being the Kali-yuga as it specifically manifests in the western world; as a necessary consequence, therefore, it invoked a higher Rigor, and ultimately a higher Mercy, than can be fully intelligible on the plane where that Rigor manifests. Schuon is well known for his paintings of radiant female nudes, many of them representing Native Americans, which are collected in his two books ***Images of Primordial and Mystic Beauty*** and ***The Feathered Sun***. Since representations of the nude human form run contrary to the Muslim ethos and *shari'ah* on several levels, what can we conclude regarding the production of such images by a self-described Traditionalist and Sufi shaykh? At the very least I believe that in his act of producing them he invoked certain valid metaphysical principles and latent spiritual possibilities, though in their Wrathful rather than their Merciful forms.

In ***Language of the Self*** (Madras: Ganesh & Co., 1959), in the chapter "The Sacred Pipe and the Red Indians," Schuon writes:

> There are . . . particular reasons why the wisdom of the Redskins should be of interest to Hindus and

CHAPTER THIRTEEN

> these rest upon the truly primordial nature of the tradition in question, which in many of its expressions as also in its manner of reading deep truths through the signs of Nature is highly reminiscent of India in Vedic times. Similarly, the cosmological lore of the American Indians exhibits many striking analogies with corresponding Hindu doctrine ... the American Indians, though accidentally so named by the early European invaders ... well deserve the title in view of a spiritual kinship that makes all true traditions one and all noble peoples Aryas.

There is nothing false in this statement as it stands. Yet the actual form taken by Schuon's Primordialism manifested definite errors on the level of ethos. Specifically, his notion of "sacred" nudity, which he apparently saw as a central symbol of his Primordialism, seems to be based on a confusion between the nudity—sacred or profane—of the Hindus, and the nudity—sacred or simply matter-of-fact—of the American Indians. The naked human form can symbolize a number of things: unadorned Truth, especially the truth of the Unmanifest, as in the case of Buddhist iconography or the Shaivite sadhus of India; the opposite but closely related quality of spiritual poverty before God, as with Job, or the Lakota warrior who "laments" for a vision; heroic exposure to danger, as in the case of the Norse berserker and the Greek warrior or athlete; sacred or profane eroticism; the metaphysical significance of the human form as such, as with the graphic images of William Blake; and the healthy simplicity of nature as opposed to the artificiality of civilization, as with Diogenes the Cynic or the Germanic "back-to-nature" movement.

CHAPTER THIRTEEN

The contemporary Plains Indians are fundamentally modest. Michael F. Steltenkamp, in ***Black Elk, Holy Man of the Oglala*** (University of Oklahoma Press, 1993), which covers Black Elk's later life as a Catholic catechist, tells of the time when the actor David Carradine (of *Kung Fu* fame, the 70s TV series about a self-effacing yet badass Chinese martial artist wandering through the American West) visited the Lakota. Thinking he was among "nature worshippers" or "primordial hippies," he doffed his clothes to go skinny-dipping in the river. Predictably, his hosts were shocked. Among today's Lakota, nudity is ceremonial, and almost exclusively male; outside this context, it is considered immodest even for a man to remove his shirt. (Can you imagine a Traditional Native American in a short-sleeved shirt and Bermuda shorts?)[5] In the case of the plains Indians, male nudity, or more often partial nudity, represents either poverty before God or, as with the Greeks, the spiritual potency of the warrior who willingly exposes himself to danger. Consequently the nude apparition of White Buffalo Cow Woman to the Lakota was power-

ful, dangerous, *wakan*; it was a radical break with everyday reality, and as such it represented, on one level, a theophany of the Formless Absolute. Female nudity among the Hindus, however, is inseparable from an (ideally) sacred eroticism, at least in earlier times—an eroticism that is implicit, though veiled, in Islam as well—which is poles apart from the fundamental sobriety and stoicism of the Plains Indians, a sobriety that is normally broken

---

[5] I did, however, once encounter a Native American dressed in exactly this way, on the occasion when I and my wife drove Prof. Huston Smith to a motel in San Francisco's Fishermen's Warf, where he videotaped what can only be called "a TV commercial for peyote" for a group called Dreamcatchers. (Peyote, breakfast of champions.)

CHAPTER THIRTEEN

only by the "Dionysian" ecstasy of the warrior. A Lakota nautch dancer or singing-girl in the Hindu or Arabic style is simply inconceivable. Unlike the nudity of the Native Americans, that of the Hindus is inseparable from elaborate, civilized dress; it is based not on a primordial simplicity but rather on the act of "divesting," with all the symbolism this implies, in terms of both eroticism and the spiritual Path.

The manifestation of White Buffalo Cow Woman relates to eroticism too, but in a different sense. When she appeared on the prairie before two Lakota braves, one of them wanted to rape her, while the other recognized her as *wakan*, holy; the would-be rapist was struck down; the pious

brave became her messenger. In this legend we can see precisely how *Mahamaya* manifests as either *Vidya-maya* or *Avidya-maya* according to the "eye of the beholder." (The Hindu doctrine of *Maya* is roughly equivalent to the Sufi teaching that Allah is both veiled by His manifestation and manifests Himself by means of His veil, and to the allied teaching that He can and will misguide those who refuse His guidance, as is indicated in the Fatihah of the Qur'an by the words *Guide us on the straight path/ The path of those whom You have favored/ Not the path of those who earn Your anger, nor of those who go astray*.) Unlike the nudity of the Hindus, therefore, the nudity of White Buffalo Cow Woman served to make a radical separation between lust on the one hand and holy awe on the other. Like that of the Eastern Orthodox "nude saint," Mary of Egypt, a reformed prostitute, it had less to do with the explicit "tantric" purification and elevation of sexual energy to the level of Divine contemplation than with an ascetical mortification of the passion of lust— although these two are not entirely unrelated.

It is my belief that Schuon erroneously confused the stoic nudity of the Plains Indians, the sacred erotic nudity of the Hindu Tradition, and the modern "back-to-nature" nudism of the Teutonic race. It is certainly true that all these manifestations spring from a single archetype, since in any "Golden Age" worthy of the name they would not yet have grown apart. But it is just as certain that these elements are incompatible under present cosmic circumstances. Schuon's appreciation for "sacred" nudity in his paintings and the ideology surrounding them was perhaps true in another world but in this world, in this age, in either Dar al-Islam or the post-Christian west, it was, and is, an error. Its symbolism remains valid and may thus be effective in the *batin* (the inner), but there is no way it can be practiced in the *zahir* (the outer) without seriously negative consequences.

In the videotaped interview mentioned above, Schuon made the statement that the pre-Islamic tradition of circumambulating the Kaaba in the nude—strictly analogous to the nude (or semi-nude) dance of King David before the Ark of the Covenant—had been discontinued by Muhammad (peace and blessings upon him) because it was too late in the cycle for such things. These practices had lost their primordial innocence and could only inflame the passions. Some practitioners of the tantric "left-hand path" have felt free to ignore this principle, and may indeed have justified their audacity by their high spiritual attainments. However, as is shown in the **Kalika-purana**, not even Shiva, insofar as he partakes of form as a member of the Trimurti, is the detached and impassive master of his own *Maya*. The same truth is depicted

CHAPTER THIRTEEN

in the tantric icon where *Shakti*, appearing as the goddess Kali wielding a naked sword, dances on Shiva's prostrate form.

The double aspect of *Maya*, *vidya* and *avidya*, also appears in the New Testament as the dance performed by Herodias' daughter, whose name according to tradition was Salome, "peace." Tradition further recounts that during her dance she progressively divested herself of seven veils, which is clearly symbolic of a step-by-step disidentification with the world of manifestation, moving from the gross to the subtle, the seven veils being strictly analogous to the five Vedantic *koshas* or "sheaths" of the *Atman*. She danced only one dance; yet its effect was double. Insofar as she was the *Shakti* of Herod, the tyrant ego, she inflamed the passions and caused the murder of a prophet, the violent and total denial of the reality of Spirit; in this guise she represented the temporary and destructive peace which comes from giving in to the passional self. Salome, however, was also (esoterically considered) the *Shakti* of John the Baptist, and as such represented the peace of certainty, i.e., Holy Wisdom. Insofar as her dance can be imagined as taking place before John as well as Herod, her act of divesting symbolizes a mortification of the passions, a turning away from the world, a transcendence of the created psyche, a realization of the uncreated Spirit, and ultimately the nakedness of the Formless Absolute. This transcendence of form is represented in a parallel way by the beheading of the Baptist, which (as in Sufism) symbolizes the transcendence of discursive, cerebral consciousness and the realization of unitary, cardiac consciousness. Both Herod and John lost their heads when Salome danced—Herod in the name of a lower principle, John in service to a higher. *Maya* does not neatly differentiate herself into *avidya* (ignorance) and *vidya*

(Knowledge) for our convenience; her dance is only one. The division she inevitably produces is always according to the spiritual center-of-gravity of the beholder, who will be oriented either toward Wisdom, which understands itself and passion too, or toward passion, which understands neither Wisdom nor itself.

Anyone familiar with the many failed attempts to bring together "sacred sexuality" and mystical realization in our times is in the presence of a blindingly clear example of precisely this division: the separation of the Sheep and the Goats, not only in the realm of the moral will but also in that of the contemplative Intellect. This separation is so radical that, in my opinion, it stands as an eschatological sign. Whoever can accept the intrinsically sacred nature of Eros without inflaming the passions, whoever can mortify the passions without freezing and suppressing Eros, may be considered to have joined the ranks of those western quasi-tantric practitioners known as the Fedeli d'Amore. In these fierce last days of the Kali-yuga, this is the most rigorous Path of all.

Truth and Beauty, Love and Will: Some Serious Doctrinal Errors

In Schuon's ***Gnosis, Divine Wisdom*** [Perennial Books, 1990; p. 70] the following passage appears:

> One can love something false, without love ceasing to be what it is; but one cannot "know" falsehood in a similar way, that is to say knowledge cannot be under illusion as to its object without ceasing to be what it is; error always implies a privation of knowledge, whereas sin does not imply a privation of will.

CHAPTER THIRTEEN

This, in my opinion, is a monumental error, one that clearly demonstrates that Schuon sometimes reduced love to mere subjective sentiment, whereas Guénon clearly understood it as an objective metaphysical principle. Anyone who has ever struggled against the passions—a word that is etymologically related to *passivity*, indicating that we fall under the power of the passions simply by irresponsibly letting things slide—knows what a radical weakening of the will sin represents. In the words of St. Paul in Galatians 5:17, "For the flesh lusteth against the Spirit, and the Spirit against the flesh: and these are contrary the one to the other: so that ye cannot do the things that ye would." It is certainly true that a darkening of the Intellect can be an immediate and all-pervading privation, like a cloud swiftly covering the face of the sun. But sin most certainly is a privation of the will and nothing else. When the intellect is darkened, the will becomes weakened and imbalanced—just as, when a cloud covers the sun, there is a diminishment of heat as well as light. As in the well-known etymology of the word "sin," the will "misses the mark" because the mark can no longer be clearly seen; every privation of the Intellect results, therefore, in a privation of the will. The imbalance of the will that is sin manifests either as deficiency—sloth or envy, for example—or as excess, as in the case of gluttony, lust, or anger. Both deficiency and excess, however, are privations vis-a-vis the plenitude of the will, which is fully itself only in its complete submission to the Intellect. This privation of the will may manifest as a progressive degeneration rather than the sort of sudden eclipse that affects the Intellect that embraces error—as, for example, in the case of a man whose integrity and life-energy are increasingly drained by his attempt to "sincerely" love a manipulative woman—but a privation of the will is precisely what it is, and nothing else. Furthermore, to claim that the Intellect in error simply ceases to be what it is is not strictly accurate either (as Schuon himself points out elsewhere), since error, as a privation, can never be absolute, and can therefore never completely veil the Intellect, which is nothing less than a ray of the Absolute Itself. Every doctrinal heresy is based on the perversion of a real principle; error is seductive because it always contains an element of Truth.

The Intellect in error "ceases to be what it is" in the sense that it loses, first, the knowledge that "this 'I' is God," and secondly its reliability as a guide, which is disastrous since "this 'I'" is now not God but merely my own benighted ego-self, in desperate need of guidance. But for all that it still remains a virtual theophany: In the words of the Qur'an, *God guides aright whom He will, and leads astray whom He will* [Q. 35:8], which means that Divine guidance remains virtually present even in error, though in an inverted way, in the sense that those who are unwilling to learn their lessons will become object-lessons for others—and possibly eventually for themselves as well, if they can survive the rigors of the test and awaken to its meaning. The constellating of error to the point where it becomes intelligible *as error* is also a function of the Intellect, even though the ones who remain within the error in question cannot benefit from this function, except via the rigors of Divine Justice; as William Blake succinctly put it, "to be in error and to be cast out is part of God's plan." (In **The Eye of the Heart**, maddeningly enough, Schuon contradicts his principle that "knowledge cannot be under illusion as to its object without ceasing to be what it is" by asserting on the contrary that "deviated intelligence is still intelligence, unless this were denied by having recourse to some new term which defined intelligence as related to truth alone...." No new term is necessary, however, seeing that an intelligence that is not related to truth alone is obviously not intelligence at all but rather delusion and stupidity. Here Schuon apparently identifies "intelligence" with mere mentality, if not with an infernal cunning that delights in darkening the minds of its victims. He inexplicably defines "intelligence" as some vague faculty or entity that has nothing to do with the Intellect as he usually characterizes it—namely the *Nous* that is one in essence with the transcendental Truth it contemplates—or even with sound rational thought as the lower reflection of this *Nous*. It is only in this inverted sense that the mentality of demons, who from the Christian point of view are fallen angels, can be described as "intelligent," since they have no interest in the truth per se beyond determining how they might best pervert it; in this light the notion that "deviated intelligence is still intelligence" appears as something on the order a demonic suggestion designed to destroy intelligence itself.)

In the passage quoted from **Gnosis, Divine Wisdom**, as well as many others, Schuon identifies love and will, though sometimes the dyad "intellect; love/will" is replaced by the triad "intellect; affections; will." Both formulations, in my opinion, are valid in their respective contexts. But when Schuon says, "One can love something false, without love ceasing to be what it is," what is being implied? What exactly is the "false object" of a "true love"? According to a doctrine of Maimonides, with which I agree, "Love is the highest form of Knowledge"—but a love that can become attached to a false object and supposedly come to no harm is not itself a mode of Knowledge at all. And love of a false object is obviously no longer Love in the fullest sense. Love of the ugly, for example—seeing that ugliness is not a positive element of Being but simply a privation of Beauty—is really concupiscence. It is a flight from God into the shadows of the self-regarding ego which is at the same time a flight from oneself, both an act of self-worship and a state of unconscious and "projected" self-loathing. An exception may be made in the case of a conscious and penitential contemplation of the Divine within an object in spite of its ugliness, as when we must grant that even the worst criminal is made in the Image of God, even if he has spent his life profaning that Image; such contemplation secondarily involves a witnessing of the Divine Wrath by means of the ugliness itself. But in neither case is the ugliness attractive. Rather, it is all the more loathsome when seen against the radiant background of the Divine Self-Revelation in Man, and under the wrathful shadow of Divine Justice invoked by this very contrast. An attraction to ugliness is not a love of the ugly; this is intrinsically impossible. It is rather a hatred of Beauty—an attack upon God.

But if God, Who is absolutely loveable, is immanent in all forms, and if we are commanded, in Christian terms, to love even our enemies (which, of course, entails the clear realization that they are indeed our enemies), then no object of love possessing positive existence is intrinsically false in every sense. True Love loves whatever is real, and has no relationship with anything unreal; we cannot truly love evil because evil is not a mode of Being but only its privation—as ugliness is a privation of Beauty. So "falsity" must inhere in a partial veiling of the Intellect, a distortion of perspective, as when we love the sin, not the sinner, or follow the Divine Light as reflected in the mirror of manifested forms in such a way that we are led not toward but away from the Source of that Light; to love a negation that possesses no positive Being is nothing but a delusion, and consequently not a form of love at all. Furthermore, the objective knowledge that a given object will delude us if we pursue it is not an attribution of intrinsic falsity to the object itself considered in terms of its positive existence, otherwise God would not be able to know it as an aspect of His own Being, in which case it would not exist. It is rather an insight into the essentially privative aspect of the domain of contingencies, as well as a sober realization that we, in our limited, contingent selves, are not God, and consequently cannot, as God can, look upon all things in the realm of manifestation and come to no harm. In other words, false attraction can only be a privation of the Intellect, not of any of its contingent objects, privative though they be when considered in their contingency alone. If we see something as it really is, we will know that what we see cannot be intrinsically false in every sense because we will know its privations and distortions as testifying to the very Truth by which we can discern them; if we love something that is effectively false for us in view of our own contingent limitations, this indicates that we do not or cannot see it as it really is, that we fail to know the essence of it as one of God's infinite Names—in this case one of the Names of Wrath. To see something as it is to see "with the eyes of God," and God sees only Truth—only Himself. Consequently God loves all He sees, even though a sentient being who does not love Him in return will experience this love only as wrath. Since He is omniscient, His Intellect is never veiled or diminished, consequently He is not subject to false attractions. Therefore the attraction of the will to an unhealthy object—as Schuon (from time to time) seems to imply—is first and foremost an intellectual shortcoming, a distortion of perception; it is not an overpowering of our will by the object in question. Prostitutes do not kidnap us by imposing their privations and distortions on us, since if we were fully aware of these limitations they would function as elements of knowledge and consequently as salutary warnings; rather, they seduce us through our own false projections. It is therefore incorrect to say that love can become attached to a false object and still remain love, because love for a false object is inseparable from a veiling of the Intellect, and is therefore based on a deficiency in Knowledge—and if we cannot know a thing as it really is, or do not want to know it, then we cannot truly love it. Consequently Schuon is in manifest error when he denies that sin is a privation of the will, since every such privation has its roots in a privation of the Intellect, which Schuon accepts as a true possibility. The privations of the will do not present the same appearance as intellectual distortions, distortions such as "fascination" or "attraction to the false" (Schuon seems to understand this), but rather manifest as "weaknesses," "obsessions," and other imbalances that are secondarily derived from these primary intellectual errors, which in turn are inseparable from the submission of the will to the ego rather than to the Intellect. But unless I mistake him, Schuon is here implying—whether or not he realizes it—that even if the Intellect is in error, and so has "ceased to be itself," the will remains sovereign and unaffected. This, however, is not the case. Since the Intellect is hierarchically superior to the will—will being identified with love by Schuon in the present passage, and elsewhere—the privation of the Intellect which is error is necessarily the source of the privation of the will which is sin. To believe that love can remain unaffected by its attachment to a false object—that is, to an object perceived in a distorted way due to a darkened Intellect—is to fall into what Schuon calls the error of "sincerism," the belief that subjective sincerity or earnestness can obviate the negative consequences of objective error. Love of a falsely-perceived object, which will most likely be falsely perceived because we have not developed sufficient *apatheia* to allow us to steadily contemplate it, without cowering, as a theophany of Wrath, begins in the Intellect and subsequently affects the will; such false sincerity represents a kind of collusion between the darkened Intellect and the concupiscent will that can perhaps best be described by the word "dishonesty." And the pernicious notion that the will can remain sovereign and unaffected even if it acts in the service of intellectual error is inseparable from the idolatrous "voluntarism" Schuon so often criticizes. Suffice it to say that if Schuon had understood that the proper use of the will is submission to the Divine decrees, rather than indulged in an antinomianism that he falsely believed (as so many others have) to be the privilege of the gnostic, the *arif*, he would have understood exactly how sin most certainly is a privation of the will, and understood it in the most concrete and rigorous terms imaginable.

So here Schuon's placement of Knowledge above Love,[6] entirely legitimate from one perspective, given that Love is the root and

---

6   It is equally possible, from a different perspective, to place Love above Knowledge, as long as Love is defined not as sentiment but as full and intimate contemplation of, and union with, the object of Knowledge. This hierarchical relationship between Love and Knowledge appears in the angelology of Dionysius the Pseudo-Areopagite, who places the Seraphim in the highest of the nine choirs and the Cherubim in the second-highest. The Seraphim are those angels in whom Knowledge and Love are seamlessly united, whose eternal function is to praise God with a perfect Love that is inseparable from perfect Knowledge. In the Cherubim, on the other hand, Knowledge has begun to be differentiated from its highest expression in and as Love, and now oper-

CHAPTER THIRTEEN

Knowledge the flower—even though the "higher" flower cannot subsist if separated from the "lower" root but must wither and die—casts its inverted shadow: the doctrine, intrinsic to a false romanticism, that although love may be "blind," it still remains sovereign, and so "conquers all." If love is still true when attached to a privative and falsely-perceived object, if it remains unaffected by the darkening of the Intellect, then raw unenlightened affection, not Intellect, is king: a blind king, ruling a kingdom where Eros is a law unto itself, where every attraction to whatever object is self-justifying. This "doctrine" of love-independent-of-the-Intellect as sovereign is certainly not always asserted by Schuon; it is in fact often criticized and rejected by him as "sincerism." But even though he does not "officially" assert it, it is nonetheless clearly implied in the above passage. And this implied assertion has everything to do with Schuon's doctrine that "the theophanic quality of the human body resides uniquely in its form, not in the sanctity of the soul inhabiting it" [*From the Divine to the Human*: World Wisdom Books, 1982; 92] and "outward Beauty, even when combined with inner ugliness, testifies to Beauty as such" [*Survey of Metaphysics and Esoterism*]. True! But this doctrine, though true, and therefore a valid element of a legitimate spiritual Way, desperately needs to be balanced by the compensatory doctrine that the very same beauty is either *vidya-maya* or *avidya-maya* depending upon our purity or impurity of heart, that if one is attracted to that vicious soul by means of the beautiful body it inhabits, one "will not come out again until he has paid the last farthing" [Matthew 5:26]. Schuon's "*Shakti*"

---

ates as an independent principle. In a condition of rebellion against God, the *fallen* Cherubim work to instigate delusion and false doctrine, while the role of the fallen Seraphim is to inspire pride and hate.

CHAPTER THIRTEEN

paintings portraying radiantly beautiful female nudes (done in a style reminiscent of Nicholas Roerich) effectively render the female form as a living symbol of the Divine; my problem with them is not based so much on what is portrayed but on what is left out. If this is the Kali-yuga, then where is Kali? Where is the bloody-mouthed hag with the necklace of human heads? Without an honest presentation of the dark side of Eros, the image of the paradisiacal Eros remains vulnerable to the insidious influences of what is denied. Every rose has its thorn, every paradise its angel with a flaming sword; they are there to protect "the soul of sweet delight" (Blake) from the crassness and lust of this world. Without a teaching that elucidates Eros in its false forms as well as its true ones, its rigorous aspects as well as its merciful ones, a strict puritanism would be the wiser course. There are plenty of traditional sources—Grimm's fairytale "The Goose Girl," for example—which remind us that the outwardly attractive woman is not always the True Bride, a doctrine that is valid in gnostic as well as emotional terms. Popular culture also recognizes this truth, its classic cinematic statement of it being *The Blue Angel* starring Marlene Dietrich. But it is Shakespeare, not surprisingly, who ultimately says it best.

In ***The Merchant of Venice***, Portia (Divine Wisdom) has concealed her portrait in one of three caskets, one of gold, one of silver, and one of lead. She is then approached by three suitors. The expansive, foolish one chooses the gold casket: wrong. The cold, calculating one chooses the silver casket: wrong again. But the true bridegroom, Bassiano, chooses the leaden casket, and in so doing becomes a type of Christ, who endured the *tamasic* heaviness of the material world, death on the cross, and the

CHAPTER THIRTEEN

harrowing of hell to save us. Within the lead of radical *kenosis*, Bassanio finds the portrait of the True Bride. "You that choose not by the view" says Portia, "chance as fair, and choose as true!" And we need to listen as well to her verse dismissing the Prince of Morocco, the vain, inflated suitor, whose character reminds one of the Islamic legend that it was the peacock—narcissistic aestheticism—who introduced the serpent into Paradise:

> All that glisters is not gold,—
> Often have you heard that told:
> Many a man his life hath sold
> But my outside to behold:
> Gilded tombs do worms infold.
> Had you been as wise as bold,
> Young in limbs, in judgment old,
> Your answer had not been inscroll'd:
> Fare you well; your suit is cold.

Only the man, or woman, who thoroughly understands this can look upon Beauty naked, and know it as Wisdom. To teach "Beauty is the splendor of the True" without at all points immediately balancing it with "all that glisters is not gold" is to invoke *avidya-maya*, ultimately leading to the veiling of the Intellect and the corruption of the will. Schuon says: "The serpent is to be found in Paradise because Paradise exists. Paradise without the serpent would be God." True!—but watch out for that Serpent.

Beauty of body is indeed a theophany, and when Schuon exalts it, he is speaking truth, a truth which is a necessary and legitimate compensation for the ascetic hatred of beauty—as exhibited, for example, by the beautiful Christian saint who disfigured her face to discourage her many suitors—as well as the general hatred of beauty, or even fear of it, which is an inescapable aspect of the collective human soul in these latter days. But someone whose intellect is pure and whose will is virtuous will necessarily experience a beautiful body that is coupled with a vicious soul as anomalous and inappropriate, this reaction being the trace within us of our primordial or Edenic state, when physical Beauty was the direct manifestation of Virtue, as Virtue was of Intelligence. A beautiful painting discovered in a garbage dump is a similar anomaly. Anyone of sound sensibilities will, upon encountering it, have two reactions: "What a beautiful work of art!" and: "What is such a beautiful work of art doing in a garbage dump?" Furthermore, if two exhibitions of beautiful paintings were announced, one taking place in a museum and the other in a garbage dump (something which is far from impossible nowadays, and may already have taken place, given the idolatry of ugliness of the contemporary art world), the person of sound sensibilities will choose the museum over the garbage dump, every time. The quest for beauty in human form, if it is a true quest, combining sincerity of intention and a goal which is one with objective Truth, must be the quest for the fullness of beauty: beauty of body, beauty of soul (virtue), and beauty of Spirit (intelligence). This full appreciation for beauty in all its human forms is revealed in the following passage by Ibn al-'Arabi, from his ***The Interpreter of Ardent Desires*** (***Tarjumán al-Ashwáq***), where he extols the beauties of Nizam, the lovely young daughter of his host in Damascus:

> Now this shaikh had a daughter, a lissome young girl who captivated the gaze of all those who saw

CHAPTER THIRTEEN

her, whose mere presence was the ornament of our gatherings and startled all those who contemplated it to the point of stupefaction. The magic of her glance, the grace of her conversation were such an enchantment that when, on occasion, she was prolix, her words flowed from the source: when she spoke concisely, she was a marvel of eloquence: when she expounded an argument, she was clear and transparent. If not for the paltry souls who are ever ready for scandal and predisposed to malice, I should comment here upon the beauties of her body, which was a garden of generosity. . . .

I took her as a model for the inspiration of the poems contained in the present book, which are love poems, composed in suave, elegant phrases, although I was unable to express so much as a part of the emotion which my soul experienced and which the company of this young girl awakened in my heart, or of the generous love I felt, or of the memory which her unwavering friendship left in my memory, or of the grace of her mind or the modesty of her bearing, since she is the object of my Quest and my hope, the Virgin Most Pure.

Those who aren't in quest for Nizam, those whose ideal is something less than the fullness of Beauty, have embarked on a centrifugal course. The fruit of the Tree of the Knowledge of Good and Evil has a degree of beauty, since it is a partial reflection of Beauty Itself: this is the grain of truth in the Serpent's lie that those who eat of it will become like God. But it is not the fullness of Beauty; it is not the Tree of Life. A man who rests content with the beauty of body alone will necessarily experience it as *avidya-maya*. In contemplation of it, his virtue will become corrupted, his intelligence darkened. This is why it is spiritually incumbent upon us, when encountering a beautiful body coupled with a vicious soul, not to deny that this beauty is a revelation of Divine Beauty, but to turn away from that beauty in its incomplete and distorted form, just as one would not, in order to contemplate a beautiful painting, spend several hours in a garbage dump. One would either remove the painting from the dump, or, if this were not possible, turn and leave the premises.

An exception to this imperative not to look upon spiritual ugliness of soul is the saint or spiritual guide who must attend to all aspects, Spirit, soul and body, of the pupil he is commanded by God to enlighten and sanctify—a process which entails, on the guide's part, a vicarious suffering, from a higher level of integration, of the comparative disintegration of the soul in his charge. Even simple charity may require the same thing of any of us, at least on occasion. And part of the charisma granted the one whose duty it is to spiritually purge others within a context of guidance may be to contemplate, in a person whose soul is sick, physical beauty as a theophany of the Essence, thus putting that person at least virtually in touch with the spiritual integration he or she has heretofore failed to achieve, as in the case of the Sufi saint Ruzbehan Baqli, who fell in love with a singing-girl just long enough to awaken her to the Divine Beauty which had been veiled from her by her own profane relationship to beauty, after which God removed his infatuation. But this doesn't mean we can simply tell someone who has used his or her beauty in the service of a crass power-motive or a narcissistic self-worship, "your physical beauty is a manifestation of God, but you aren't living up to it." The person in question must first be convicted of their ugliness of soul, and their beautiful face in the mirror is not what will so convict them; only shame in the face of the Divine Beauty can accomplish this task. As is shown in Oscar Wilde's allegory *The Picture of Dorian Gray*, in such cases the truth of the actual situation would be better revealed if the outer form were not beautiful.

Schuon often seems to identify the beauty of the human body with the beauty of nature. The manifestation of God through the human body, however, is on a different ontological level, and obeys different rules, than His manifestation in other natural forms. Men and women are not noble lions and beautiful gazelles—they are men and women: body, soul, and Spirit. The viciousness of the tiger is not at odds with its beauty, since they together manifest the mystery that God's Rigor is inherent in His Beauty, and His Beauty implicit in His Rigor. But in the case of the human being, beauty of form and viciousness of soul are at odds. If we are blind to this truth, if we forget the warning from the *I Ching* (Hexagram 58, "The Joyous") that "sincerity toward disintegrating influences is dangerous," if we turn aside from the quest for the fullness of beauty to contemplate beauty of body coupled with viciousness of soul, then our awareness will necessarily be diverted away from the viciousness, which is repulsive, and toward the beauty, which is attractive, the result being that we will begin to see the person in question not as a human being but merely as a body, albeit a body which is also, and legitimately so, a virtual theophany. At this point, we have become partners-by-default of the Manichaeans, or the Gnostics, in that we have introduced a radical dualism between body and soul, and have also forgotten in the process that a viciousness of soul will always leave traces—sometimes subtle, sometimes grossly obvious—in the gait, in the physiognomy, in the tone of voice. Furthermore, the attempt to contemplate Beauty as separate from sound traits of soul such as justice, compassion, humility, and courage is to transform it from a manifestation of Divine Gentleness, Innocence, and Mercy into one of Divine Wrath: there is nothing more wrathful than a cold beauty, like that of the cobra hypnotizing its victim, which doubtless attracts, but attracts only to destruction. And it is not essentially lust which is attracted to such cold beauty—it is pride. The belief that one can separate beauty of form from viciousness of soul, and contemplate it in isolation while coming to no harm, is inseparable from the sort of pride which believes that, through power alone rather than through intelligence and virtue, it can extract the juice of life and discard the rind. Schuon is aware of the dangers of unchastity in the contemplation of the beauty of the human form; he is much less aware—at least one gets this impression—of the dangers of aesthetic pride.

And what becomes of the human soul which is ignored and neglected in the name of a contemplation of the human body? If we do not see others in their full humanity, we "murder" them, and destroy as well the fullness of our own humanity. As beautiful bodies whose souls remain invisible to us, they may be supports for our own contemplation of God—on a temporary basis—but it will become progressively less possible for us to imagine them as contemplators in their own right. We forget that the "I" within

CHAPTER THIRTEEN

us, though obviously unique, is mysteriously one with the equally unique "I's" within them; consequently, what Schuon calls "the enigma of diversified subjectivity" becomes veiled; the beautiful objects in question are transformed from living theophanies of the Divine into dead possessions of the ego.

The Traditionalist School, as we have pointed out above, is often identified with an exaltation in principle of Knowledge above Love. And even though Schuon, depending upon the perspective he adopts, sometimes places Love hierarchically beneath Knowledge, sometimes presents them as intrinsically complementary, and sometimes even admits (as in *Spiritual Perspectives and Human Facts*) that Love is in practice more important since Knowledge is the fruit of Love, the primacy of Knowledge remains a central tenet of the School. But if "Knowledge is Power," the danger in exalting Knowledge above Love is that the one questing for God through Knowledge, when seeking his bride, may make the mortal error of ignoring Love, and choosing Power instead—of capitulating to a crass power-motive that, on the human level, can have no more revealing symbol than that of a man or woman with a beautiful body and a vicious soul. The whole question of whether *jñana* or *bhakti* is paramount in the spiritual life may make it seem as if there were an inherent conflict between Knowledge and Love, an all-too-common delusion that might be described as Satan's greatest masterpiece—whereas the true conflict, the greater *jihad*, is not between Knowledge and Love, but between the spiritual union of Knowledge and Love and the ego-based power-motive that would separate them. As we have already pointed out, Ramana Maharshi said that "imperfect *jñana* and imperfect *bhakti* are different; perfect *jñana* and perfect *bhakti* are the same." If the questing Knight is Knowledge, and the abducted Princess, Love, then the Dragon who holds her captive is the will to power, operating both through intellectual pride (within the Knight) and seductive manipulation (within the Princess). When the power-Dragon is slain, this truth can be known; when the will is purged of pride through full submission to God, Knowledge and Love unite.

Perhaps the most vulnerable point in the Traditionalist School to attacks by "the rulers of the Darkness of This World" lies in the realm of the affections. This vulnerability is reflected in Schuon's tendency to over-identify Love and Will, and consequently to separate Love from Intellect in too radical a manner—a stance certain other sages, notably Ramana Maharshi, have cautioned against. Though in some places Schuon posited an "intrinsic *bhakti*" that is inseparable from *jñana*, and understood that there is such a thing as *parabhakti*, a devotion to God transcending subject and object, elsewhere he made a sharp and somewhat arbitrary distinction between a purely voluntaristic *bhakti*, ardent and sentimental, and an exalted *jñanic* impassivity that puts one in mind of the lines of W. B. Yeats, "Cast a cold eye/ On life, on death." This uneasy tension between Love and Knowledge may have led him to forget, at times, something Dante so magnificently demonstrated in his figure of Beatrice: that the object of True Love must necessarily be Truth itself.

Schuon, however, in his better moments, knew this. ***In Survey of Metaphysics and Esoterism***—unhampered by his intent, valid on its own level, to criticize the excesses and shortcomings of a voluntaristic and sentimental *bhakti*—he presents his most

CHAPTER THIRTEEN

complete teaching on the relationship between Love and Knowledge:

> Fundamentally, we would say that where there is Truth, there is also Love. Each Deva possesses its Shakti; in the human microcosm, the feeling soul is joined to the discerning intellect, as in the Divine Order Mercy is joined to Omniscience; and as, in the final analysis, Infinitude is consubstantial with the Absolute.

Nonetheless, as should be painfully clear by now, Schuon's hold on this doctrine was shaky and intermittent; and seeing that his ambiguity as to the relationship between Love and Knowledge is perhaps the central weakness of his entire teaching, it will not be out of place to recapitulate my critique of this ambiguity in a more concentrated form, as follows:

If a true love of a false object is possible, then love is totally divorced from knowledge; it is reduced to mere sentiment and passion, the kind of passion it is possible to feel for any idol you could name. This also inevitably implies, without explicitly declaring it, that a knowledge devoid of love might nonetheless be a complete intellective *gnosis*, which is certainly not the case. In reality, true Love is a mode of Knowledge, just as complete Knowledge is a mode of Love. Nor does a knowledge affected by error immediately become total darkness or total error. There are many valid forms of knowledge that still fail of perfection—logic in comparison to Intellection for example—and even an intellect that is fundamentally oriented toward error will retain certain elements of truth, without which it would be totally negated as a human faculty, as for example the sort of incomplete Intellection that generates heresy, seeing that heresies always contain traces of true doctrine and would have no attractions without them. Likewise the love of a corrupt object that is mis-conceived as totally pure or sincere may nonetheless possess elements of generosity, compassion and self-sacrifice. All of these virtues will exhibit defects, however, because any love that is not fully aware of the elements of falsity in a false or partially false object is in a state of privation, the same sort of privation that an incomplete knowledge will suffer when it imperfectly contemplates a total Truth. And a will affected by sin will certainly exhibit privation, since no will that is not initially deluded as to its object, based on a pre-existing privation of the Intellect, is capable of choosing sin. This truth is dramatized in Genesis by the fact that the lies of the Serpent, symbolizing the perversion of the Intellect, first influence Eve, a symbol of the affections; only then does Eve induce Adam, who symbolizes the will, to eat of the fruit of the Tree of the Knowledge of Good and Evil. And beyond this, there is no question that sin itself introduces a further privation into the will by weakening it in its power to reject sin and choose virtue; only a will that freely chooses virtue, based on a true Intellection of the essence of a particular virtue as a Name of God, can be without privation, seeing that Intellection is inseparable from *certainty*, and the fundamental power of the will is certainty and nothing else. Sin and error are rebellions against Love and Truth respectively, or rather against the God in Whom Love and Truth are one; consequently both of them have an aspect of "mortal sin," defined as the immediate veiling of Reality and the swift cutting-off of the grace of God. Yet as *vices*, as habitual dispositions of the soul toward sin and error, they develop gradually, exhibiting many intermediate stages between complete darkness and total light;

this is why the Sufis understand "the greater *jihad*," the struggle against the passions and delusions of the *nafs al-ammara bi'l su*, "the soul that commands to evil," as being just as integral to the spiritual Path as is *kashf*, the immediate unveiling of Divine Truth. And perhaps the most central delusion to beset Schuon's whole enterprise was the passion to concentrate almost completely on *kashf*, gnostic unveiling, to the detriment of the work of educating the *nafs* and purifying the Heart, in the apparent belief that "if you've *got* the Truth you don't need to purify the Heart, since the Truth Itself has already done that for you." This might well have been Schuon's actual interpretation of a saying of the Hindu *rishis* that he often liked to quote, "there is no lustral water like unto Knowledge." True! But such Knowledge needs to be *applied to the work* of purification, not simply taken as indicating that such work is no longer necessary; it is here that the almost entire lack in Schuon's teaching of *a theology and praxis of the will*—such as is well expressed, for example, in the works of the famous Sufi al-Ghazali—appears in its most destructive guise. Without the work of purifying the Heart of the veils that obscure the Spirit within it, the *gnosis* of higher spiritual realities can never be stable. In the absence of a dedication to such work and a method that effectively serves it, our initial *identification* with the Truth we have seen, in an overwhelming flash of revelation, will generate a powerful spiritual complacency—this being one of the more delusive aspects of the sin of *sloth*, namely *sloth masquerading as contemplative impassivity*—until such complacency ultimately degenerates into a terror of the affections and a darkening of the mind. Be that as it may, Schuon never tired of emphasizing the need for constancy in prayer and invocation of the Name of God, which on the Sufi path is the essential method of deepening one's intuition of the Presence of Allah and applying it to the work of transforming the *nafs al-ammara bi'l su*, the passional soul, into the *nafs al-mutma'inna*, the soul perfectly submitted to God's Will, by means of the purification of *al-Qalb*, the Spiritual Heart. If Schuon's followers have found this doctrine and method in his teaching, and dedicated themselves to it wholeheartedly, then more power to them.

Schuon on Judas

Some years ago a controversy swirled in and around the journal *Sophia* (edited by Seyyed Hossein Nasr) relating to Schuon's claim, in his last prose work published in his lifetime, *The Transfiguration of Man*, that Judas Iscariot "could not have been a fundamentally bad man." I would now like to give my opinion of this controversy, since it touches upon the sometimes uneasy relationship between metaphysics and theology. I accept the criticism of John Stevens, who first took issue with Schuon's belief that Judas might be saved after remaining in Purgatory until the end of time, since Jesus Himself said that it would have been better for Judas if he had never been born, something that cannot be said of any soul destined for glory, even after an aeon of purgation; Schuon's belief in the possibility of Judas' salvation thus runs directly counter to Christian scripture and tradition. And if this is true, and if it is also true that Revelation and Intellection are essentially equivalent, as he apparently taught—although, as we have seen, his "Revelation is an Intellection of the macrocosm; Intellection is a Revelation of the microcosm" is susceptible to other interpretations—then by what authority could he assert that Judas was saved against the plain meaning of Scripture? As I see it, only a new Revelation could have granted him that power, and Schuon always denied (as least publicly) that he had brought such a Revelation—though certain of his followers, if indeed they proclaimed him an Avatar as has been asserted (whether or not he himself made this claim) might have intended to imply that he did. Nonetheless, given Schuon's great depth of metaphysical discernment, I find myself unwilling to let it go at that. He apparently had a "private revelation" of some kind that told him Judas was saved, and the only way I can make sense of this, though not with any degree of certainty, is to take it as an obscure intuition in his extreme old age, not of the salvation of the individual soul of Judas on the plane of form, but of the reality of the *apocatastasis*, when all *lokas*, paradisiacal or infernal, are absorbed into their Absolute Principle at the end of the cosmic cycle. This is certainly in line with the Qur'an's repeated emphasis (which, incidentally, could be one way of "saving" Origen's doctrine of universal salvation) that *Unto Allah belongs whatever is in the heavens and whatever is in the earth; and unto Allah all things are returned* [Q. 3:109]—to which Q:13:15 adds: *willingly or unwillingly*. Because to say, supposedly based on metaphysical discernment, that the soul of Judas was saved in individual terms, which is what Schuon actually asserted, is to make metaphysics an enemy of theology, thus placing it on the same level as theology—not to support an orthodox dogma, however, but to proclaim a heresy. The real use of metaphysics is not to contradict theology but to transcend it, just as the doctrine of the *apocatastasis* transcends the dogmas of the particular and general judgments, but must never be used to deny them. The Noble Qur'an says, in some places, that there is no escape for damned souls from the Fire, but it also emphasizes in many other places [cf. Q. 3:109 et al.] that all things return to Allah. Thus it

CHAPTER THIRTEEN

is clear that, although the universal restoration of all things in Allah's Eternity is a true doctrine in Islamic terms, it must be taken in a higher and more metaphysical sense than the temporal "eternity" of the Fire; Schuon himself, in the chapter "Universal Eschatology" in *Survey of Metaphysics and Esoterism*, spoke of the dark perpetuity of Hell as being on a vastly different level than the Eternity of God. Nonetheless this universal restoration, which is related by implication to Schuon's doctrine that even evil "contribute[s] in its fashion to the equilibrium of the phenomenal order," cannot be correctly understood without Jesus's warning in Luke 17:1 that "It is impossible but that offenses shall come, but woe to him through whom they come!"

Be that as it may, it turns out that Frithjof Schuon's rehabilitation of Judas Iscariot, reminiscent of a similar attempt by George Ivanovitch Gurdjieff, is of more than mere "academic" interest, seeing that the Vatican, on Maundy Thursday, 2021, issued a statement to the effect that "Judas could not have been a fundamentally bad man"! Schuon himself, in an article in his journal *Studies in Comparative Religion*, lamented that the Catholic Church was being destroyed, but nobody seemed to care. Did he himself later unwittingly become one of the agents of that destruction?

Flow and Ebb

In an unpublished statement I once read, Frithjof Schuon described himself (if I remember correctly) as God's chosen instrument for the revelation of the perennial philosophy at the end of time. This strikes me as the simple truth—as long as we add the codicil that Schuon also generated the type and degree of error that only

CHAPTER THIRTEEN

those destined to understand the perennial philosophy would be able to see through. That instrumentality was clearly shared by his pre-eminent colleagues and predecessors: Titus Burckhardt, Martin Lings, René Guénon, and Ananda Coomaraswamy. The immense overflow of wisdom represented by these five would be rare in any time, and is almost inconceivable in times like ours. And yet it happened. When God decides to release a spark of His Wisdom into this world, even the rocks in the dry riverbeds open their mouths and speak. With a ruthlessness that respects no obstacles, that Word is spoken in the place and time destined for it—and if it is not heeded, then so much the worse for the heedless! And yet such wisdom cannot be openly declared in times as dark as these without casting a shadow of serious error.

Frithjof Schuon was the chosen servant of this kind of ruthlessness. As a poet, I know something of what it means to be ridden by an inspiration that for as long it lasts dominates all other values: prudence, compassion, psychological balance, one's duties to one's friends and loved-ones—all are commanded imperiously to clear out of the way when the Word announces itself, when it picks up its chosen instrument and shakes it till the bones rattle, in order that a faint echo of that Word as originally spoken might fall on human ears. I also know how much one must pay, sometimes, for such inspirations, possibly over a period of many years. Just because a celestial inspiration chooses to make use of us, we are not thereby exonerated on the personal level from whatever temptations we may be led into in the process, or whatever damage we may do to our own soul or to the souls of others. And when such an inspiration comes paired with its own negation and counterfeit, the price that must be paid for those called to separate the wheat from the chaff in the case of such manifestations is even higher. Only the prophets are fully defended by God from the negative consequences of inspiration, and Frithjof Schuon was most certainly not of their number.

The visionary poet is all too often suspended between the glory of his art and the degradation of his circumstances—Dylan Thomas is a case in point. Likewise the gnostic whose knowledge has come to him more through quasi-poetic inspiration than as the fruit of piety and ascetic discipline is suspended between a powerful spiritual glamour and a hidden spiritual disgrace. If he recognizes this disgrace, takes it as an abasement imposed by God as "payment" for his act (as it were) of appropriating spiritual truth without full Divine sanction, then his inspirations may ripen into true *Ma'rifa*, true *gnosis*. Conversely, if he succumbs to the temptation of using the glamour of his inspirations as a way of hiding from both himself and others the degradation that is their inevitable shadow, that behind-the-scenes degradation will only grow. Simultaneously his insights, while losing none of their glamour, will gradually become more distorted and delusive. And given that a contemplation of one's inspirations is highly pleasurable, and of one's degradation extremely painful, this will be a very difficult temptation to resist. In the words of the Qur'an [26:224–27]:

As for poets, the erring follow them.

Hast thou not seen how they stray in every valley, And how they say that which they do not?

CHAPTER THIRTEEN

Save those who believe and do good works, and remember Allah much, and vindicate themselves after they have been wronged.

Those who do wrong will come to know by what a (great) reverse they will be overturned!

To be given true inspirations, especially Divine ones, that are not matched by one's strength of character and purity of heart, is to be wronged in just this sense. The human vessel, in terms of its formal limitations, is intrinsically unworthy to receive such gifts—though, as Schuon correctly points out, in terms of its essence the human form is "naturally" designed to host a "supernatural" content. This, however, does not justify presuming upon our intrinsic affinity for the Truth as if that Truth were "easy." We must never be so foolish as to take the gift of Divine Wisdom as no more than a kind of personal good fortune, but must always compensate through piety and gratitude for the debt implicitly incurred by such bounty, thereby transforming "cheap grace" into "costly grace." To become host to a Knowledge that is infinitely higher than one's mere humanity is to be abased in the face of Majesty of God; without such abasement we will be hard-pressed to realize that deeper level of the human essence where *gnosis* is a God-given birthright. Those who are unwilling to prostrate before this Majesty, who are ungrateful for God's gifts because they take them for granted, have seriously wronged themselves, and can only ultimately vindicate themselves by embracing the abasement that such treasures carry in their train, thereby exchanging the chastisement of humiliation for the virtue of humility.

CHAPTER THIRTEEN

Martin Lings, in *What Is Sufism?* [University of California Press, 1977], has this to say of the Spiritual Path:

> From time to time a Revelation "flows" like a great tidal wave from the Ocean of Infinitude to the shores of our finite world; and Sufism is the vocation and the discipline and the science of plunging into the ebb of one of these waves and being drawn back with it to its Eternal and Infinite Source.

The writings of Frithjof Schuon took the form of a great flow of what one is almost tempted to name "Revelation"—though of course this word should be strictly reserved for revealed scriptures and religion-founding prophets and avatars; and Schuon himself always denied, at least publicly, that he came to bring a new religious dispensation. But it appears that this very inspired or quasi-revelatory quality of Schuon's mission sometimes threw the methodical traversal of the spiritual Path itself into the shadows. When the great image of Metaphysical Truth is unveiled for all to see, it dazzles. What we witness with such ease and inevitability we think we have actually attained, since everything other than the splendor of this Truth has fallen into the shadow of it, resulting in the sort of false enlightenment that Jean Borella, in *Guénonian Esoterism and Christian Mystery*, has named "the aesthetic identification with the Essence," which he believed Frithjof Schuon had been affected with. And when the power of *vidya-maya* that was initially dominant in this great unveiling retreats, as it now certainly has in Schuon's case, we (or some of us) are left with nothing but a memory, a paralyzing memory that tempts us to keep "returning" to the smoking crater left behind by the great explosion instead of taking care of the business at hand: the destruction, not through Intellection alone but through Intellection applied as sacrifice, of anything that would veil this Truth in our own souls, of all the weaknesses and obsessions and passions and illusions that were hidden from us in the shadow of that great Light. I can of course only speak with any degree of authority of the effect his teachings have had on me, on someone who read his books but never adopted his spiritual practices because he never came into the sort of initiatory or quasi-initiatory relationship with him that would theoretically make such practices effective. After a certain point, the only way I could continue to assimilate the great truths Schuon revealed was to criticize his errors according to his own criteria, both in the context of his writings and in response to my own temptation to embrace those errors, hoping that they might exempt me from facing my own personal darkness, from taking the necessary steps required by the spiritual Path. No matter what visions we may have seen, we are poor in everything but our poverty. Only God is *the Rich* [Q. 47:38], and consequently it is only our intrinsic poverty that can put us in effective touch with the wealth of the Divine Nature. We may be able, God willing, to receive something out of the great store of those riches, but we can never possess what we have received in our own right. And if we are unfortunate enough to have been given more intellectually than we can assimilate existentially, then we have gone into debt to Reality itself—a debt that only spiritual poverty united with penitential suffering can pay. Nothing but a keen recognition that we are *the Poor* [Q. 47:38], not simply our receptivity to the great aesthetic image of Spiritual Truth that has become available to an increasing number of us in these latter days (whatever our degree of spiritual qualification or the lack of it) due to the thinning of the veils of terrestrial existence, will show us what it means to be the *fuqara*, the "poor in spirit."

Schuon as Shiva; his *Shakti* as Kali

We have considered a number of instances of both ambiguity and outright error in the content of Schuon's teachings; now it is time to consider his writings in terms not of their content, but their form.

Because of his immersion in the *Maya* of the Absolute at an extremely high level, Frithjof Schuon was a writer of immense doctrinal volatility, a fact that is not readily apparent due to the extreme sobriety and elevation of his teaching; the very magisterial certainty of his expression has worked to hide this volatility. I do not mean to imply by this that Schuon's certainty was not in most cases justified, since it clearly arose in many instances from direct Intellection; it's as if we sometimes hear him reading the text of the Truth Itself, just as you or I would read from a printed page. But whoever reads him critically rather than "devotionally" will repeatedly encounter formulations seemingly so one-sided that they appear as errors—formulations that are often (though not always) triumphantly compensated for in the next sentence and resolved in a greater synthesis. Schuon's writing is thus supremely dialectical; he takes various "sides" of a given question, both to demonstrate the necessary suppleness of metaphysical expression as opposed to the dogmatic theological crystallizations for which it compensates, and to "triangulate" the truth of the matter on a higher dialectical level through viewing it from multiple standpoints. Thus his seeming contradictions are most often revealed as the necessary elements of metaphysical paradox—though not in every case. Verbal formulations may endlessly approach metaphysical Truth but they can never ultimately encompass It; the inescapable paradoxes of metaphysical expression are the sign that the Object of metaphysics must always transcend even Its own highest expression.

Unfortunately, not all these dialectical cycles are completed within the space of a single paragraph; sometimes it will take years for Schuon to formulate the antithesis to an earlier thesis, and thereby reach a higher synthesis—not to mention the fact that sometimes he never reaches it at all. And over the period of those years, for those who have read only one or two of his books, that uncompensated first thesis remains at best an unanswered doctrinal imbalance, and therefore (in effect) an error. Nor are Schuon's apparent errors always the product of necessary metaphysical paradox; sometimes they are just outright contradictions. As we saw above, in **Logic and Transcendence** (1975), Schuon denies that the action of the priest, by the power of the Holy Spirit, effects a substantial change in the species of the Eucharist, and then affirms it (more or less) in **In the Face of the Absolute** (1984). These two statements are not paradoxical or dialectical, but simply opposed; anyone who accepts both without noticing the contradiction between them, because "whatever the master says must be true," has jeopardized his or her capacity for intellectual objectivity. (Other examples could be cited, and they are definitely worth collecting.) But because Schuon writes on so high a level, almost unique in our time, it is hard for us to make out the gradual changes in his thought, or discern the contradictions in it. And contradictions, especially unconscious ones, have a paralyzing effect not only upon the intellect but also upon the affections and the will; as Titus Burckhardt points out in ***Alchemy: Science of the Cosmos, Science of the Soul***, the hidden contrary of psychic volatilization is psychic petrification, these two conditions often being present at the same time in the same soul. Schuon speaks in several places of the power of the Divine Feminine to melt the hardness of the human ego; nonetheless, whenever *Mahamaya* is unfolded, the dark side of the archetypal Feminine Principle (which, as we have already seen, Schuon rarely confronts) is necessarily also present—the transpersonal petrifying-power—the Head of the Medusa. On the conscious level everything is immersed in the flow of life; simultaneously the unconscious is menaced by the fear of death. The subliminal contradiction between these two states is capable of producing a profound psychic paralysis that some of Schuon's followers and readers appear to have been affected by—myself included; it is a paralysis that I had to repeatedly overcome during the writing of this book. I see this as one of the potential pitfalls of an aesthetic contemplation of metaphysical truth in which the will is not engaged. A disengaged will is weakness incarnate, and therefore must encounter fear—the fear of Kali, the Goddess of Fate; a weak or damaged will (one of the signs of which is an impulsive willfulness) is necessarily ruled by Fate, to which it often has a *fatal* attraction.

One can legitimately see Schuon's dialectical swings, sometimes taking years to complete and sometimes never completed at all, as an imperfection in his mode of expression. But in reality they are much more than that. If we consider the form of his expression rather than its content, particularly its quality of relentless *Maya*, we will see that Schuon was commanded by God to tell the truth in a way that would necessarily result in error, apart from any errors of his own. Thus we may discern in his Marian spirituality precisely the advent of the eschatological Virgin, who also showed her rigorous and apocalyptic face at Fatima, LaSalette and Akita, and elsewhere in our time. In the case of Christ's first advent, the universal *Maya* or *Shekhina* of the Absolute, via the Virgin Mary, provided the necessary Matrix for the Incarnation of Christ as Redeemer. Schuon's role, however, was to herald, and in part initiate—as the presence of the same universal and ever-Virgin *Maya*—the manifestation of the Matrix that will allow for the appearance of Christ the Judge, of the eschatological Rider on the White Horse, who is equally the Saoshyant of the Zoroastrians, the Mahdi and the Prophet Jesus of the Muslims, the Maitreya of the Buddhists, and the Kalki Avatara of the Hindus. This archetypal role of the Virgin as the Matrix of universal manifestation and dissolution, which appears in the human microcosm as the perfect submission and receptivity of the soul to God's Sovereign Word, is one of the things that justified the great Sufi Ruzbehan Baqli in characterizing Maryam the mother of Jesus as "the Mother of all the Prophets," each of whom brought a different aspect of that same Word. Whether Schuon himself, who believed he had been chosen for his role of latter-day revealer of the *philosophia perennis* by the Virgin Mary, willingly submitted to that Word or was simply dominated by it in ways that he did not fully understand, is an entirely different question. Be that as it may, to unfold the universal *Maya* of the Absolute at the tail-end of the Kali-yuga, under conditions that all but guarantee it will generate error to the very degree that it unveils the Truth—not excepting the final error of *al-Dajjal* or

CHAPTER THIRTEEN

Antichrist—is precisely to herald the coming of the Hour; it is to call for the separation of the Sheep and the Goats, according to the teaching of the Qur'an that *Allah guides aright whom He will and leads astray whom He will* [Q. 35:8]. In Schuon one discerns both the wheat and the tares—which Jesus says will be allowed by God to grow up together until the arrival of the Hour [cf. Matthew 13:24–30]—in their most fully-developed and terminal form on the intellective plane. The wheat certainly predominates in the content of his teaching; the form of his teaching, however, coupled with his own pretension, at least as reported by some of his closest associates, to be the "Seal of the Sages" along with various other exalted titles, was as if expressly designed by God to allow the tares to grow up along with the good grain, error along with Truth, so that those who are humbled in the face of Truth will be fed by the wheat, while those bound to error by the chains of their pride will follow the tares into the Fire.

Frithjof Schuon was greatly influenced by Kashmiri Shaivism; consequently his "eschatological" function was in my opinion related in some ways to the myth (he himself recounts it) that when Shiva opens his Third Eye the world is burned to ashes. Schuon's most immediate precursor, outside of René Guénon, in the orthodox understanding that a multiplicity of religions are valid and sent by God, was Ramakrishna, who worshipped Kali, the *Shakti* of Shiva, the Goddess of Destruction, though most often in her positive and merciful form. In Ramakrishna's realization of God through the Christian and Muslim forms in addition to the Hindu one, as well as in Schuon's annunciation of the Transcendent Unity of Religions and his magisterial presentation of the esoteric doctrines of almost all of them, we may discern signs of the approaching end of this cycle of manifestation. As we have already pointed out, the doctrine of the Transcendent Unity of Religions, true as it is, cannot be announced to a world ready to believe it but not capable of understanding it without giving aid and comfort to those who are working to homogenize the world's faiths into a One-World Religion, and consequently destroy them all, partly by means of a Satanic counterfeit of this very "meta-doctrine." And the destruction of the Revelations that give humanity access to the transcendental dimension must result in the destruction of the world, since humanity is the central and "axial" being who maintains the connection between terrestrial existence and its transcendent Source; if we lose this function, which we cannot remain faithful to in any stable way outside the framework of some Divine Revelation, the earth will fall. And it is abundantly clear that God wills that the Transcendent Unity of Religions, for all its inescapable dangers, be proclaimed in our time.

But when Shiva opens his Third Eye so as to "see through" the world-illusion, this does not in and of itself destroy the form of that illusion; the Eye of the Intellect is just as capable of seeing *Mahamaya* as *vidya-maya*, thereby witnessing all manifest forms in their "metaphysical transparency" as the manifestation of the *Atman*, and thus affirming them, as it is of knowing all forms as *avidya-maya*, as a veil over the *Atman*, and thereby destroying them in the fires of a universal *nirvikalpa samadhi*. No: The world is destroyed when Shiva opens his Third Eye because when he does so his *Shakti* begins to dance. When that Eye is closed it sees the Unitary Absolute alone, beyond the *dvandvas*, the pairs-of-opposites; when it is open, it sees the pairs-of-opposites *as* the

Absolute, and understands them not as fixed poles or dichotomies but as dynamic polarities—as waves—as Universal Vibration. Consequently the world is volatilized, transformed from matter into Energy. (The German word for "woman," *weib*—cognate with the English words wife, wave, weft, and vibrate—reveals the same primordial understanding of the Divine Feminine Principle as *Shakti*, Vibration, Energy.)

The dance of Shiva's *Shakti* is woven on the loom of the most primordial of the pairs-of-opposites, more primordial than Good and Evil, or even Truth and Error—that of Transcendence and Immanence (which according to Schuon are prefigured in the Absolute and the Infinite, though these in themselves never appear as opposites). The universe both is and is not God; *Mahamaya* both is and is not Shiva. The wavelike quality of manifestation, and consequently its nature as *Maya* or "truly-existing illusion"—something that, according to the traditional simile, is "like a rope mistaken for a snake"—results from the fact that it exists in one sense and does not exist in another, which is why we see it as always coming into and departing from existence. This is the import of the Islamic Asharite doctrine of "occasionalism," which maintains that God creates, destroys, and recreates the entire universe in each separate instant, this being the cause and essence of its vibratory nature, symbolized and invoked in Hinduism by the syllable *Om*. When this vibration increases in frequency, and consequently becomes more subtle, it indicates a progressive approach to the understanding that God's universal manifestation simultaneously is and is not. And when this simultaneity is fully realized, resulting (in Buddhist terms) in the vision of *tathata* ("suchness") as one with *shunyata* ("emptiness"), vibration itself is transcended; existence and non-existence are seen to be the same thing; *Shakti* melts back into Shiva; God Alone remains. This is what is known as "the end of the world."

Thus we may understand Schuon's doctrinal inconsistencies as a manifestation of *Shakti*, of *Maya*. And to the degree that they sometimes harbor petrifying and paralyzing contradictions, the dissolutionary power of *Shakti*, in the guise of Kali, is automatically invoked to provide the necessary compensation. When *Mahamaya* unfolds her power it becomes impossible to make consistent doctrinal or strategic sense out of what she manifests; she is the source of our every idea or plan of action; at the same time she transcends them all, confounds them all. And she also employs whatever conception we may become attached to in order to sweep us away into the particular *loka* where that conception is the ruling principle; this is how she functions as Judgment. *Mahamaya* only serves *moksha* or Liberation if we fully awaken to our intrinsic inability to make systematic sense of her; this is part of what Abu Bakr was alluding to when he said "to know that God cannot be known is to know God," and why some Sufis consider *bewilderment* to be the highest spiritual station. And if we then put this realization into concrete practice through the method of continually and consciously letting go of our conceptions of the Absolute, as generated by the Absolute, in the face of the Absolute—the Sufi term for this being *fikr*, sometimes translated as "contemplation"—then we will be purified of delusion, obsession, and self-will, and learn the true meaning of *Islam*: submission to the Divine Will. No longer will we attempt to use our spiritual perceptions and creative imagination to articulate metaphysical truths for the purpose of avoiding submission, because we will have understood that true and established *gnosis* or *Ma'rifa* is the fruit of submission, not the other way around—submission to both the norms that God has laid down for everyone and to the dance of His mysterious Will operating in our own lives in each separate moment of time, a Will that is not required to satisfy our own notions of consistency, and in any case never wills the same thing twice. And while it is our duty to seek consistency to the best of our ability by affirming Schuon's truths and refuting his errors as thoroughly and rigorously as we can, ultimately the only way we will be able to follow his teaching to its final limit is to sacrifice him as teacher. We can only legitimately perform this sacrifice, however, if we have truly reached the station where it is called for—a station symbolized by the dance of Kali on the prostrate form of Shiva. When this station has been reached, it is time to stop trying to affirm or deny or evaluate the indications and pass on to the Indicated—to take our attention off the finger and turn it instead to the Moon. To do this is to transform whatever *avidya-maya* may adhere to Schuon's teachings, and to our own souls, into *vidya-maya*, and thereby enter into the "quintessential esoterism" that it was his stated intent and mission to teach, regardless of whether we think he triumphantly fulfilled that mission or wretchedly betrayed it. If you see the Buddha—kill him.

The Uses and Misuses of Comparative Religion

As was pointed out above, Frithjof Schuon disagreed, in the name of Intellection, with various orthodox Christian and Islamic doctrinal formulations, while continuing to assert that Intellection is intrinsic to orthodox Tradition, seeing that "Revelation is an

CHAPTER THIRTEEN

Intellection of the macrocosm." In order to deal with the problems created by this approach, he made a rather facile distinction between the "Esoteric Christian (or Muslim)" and the "Christian (or Muslim) Esoterist," with the second category considered the higher and more inclusive. The first category includes those whose esoterism remains within the framework of a single Revelation, while in the case of the second category, where "plenary esoterism" holds sway, esoterism comes first, as it were, and the particular revelation that is followed, second. I certainly accept the reality of plenary or quintessential esoterism insofar as it represents *gnosis* or *Ma'rifa*—the direct knowledge of God and the universal metaphysical order—given that God is not limited by His various Self-Revelations either to a particular dogmatic formulation or to a single Tradition. God sends Revelations but Revelations do not bind God. His Revelations are binding upon us and have the power to save us, but God Himself has no need of them. But I do not accept everything Schuon presents as plenary esoterism—by which I mean that any metaphysical formulations which contradict orthodox dogma rather than providing an esoteric hermeneutic of it are entirely out of place. And one implication of this is that while plenary esoterism certainly embraces all the Revelations on the level of the highest potential realization (given that the Truth is One), any "generic" esoterism that "transcends" the particular faiths in the sense that it strictly adheres to none of them will necessarily be inferior, in practical and spiritually operative terms, to an esoteric doctrine that faithfully conforms to the principles, terminology, symbolism, and authorized practices of a single God-given Revelation. "Exclusivist" esoterism may accidentally produce a narrowness-of-outlook that remains relatively ignorant of the esoterisms of the other Revelations, but what is lost in terms of horizontal breadth is more than compensated for by vertical penetration and one-pointedness, these being aspects of "the one thing needful." In other words, in terms of concrete realization if not outward expression, the only way to access plenary esoterism—barring the rare exceptions allowed by the principle that "the Spirit bloweth where it listeth"—is to pass through, and beyond, the center of one the "provincial" esoterisms of the Revealed faiths. Those who may happen to reach the threshold of the Absolute by the unpredictable election of the Spirit rather than any Traditional Path are literally "exceptional," like the *pratyeka buddha* in the Buddhist tradition: they possess no vehicle that would allow them to effectively and operatively transmit what they know. As for the vast majority of those spiritual seekers who understand that the well-traveled highway to Absolute Truth lies in Tradition and nowhere else, the words of the Prophet Muhammad, peace and blessings be upon him, clearly apply: "Enter houses by their doors."

In my opinion, comparative religion has two legitimate uses. In terms of the first, the fact that a particular Tradition may express a given doctrine more clearly than a different Tradition, a doctrine that all Traditions nonetheless hold in common in one form or another, can serve to throw light on a doctrine that one's own Tradition certainly embraces but which nonetheless remains in a more-or-less implicit or latent state. For example, the Vedantic doctrine of the *Atman*, the Indwelling Absolute Witness, can reveal greater latent depths in the Islamic prophetic *hadith* "He who knows himself knows his Lord" and throw a clearer light on *Al-Shahid* (the Witness) as a Name of Allah, as well as (in Christian terms) on St. Paul's "it is not I who live, but

CHAPTER THIRTEEN

Christ lives in me." This "triangulation" of a given principle in terms of more than one faith also has the effect of demonstrating how metaphysical doctrines are not simply discrete items within "culturally-conditioned belief-systems," but refer to objective realities that lie beyond the realm of belief entirely. This is an important compensation for the postmodern tendency to reject all universalism of Truth in the name of the provincial beliefs and attitudes of self-referential ethnic or religious communities, since "God" Himself, at the end of this road, is no longer recognized as one of the many Names, appearing in all human languages, that refer to the One Objective Truth, but is reduced to merely one more culturally-determined belief or "god" among many, a concept that no longer satisfies the definition of "God" as the Supreme Being. The second legitimate use of comparative religion is to demonstrate, via the recognition that certain central doctrines held by different faith Traditions are incommensurable on the plane of form (something Schuon himself pointed out in ***Christianity/Islam: Essays on Esoteric Ecumenism***), that the Unity of Religions is truly transcendent, not psychological or cultural or socio-historical. The fact that the doctrinal formulations of the respective Traditions become increasingly similar as we approach their esoteric centers demonstrates that metaphysical principles are not simply elements of this or that limited, relative worldview; that perfect unanimity is never in fact attained on the plane of form demonstrates that the Traditions meet not in some humanly envisioned meta-doctrine, already extant or yet to be developed, that is somehow expected to be spiritually effective once all the bugs are ironed out, but in God Alone.

CHAPTER THIRTEEN

Frithjof Schuon was a truly great metaphysician; consequently, his errors were also great. I believe it is time to confront these errors, not in order to damn him root and branch (which is God's prerogative in any case, if He chooses to exercise it) but to save what is best in him. And if we do, we will find in many cases that Schuon himself is our greatest ally. Frithjof Schuon said virtually everything; he was in effect a human explosion of metaphysical expression with few parallels in human history. However, the turbulence unleashed by that explosion resulted in certain errors and contradictions that—if we are willing to follow principles, not persons, seeing that "there are no rights superior to those of Truth"—we might now be able to face, evaluate, and put right.

For years I believed I had learned certain important principles from Frithjof Schuon: that metaphysical discernment, while it might provide an esoteric exegesis of Traditional theological dogma that some "exoterists" would be likely to see as heterodox, can never contradict that dogma; that syncretism is disallowed from the outset; that when treating of a particular revealed religion we must speak of it in its own terms, or at least in terms of its greatest theologians and saints and sages, rather than immediately importing concepts from different revelations or from "pure metaphysics" whenever we encounter an orthodox doctrinal formulation we don't feel comfortable with; that "esoteric ecumenism" should be limited to areas where, based on our metaphysical discernment, we can be certain that two or more Traditions are speaking, from their own differing perspectives, of one and the same principle; that this esoteric ecumenism cannot be simply applied to every orthodox dogma, some of which will remain totally irreconcilable on the plane of form with dogmas

CHAPTER THIRTEEN

from other Traditions; and consequently that the Transcendent Unity of Religions is truly *transcendent*: the God-given Paths are perfectly reconciled only in the Absolute itself. Passages that support these principles appear in many places in Frithjof Schuon's opus; and yet, as we have seen, Schuon himself did not always follow them. And the most puzzling thing to me is: why didn't I see this before? Was it because Schuon's followers, particularly Seyyed Hossein Nasr, Martin Lings, Marco Pallis, and Titus Burckhardt, were in fact more Traditionalist than Schuon himself? Or because among my main contacts with the Traditionalist world were Alvin Moore Jr. (Eastern Orthodox Christian and godfather to the Traditionalist writer, Dr. James Cutsinger) and Rama Coomaraswamy, who, as fully committed Christians, were Traditionalist to the core? In any case I have now been forced to conclude that I took certain things from Schuon that suited my own intellectual needs and spiritual destiny, and left other things behind. Schuon made me a "non-exclusivist Traditionalist"—one who remains strictly faithful to one Revelation while not denying the validity of others—even though he himself (for good or ill) did not limit himself to Traditionalism in this sense. In other words, while I am able (legitimately I hope) to discern real parallels between different Revelations on the esoteric plane, I am also capable, and actually compelled, to adopt an exclusively Muslim perspective when speaking of Islam, an exclusively Christian perspective when speaking of Christianity, though I am still not certain that I practice this perfectly. I can apparently do this without becoming involved in irreconcilable contradictions, or radical dishonesty, because I have realized on an existential level that God is the Source of all the orthodox Revelations, and that when the Absolute expresses Itself in terms of the relative It must do so via multiplicity, a multiplicity that only appears as contradiction when we foolishly attempt to reconcile forms that, as Schuon himself points out, exclude one another by definition, in the same sense that a lion or a peacock or a bull cannot at the same time be an eagle. We can easily accept a multiplicity of living species or human racial groups; it is much harder for us—understandably so—to accept a multiplicity of orthodox religious doctrines that contradict one another on the plane of form. And this is as it should be. We must not glibly enumerate differing doctrinal formulations related to the Absolute on a simple "phenomenological" basis, on pain of falling into a mere horizontal catalogue of "the various beliefs that human beings have entertained throughout history," the sort of comparative religion that relativizes the theological and metaphysical contents of the Revealed faiths, and thereby acts to destroy them. When considering and speaking of more than one Divine Revelation, we must constantly refer them back to their Principle and Origin, to the Absolute itself, or else encounter one or the other of a pair of hopeless traps: either that bottomless pit, of which postmodern academia is one province, where all divergences in doctrine or worldview are taken as absolute and so must generate "quasi-absolute" contradictions as soon as we compare them, or that rarefied stratosphere where all doctrinal similarities are absolutized, thereby relegating the providential particularities of the separate Traditions to a second-class status, if not deconstructing them entirely. As Ibn al-'Arabi put it (even though he was speaking on a much higher level than mere "interfaith studies," which did not exist in his time): "there is war between the Names of God." Nonetheless he also made clear that these names are not the "parts" of the One God, Who is in no way divisible, but refer in

CHAPTER THIRTEEN

every case to His Absolute Trans-formal Essence and nothing else, since (as should be obvious), God cannot go to war against Himself.

In view of the need to avoid both postmodern fragmentation and universalist syncretism in the field of comparative religion—which Frithjof Schuon certainly attempted to do, though far from perfectly—I believe that the doctrines of Ibn al-'Arabi can help us purify Schuon's teachings of the increasingly worldly universalism and antinomianism that his enterprise ultimately became infected with. Furthermore, once we have come to both a true understanding of Schuon's valid insights and a thorough discernment of his errors and contradictions, we will be free to apply the valid aspects of his metaphysics to a deeper understanding of the dogmas of the revealed faiths in their providential multiplicity from the standpoint of the Unity of Truth, rather than simply preserving them in the form of "systems of thought" that can be supposedly be objectively researched and studied by nonbelievers alone, as if they somehow lay outside the authority of the Revelations that produced them. It is crucial that this metaphysical understanding be both deepened and brought into line with orthodoxy, in view of the fact that some people (Patrick Laude for example) are already envisioning the emergence of a universalist "meta-doctrine" based on Schuon's works—a paradigm that, given sufficient patronage from the globalist elites, might take the place of the revealed faiths. However, in order to apply the balanced critical evaluation of Schuon's metaphysics that I am suggesting, we will need to have reached—partly with Schuon's help—a type and degree of metaphysical certainty that is not founded on a simple "belief"

CHAPTER THIRTEEN

in his ideas. Armed with this discernment we will be empowered to carry on both an esoteric exegesis of the orthodox dogmas of the Revealed religions in light of Schuon's metaphysics, and an "inquisition" of Schuon's formulations according to the norms of those Revelations, so as to determine whether a particular formulation of his is truly esoteric or merely heterodox, whether it metaphysically expands and deepens our understanding of orthodoxy or simply contradicts it. God is equally the Inner and the Outer; we cannot limit "confessional" orthodoxy to mere exoterism, any more than we can—as those whose viewpoint is intrinsically exoteric so often have—see all esoterisms as heterodox. Just as it is the role of metaphysics to save theology from literalism and idolatry, so it is the function of theology to preserve metaphysics from error. If metaphysical speculation wanders away from orthodox theology in the horizontal dimension it enters the outer darkness, but if it cleaves to orthodox dogma as faithfully as any confessional exoterism does, it will find itself able to greatly expand and widen and deepen such dogma in the vertical dimension—without thereby being forced to deny the validity of the other orthodox Revelations—and thus fulfilling its own proper function. If we can imagine a way to apply Schuon's magisterial insights to this task, we might eventually find ourselves able to plumb the depths of the orthodox faiths as never before, while at the same time protecting these precious Revelations from the widespread syncretistic tendencies (often backed by powerful globalist patronage supporting the development of a One-World Religion) that is abroad in today's world. If we call ourselves Traditionalists, let us fully engage with the Traditions, damaged and darkened though they be in these latter days, and not take our hopefully valid understanding of universal metaphysical principles, as rare and exalted as this understanding may be (at least in the abstract), as an excuse for not doing so. Spiritual Truth is a great expanse, but it is reached through the eye of a needle.

Frithjof Schuon, Purgatory of the *Arifun*

Among our acquaintances in the Traditionalist world, my wife and I were privileged to know Dr. Rama P. Coomaraswamy, son of the "co-founder" of the Traditionalist School, Ananda K. Coomaraswamy, during the last years of his life. Rama was Mother Theresa's cardiologist; after ill health forced him to retire from the practice of medicine he re-trained as both a psychiatrist and a Traditional *sedevaccantist* Catholic priest, in which capacity he worked as an exorcist along with Father Malachi Martin in the New York area. In response to Frithjof Schuon's wedding of a largely orthodox *theoria* with a sometimes heterodox *praxis*, Dr. Coomaraswamy told us, with an air of shock and disbelief: "This is something that has never happened before!" And what may indeed be entirely new, something possible only in the final days of the Kali-yuga of a given *manvantara* or cycle-of-manifestation, is for a metaphysician of the highest order, one superbly informed as to the doctrines, scriptures and practices of all the world's religions as only someone in the modern or postmodern age could be, to bring certain of these doctrines to a sublime level of expression, and still place himself in so many ways "above" the norms of those religions, according to the sort of radical individualism that Patrick Laude has termed "supranomian"—a sage who produced a large body of work filled with almost incomparably exalted metaphysical discourse, throughout which are scattered various passages which, while strictly maintaining their elevated tone, exhibit a degree of foolishness rarely encountered in the annals of religious writing! If this ever has happened before I've never heard of it, possibly because any similar examples were only produced in the extreme old age of earlier *manvantaras*, only to be burned, buried, drowned and vaporized in the various apocalypses that brought those ages to a close. And though Schuon may have been, at least in his own estimation, a law unto himself, due to his extreme individualism he can never stand as a law unto anyone else. Individualism has made many valuable contributions in the fields of art and spirituality, and there is no question but that Frithjof Schuon did much to illuminate the great religious traditions of the earth. Nonetheless his highly individualistic and antinomian attitude made him fundamentally incompatible with any properly "Traditionalist" worldview—and if elements of his praxis cannot be considered orthodox according to the norms of any Traditional faith, what justifies us in taking his metaphysics, though profoundly illuminating in many respects, as inherently authoritative on a plane that transcends the doctrines of every such faith, such that the foundational dogmas of these faiths might be criticized in terms of it?

In view of the inescapable contradictions inherent in the idea of "Schuon the Traditionalist" we are led to ask why God chose to confront us with such a maddening enigma at this precise point in human history! We have no right to demand explanations of the Almighty; He has His reasons for what He does that may, insha'Allah, become clear to us in the next world, if not (eventually) in this one. But in light of the fact that He is the Author of every true law, though He Himself is bound by none of them, we must wonder why He chose to confront us with a sage of the latter days who in many ways adopted the same prerogatives, acting as a profound expositor of Tradition while firmly placing himself outside it.

The danger of taking Frithjof Schuon's teachings as in some sense higher even than those of the God-given Revelations becomes apparent in Patrick Laude's book **Keys to the Beyond: Frithjof Schuon's Cross-Traditional Language of Transcendence**, which I will evaluate more thoroughly in *Chapter Fifteen* below. Laude speaks of Schuon's teachings as the potential basis for "a metalanguage that issues from traditional idioms but also transcends them." These "traditional idioms," however, could only be the sacred scriptures of the Traditional Revelations, as elaborated and commented upon by the saints and sages of those Revelations; and while Laude hopes that this metalanguage could be articulated "without claiming to supersede their respective doctrinal integrity," how could these sacred idioms be "transcended," except by means of the intuition of an Absolute Reality that transcends all forms, not simply the forms of theological dogmas, and that consequently transcends any "metalanguage" as well? And how could such a "metalanguage" transcend the Revelations without superseding them? And how could it supersede them without deconstructing them? Laude himself credits this objection when he observes that "the notion of a metalanguage . . . raises fundamental questions regarding the legitimacy of any inflection or displacement of traditional meanings." Nor are such worrisome questions pertinent and necessary only on the intellectual plane; they also intimately apply to the dimension in which the fundamental sense of the sacred holds sway, the realm in which spiritual courtesy or *adab*

CHAPTER THIRTEEN

in the presence of the Deity becomes mandatory, and where the kind of violation of the sacred that we might term "metaphysical discourtesy" consequently presents itself as a serious danger. One is reminded here of a phrase from the Zen tradition cautioning us against such discourtesy: "True—but a pity to say so." A "survey" of the religions from the standpoint of the academic and relatively secular world outside them—or from that of the "extra-religious religious philosophy" of Frithjof Schuon—may be useful, even necessary, in these times of enforced religious pluralism; yet we must never forget that any humanly-constructed view of the God-given religions that cannot in the nature of things fully participate in them must always acknowledge itself as inferior to them, no matter what degree of human genius might have produced it. It may in fact be true that the brilliance and universality of Schuon's metaphysics were commanded by God in view of the unparalleled spiritual darkness we must now contend with, just as He could have also willed Schuon's contradictions, follies, and *lapses in taste* precisely to prove that nothing can equal His authorized Self-revelations, as issued through His avatars and prophets. In any case, if we want to avail ourselves of the fulness of Schuon's teaching, we will need to take into account not only the contents of his written and visual creations but the totality of his manifestation in terms of the effects of his practice both on his followers and on the more distant circle of his "detached" observers, which together constitute a kind of "existential *koan*" filled with fascinating enigmas that beg to be elucidated and have much of vital relevance to teach us regarding the spiritual challenges we all face in this darkest of times in human history.

CHAPTER THIRTEEN

As I observed at the beginning of this chapter, and have hopefully been able to demonstrate throughout by many examples, Frithjof Schuon's metaphysics are contradictory in several ways and on more than one level. Is this a case of conscious mystical paradox or simply a lack of presence of mind? Be that as it may, unconscious or unacknowledged contradictions, proclaimed with all the authority of apparent certainty, inevitably have a paralyzing effect on those who hear and accept them. Consequently the will is not only de-emphasized as a human faculty crucial to the spiritual life in Schuon's critique of "voluntarism," it is also shackled with a contradictory metaphysic that makes it incapable of acting to conform the entirety of the human soul to the spiritual truths that Intellection reveals. And, strangely enough, it was Schuon's own teachings—certainly not alone, yet more so than any other single influence—that refined my discrimination to the point where I was able to see this. Consequently, since I have written with appreciation of Schuon's teachings for twenty years now, not uncritically but still without fully understanding the gravity of some of his errors, I must now fully deconstruct those errors to the best of my ability or incur the guilt of having led my readers astray in their spiritual lives. Frithjof Schuon is an illuminating course to take, if you can somehow find the proper criteria by which to evaluate him; taking him as an unquestioned and authoritative spiritual guide, however, is a very different matter.

But why an "illuminating course"? Why not just completely reject Schuon's doctrines as irrevocably tainted with error? Did not his great predecessor, René Guénon, try for many years to "purify" Freemasonry so as to make it a "legitimate" esoteric order within Roman Catholicism— Freemasonry which, without his being

CHAPTER THIRTEEN

fully aware of it, perfectly fits his own definition of a Counter-Initiatory organization—because he believed Christianity had lost its inner, initiatory dimension, only to give this up as a hopeless task? And isn't the attempt to disentangle truth from error in Schuon's doctrines equally hopeless? At least we can thank Schuon for refuting Guénon on this particular point when, following Dionysius the Areopagite, he defined Baptism, Confirmation, and the Holy Eucharist the valid rites of orthodox Christian initiation. In response to my own question, I answer as follows: I have chosen to "winnow" Schuon rather than simply reject him because, 1) I accept as axiomatic that God has sent more than one valid Revelation, each one foundational to a religion that continues to produce saints—saints are the proof—and because, 2) globalization has now brought these Revelations face-to-face everywhere. We desperately need a true doctrine that can make sense of this situation—spiritually, not just diplomatically—because without such a doctrine, God's several Self-Revelations to the human race will go to war with each other and tear each other apart. And as it happens, Frithjof Schuon has provided us with a large chunk of this crucial doctrine. Satan has been working overtime, however, to damage and pervert any such doctrine—for several generations if not for many centuries—precisely because an inverted form of the Transcendent Unity of Religions will be the centerpiece of the theology of Antichrist. If any of you, my readers, feel that I have made the wrong choice in adopting this course of action, I ask you to pray for me. As for those who believe I have made the correct choice—I ask you also to pray for me!

In any case it has become clear to me that my "discernment of spirits" has left much to be desired when it comes to Frithjof

CHAPTER THIRTEEN

Schuon. Due to the magisterial if not pontifical style of his writing, as well as the elevation and profundity of many of his insights, his immense mental volatility was not immediately apparent to me—and the fact that many if not most of the errors I have critiqued in this book were resoundingly refuted, on other occasions, by Schuon himself, simply goes to show how shaky his hold was on his own doctrines. If he was not in the habit of resorting to orthodox Tradition to ground and stabilize his expressions when his inspiration was operating at white heat, neither was he overly scrupulous about consulting his own past teachings. As is the case with many poets, both good and bad, the moment of inspiration was all. But while one poem cannot "refute" another written by the same poet, the same does not hold true for philosophical or metaphysical formulations.

But why, we must ask, did God allow the unparalleled mixture of profound truth and ingenious falsehood that characterized the writings of Frithjof Schuon?—God who, as the Holy Qur'an tells us, is *the best of plotters*? [Q. 8:30] As I see it, there is only one possible answer: that, in view of the fact that (in Schuon's own words) "evil ... has the positive function of highlighting the good *a contrario*," God sent Schuon as an almost inconceivably rigorous test for the spiritual intellectuals and gnostics of the final days of the Kali-yuga—not a simple, one-dimensional test like a temptation to this or that vice or passion or explicit heresy, but one that, in confronting its subjects with moral, intellectual, and spiritual contradictions that were both radical and unavoidable, (including some operating on the highest levels of metaphysical *gnosis*) apparently did so for the express purpose of preparing them to do battle with *al-Dajjal*, the Antichrist, and his ideological cadre of fallen Cherubim and their human agents. Schuon was the eye of the needle of discernment through which only the thinnest and strongest thread can pass, an incarnation of the metaphysical Symplegades. And the test he brought, and incarnated, is composed of a double temptation. Those capable of grasping not only the profundity but the *timeliness* of many of Schuon's formulations will find it extremely hard to reject his errors and contradictions, but will instead be tempted to pervert their intellectual faculties by making ingeniously mendacious excuses for them. Likewise, those who are rightly scandalized by these apparent heresies will be tempted to reject absolutely everything he said, even his wisest and most brilliant doctrines, and possibly also anything resembling those doctrines in the works of the saints and sages of the legitimate and God-given religions, if not in their sacred scriptures themselves—and, as Rama Coomaraswamy often told us, "the Devil doesn't care which side of the horse you fall off of," a proverb that is worth repeating in many contexts. This is to say that Satan, via the writings of Frithjof Schuon, apparently thought he had found a way to set Wisdom and Morality (whose other name is Love), the two inseparable poles of God's Will and Self-manifestation in this world, at war with each other, hoping thereby to wipe all true spirituality from the face of the earth. That was his plot. But God, as the Holy Qur'an tells us, is *the best of plotters*, and Satan in any case remains God's slave and agent whether he likes it or not—it being abundantly clear, from his angry protestations, that he most certainly does not like it. Therefore we can confidently assert that God sent Frithjof Schuon to impose this most rigorous of tests on the spiritual intellectuals of the latter days, one specifically designed to determine which of them have sufficient humility, insight, wisdom, courage, and

CHAPTER THIRTEEN

raw stamina to accept the Truth from the mouth of even its most contradictory vessel, while discerning and rejecting its subtlest conceivable perversions, regarding not the limitations of the vessel (though it is certainly necessary to discern them) but the Divine Truth alone. Whoever can endure the rigors of this double test, pass it, and survive both physically and spiritually, will be well fitted—I might almost say, fully *inoculated*—to enter the moral, intellectual, and spiritual jihad against the Antichrist, which is equally a battle against those Principalities and Powers who stand behind the contemporary perversions of the foundational principles of all the God-given faiths.

But what if you discover—or believe—that you have actually passed this test? What then? What if you suddenly find yourself among "the quintessential few," the anti-*Dajjalian* spiritual elite? What new and unexpected dangers might you face in that rarefied company? Schuon liked to quote St. Augustine to the effect that "all the other vices attach themselves to evil, that it may be done; only pride attaches itself to good, that it may perish"; this would make Luciferian pride not only the worst but also the subtlest of the seven deadly sins, whose effects can sometimes hide themselves more completely than those of any other.

In Catholic high school in the 1960s I was taught to "never believe that you can outsmart, or have outsmarted, the demons, the fallen angels; they are vastly more intelligent than you could ever be"; to believe that mere human intelligence could defeat demonic intelligence is to fall into the sin of pride. So if this inverted intelligence actually appears to have been outsmarted, at least in a particular arena, how should we respond? At the very least we should attribute to the invisible ministry of the unfallen

CHAPTER THIRTEEN

angels whatever power seems to have acted to expose demonic delusion, rather than taking credit for it ourselves. Years ago I coined a proverb that, while not universally true (thank God), still works as a useful warning: "Whoever believes he or she is fighting against the Antichrist is thereby actually serving him." We must never forget that whatever ability we seem to possess to counter delusion and evil is only by the Power, the Guidance, and the Will of God, which means that we will never reach the point where we can stop praying, in the words of the *Fatihah* from the Holy Qur'an:

*Ihdinas-Siraatal-Mustaqeem
Siraatal-lazeena an'amta 'alaihim
ghayril-maghdoobi 'alaihim wa lad-daaalleen*:

Guide us on the straight path
The path of those whom You have favored
Not the path of those who earn Your anger, nor of those who go astray.

Insofar as the works and example of Frithjof Schuon are the ally of those called to oppose the Antichrist, may God exalt the truth in what he wrote and thereby strengthen their resolve; insofar as his writings have, likely without either his knowledge or his consent, become useful to *al-Dajjal*, may God expose them, rebuke them, and end their insidious power to fascinate and delude. As for Frithjof Schuon himself, may his profound intuitions of the truths of God and the metaphysical order, *insha'Allah*, be his keys to Paradise—particularly in view of the function God apparently assigned him in the Divine economy of the End Times, as an invoker of judgment though not as a Judge—the role of one

CHAPTER THIRTEEN

who, often in spite of himself, made possible the discrimination between the Sheep and the Goats on the highest conceivable level of the Intellect, even if the name of the herd or fold to which he himself was ultimately destined remains hidden from us. In any case, seeing that the Almighty alone is the final Judge in all such matters, I will end this investigation with a pious wish commonly heard in the Muslim world, though one that is rather foreign to Western ears in this age of universal indiscretion: "May God keep his secret."

~~Ramadan, 2021

CHAPTER FOURTEEN

Letter to Wolfgang Smith: On Orthodoxy, Cosmology, Exoterism, Esoterism, and Frithjof Schuon

Dear Wolfgang:

I believe we both need to use what is best in Frithjof Schuon to unveil the esoteric dimension of the revealed faiths, and also to measure Schuon against the orthodox dogmas of those faiths so as to determine what in him represents a true esoteric hermeneutic of those dogmas and what is simply heterodox. And this is something that only the esoterics can do; the exoterics, as they did with Eckhart, must see everything they cannot fathom as heterodox, whereas the esoterics can understand the valid orthodoxy of their own perspective, whatever the exoterics may believe.

It is my belief that any orthodox dogma is susceptible to an esoteric exegesis, even if that dogma in part serves the need to deny an orthodox esoteric doctrine that—speaking in Christian terms—a particular Church council saw as an inopportune mode of expression that might give scandal or mislead the average believer; this is one of the implications of the notion that the Holy Spirit overshadows and guides every valid Church council. However, if the visible institutional Roman Catholic Church were to become, or if it already has become, apostate, this principle would no longer apply, since such a church's doctrinal pronouncements would no longer be orthodox.

In ***Christian Gnosis*** you speak of the pronouncement of the Fourth Lateran Council, that God created every creature *ex nihilo*, "out of nothing," from the beginning of time, as being a denial of the eternal aspect of creation, of "creation in God"—Schuon's "*maya-in-divinis.*" This denial was perhaps even intended, on the human level, to refute the notion of the eternity of the world—which, if "the world" is defined in strictly temporal terms, is of course entirely legitimate. But this formulation too can be seen esoterically. If we take *nihil* as "eternal potentiality, the being of all things in a non-determined state within God's eternity," and *creatio* as the bringing of these things out into temporal existence, then the formulation is not only orthodox, but veils a legitimate esoteric meaning, as every orthodox formulation does and must do. Certainly, time cannot begin at any one point "in" time, any more than space can have a "center" that occupies any particular point in space. But existence can certainly descend from Eternity into time—a descent that is illusory in essence, though productive of consequences that are all-too real, until such "time" as its illusory nature is realized. If "the beginning of time" is interpreted—as it certainly can be—as a descent, in terms of perception at least, from

CHAPTER FOURTEEN

Eternity into a world of time with no fixed point of beginning or end, then such a descent can certainly be seen as a "creation" or a "production" or a "drawing-out" of creatures from an absolute and non-determined Nothing into temporal existence. By the same token, when time is defined in strictly "temporal" terms—that is, in terms of past and future—it is obviously other than and opposed to Eternity; from this standpoint, creation clearly cannot be defined as eternal. But if we see time in its eternal aspect, as a succession of present moments (which anyone, esoterist or exoterist, is forced to admit that it is), each one of which is equally present, since the real present moment—the *nunc stans* of Aquinas—is One, and is *not a moment in time*, then succession itself is negated; from this standpoint, which recognizes time as eternal in essence, creation most certainly is eternal—not because it "never begins" or "lasts forever" in temporal terms, but because, when defined as God's eternal creative intent, it transcends duration. "Temporal time" does not begin or end at any fixed point; nevertheless, it is always beginning, always ending; it is mere becoming, not true and integral Being, which is why it can in no way be made co-eternal with God, on pain of dragging God Himself down from Eternity into time. "Eternal time," however—Eckhart's "simple now"—is nonetheless the very dimension in which God speaks His eternal Word, once and never again, now and forever.

Any orthodox dogma, whatever its apparent limitations, is susceptible to an esoteric exegesis—and if we can perform such an exegesis, we will be able to distinguish which doctrines presented as esoteric actually are so from those that are merely heterodox, and that consequently—like many of the purportedly esoteric doctrines of the sectarian Gnostics—simply constitute an alternate, and therefore heterodox, *exoterism*. I believe that Schuon's *opus* embraces both categories of doctrine, and that it is entirely possible for us to distinguish one from the other.

There is a perennial tendency to identify orthodoxy with exoterism alone, which is inseparable from the temptation affecting the half-awakened believer, when confronted with the limitations of exoterism, to take refuge in heterodoxy. Schuon, in a way, was "intellectually impatient" when confronting, say, St. Thomas Aquinas. If he had possessed a stable sense of traditional piety he would have shown deference to the greatest theologian of the Western Church and taken the time to penetrate his doctrines esoterically, like Eckhart did; instead, he simply became impatient, peevish, and went off on his own, relying upon his own undeniably brilliant discernment. But individual brilliance is not enough to satisfy the requirements of either theology or metaphysics; what is needed as well is a sense of Tradition, which in Schuon's case was intermittent—real, often uniquely profound, but still not entirely stable.

Sincerely,
Charles

CHAPTER FIFTEEN

Was Frithjof Schuon Really a "Traditionalist"? A Review of *Keys to the Beyond: Frithjof Schuon's Cross-Traditional Language of Transcendence* by Patrick Laude (SUNY, 2021)

Keys to the Beyond is perhaps the most exhaustive study we possess of several of Frithjof Schuon's major themes, an important resource for anyone wishing to evaluate both the strengths and the weaknesses of his teachings. The context in which Patrick Laude places those teachings in his Introduction is concerning however, at least to this reviewer.

Most of us who have been attracted to the Traditionalist perspective through the writings of Frithjof Schuon since the late twentieth century have accepted the position expressed by

CHAPTER FIFTEEN

René Guénon in his chapter "The Necessity for a Traditional Exoterism" from *Initiation and Spiritual Realization*, which—as long as we do not make the error of limiting the revealed religions to their exoteric dimension—is entirely in line with characterization of the Traditionalist way by Titus Burckhardt that I've already quoted above in *Chapter Twelve*, but which is imminently worth repeating:

> There is no spiritual method without these two basic elements: discernment between the real and the unreal, and concentration on the real [these being the last two of Schuon's Six Stations of Wisdom]. The first of these two elements, discernment or discrimination (*vijñana* in Sanskrit), does not depend on any special religious form; it only presupposes metaphysical understanding. The second element, however, requires a support of a sacred character, and this means that it can only be achieved within the framework of a normal tradition. The aim of method is perpetual concentration upon the Real, and this cannot be achieved by purely human means on the basis of individual initiative; it presupposes a regular transmission such as exists only within a normal tradition....To be precise, there is no spiritual path outside the following traditions or religions: Judaism, Christianity, Islam, Buddhism, Hinduism and Taoism; but Hinduism is closed for those who have not been born into a Hindu caste, and Taoism is inaccessible.

CHAPTER FIFTEEN

These criteria drew a firm and liberating line for us between the world of occultism, heterodox cults and New Age spirituality, and the Traditionalism of René Guênon, Titus Burckhardt, Frithjof Schuon, Martin Lings, Marco Pallis, Whitall Perry, and Seyyed Hossein Nasr. Now, however, with the publication of **Keys to the Beyond**, this distinction has to a certain degree been erased. "The very notions of *sophia perennis* and *religio perennis*," the author says, "could not but be reformulated in the context of an increasingly globalized world," and he goes on to define the philosophia perennis as "a philosophical and theological lingua franca" that "takes the fact of intellectual globalization as a starting-point and a motivating factor for the elaboration of a philosophical metalanguage." This represents a truly shocking 180-degree about-face from the original central principle of Schuonian Traditionalism, according to which Tradition is superior to zeitgeist because time is subordinate to Eternity. But now Tradition is no longer opposed to the spirit of the (post-) modern world, therefore it must be reformulated to conform to that spirit. This is nothing less than a "Vatican II" for Traditionalism. Since I cannot believe that Patrick Laude, as a recognized Traditionalist scholar, would simply drift along with the prevailing socio-political trends, such an extreme reversal in worldview must have been the fruit of either an exhaustive rethinking of the Traditionalist position, or a period of personal spiritual upheaval, or both. Yet we hear nothing at all of the process by which this radically revisionist position was reached—a lacuna I hope the author will some day fill in for us.

Traditionalism as I have known it was intended to provide a specific type of intellectual support for the contemplative life to those few who needed it, to the "pneumatic Remnant," which is why Schuon's Maryamiyya Tariqah was sometimes characterized as a "*tariqah* of solitaries." Maybe there is even a good reason now to reformulate Schuon's doctrines to appeal to the globalist intellectuals, as long as its fundamental critique of the modern world is not weakened—though it is difficult for me to imagine how this balancing-act might be achieved; on the other hand, such a move might prove spiritually disastrous, seeing that the mere abstract truism that all Traditional faiths hold many metaphysical principles in common, and thus may be posited as springing from the identical Source, must be placed on a lower ontological level than any one of the sacred *upayas* by which these truths can be concretely actualized. At the very least we need to question Laude's approach so as to make the greater Traditionalist/Perennialist world aware of the choice that now confronts it.

We should also remember that the term *lingua franca* originally referred to the use of the French language by various colonial administrations. Are the globalists actually today's colonialists? Are their colonies now the various Traditional religions? I ask this in line with my belief that the globalist elites are presently moving to co-opt and control all the Traditional religions, a perspective that first came to me while I was editing the exhaustively-researched ***False Dawn: The United Religions Initiative, Globalism, and the Quest for a One-World Religion*** by Lee Penn. Also relevant here is Christopher Lasch's monumental study of the anti-traditionalism of the global ruling class, ***The Revolt of the Elites***, not to mention the calls by Popes Benedict and Francis for the equivalent of the One-World Government, coupled with their continued liquidation of Traditional Roman Catholicism, partly through a promiscuous horizontal ecumenism that places *diplomatic* agreement with non-Christian religions above the preservation of the Christian Tradition itself.

Laude maintains that this metalanguage or *philosophia perennis* "would be nothing less than a conceptual synthesis of the world's wisdom traditions," one that would "transcend" these traditions "without superseding their respective doctrinal integrity." But can you really transcend something without superseding it, at least without transcending the dimension of form entirely, or supersede something without deconstructing it? He goes on to observe that "The current questions and challenges make the need for such a contribution particularly compelling and one that is likely to attract broader attention." But attention from whom? From the traditional authorities and exemplars of the several world faiths? From priests or monks or Traditional Sufi shaykhs? Or from academic students with a dual major in interfaith studies and international relations who do not necessarily maintain a faith commitment to any particular religion, and may even be agnostics or atheists? Laude does not seem to take into account the fact that many influential people in today's world, though they are zealously interested in religion, do not believe in God. In all this interfaith dialogue, this study of the world's religions, we must never forget that the central *raison d'être* of every true religion is not to carry on inter-civilizational diplomacy, much less facilitate the discipline of comparative religion, but—first and foremost—to save our souls. This, to use one of Frithjof Schuon's favorite phrases, is "the one thing needful."

Here is my chapter-by-chapter evaluation of Prof. Laude's book:

CHAPTER FIFTEEN

Chapter One, "Atma, Maya and the Relatively Absolute," is a luminous exposition of the essence of the Advaita Vedanta, based on the duality-in-unity of *Atma* and *Maya*; of its reverse mirror-image, the unity-in-duality of Shiva and *Shakti* in Kashmiri Shaivism; and of the interplay and essential unity between the two, which—despite their different emphases—form the basis of a central principle of Schuon's metaphysics, namely the secondary polarization of and primary identity between the Infinite and the Absolute. This chapter shows Frithjof Schuon, the universal metaphysician, at his best.

Chapter Two, "The Avataric Mystery," is a tour-de-force embracing the many perspectives from which the Absolute and the relative, the Unmanifest and the manifest, the Transcendent and the Immanent may be viewed, with the central mediating point that both distinguishes and unites them being the *avatar*, which Schuon uses as a general term embracing not only the Hindu notion of God incarnate in man but the Judeo-Islamic figure of the prophet and the Person of Jesus as the God-man in Christianity, whose Divine and human natures are "fused but not confused" in a "hypostatic union." Laude here presents Schuon as pushing an extremely subtle and intellectively-infused mental understanding of these realities so far into the mysteries—as he so often does—that his very penetrating clarity sometimes becomes a veil in its own right. One is ultimately left with the most profound formulas conceivable—formulas that are, however, in danger of blocking the way to the concrete actualization of the mysteries by their own blinding brilliance, with the result that the road into the Cloud of Unknowing, beyond which lies

CHAPTER FIFTEEN

the Reality that all mental knowledge both manifests and veils, may be blocked.

Chapter Three, "Upaya: Religion as Relatively Absolute," is where Laude considers the differences between the religions as based, in Buddhist terms, on different *upayas* or "saving means" adapted to different dogmatic frameworks, which in turn are addressed to different human needs and potentialities. I entirely agree with this. For some reason, however, Laude maintains that "the ambiguous connotations [of an *upaya*] clearly signal that the formal strategy of salvation it entails lies beyond a strict consideration of truth and morality per se. It is amoral, though certainly not immoral, since its goal is none other than the essence of morality."

This reminds me of the post I once saw on the web, where a spiritual seeker informed us that Buddhism was his favorite religion "because it has no morality." He was apparently unaware that the Buddhists consider *sila* or morality to be an essential *upaya*, and ignorant as well of the fact that, in terms of the Noble Eight-fold Path, "right intention, right speech, right conduct, right livelihood, and right effort", as essentially moral requirements, are organically related—as both causes and effects—to "right mindfulness and right *samadhi*." How could an *upaya* be "beyond a strict consideration of truth per se" if the first element of the Eightfold Path is "right view"? And how could amorality in any way bring us closer to the essence of morality? The psychopath does not see himself as immoral because he doesn't believe in morality; nonetheless he is proud to call himself "amoral" because he thinks that anyone who does believe in morality is a fool. If Laude means something else by "amoral," what exactly would that be? In view of various questions that have been raised concerning Schuon's observance of the Muslim *shari'ah*, or the lack of it, we must ask whether Laude's amorality is equivalent to antinomianism, and whether or not antinomianism, at least in certain contexts, can be considered Traditional in Guénon's sense, or if it should be classed instead as Counter-Traditional. Be that as it may, there is no doubt that morality itself is recognized as one of the most necessary and effective of *upayas* in every Tradition.

Laude goes on to say that

[Schuon is], first and foremost—an esoterist who is keenly aware of the limitations of religions as providential salvific systems. For him it is quite clear that [they] fall short, from the outset and not simply out of decay or corruption, of providing a total and disinterested conception of Reality, to the extent that this is possible given the unbridgeable gap between the Real and its doctrinal expressions.

But if this gap is indeed unbridgeable, is not every faith-tradition, no matter how venerable it might be and how subtle its metaphysics, invalidated at a single stroke? And, given that every true doctrine, considered as a necessary context for a given spiritual practice, is an *upaya*, is not every Traditional spiritual method simultaneously declared to be essentially useless? Furthermore, if the border between concept and Reality can never be crossed, what is the use of expending all one's intellectual potential in trying to come up with "a total and disinterested conception of Reality"? Since spiritual capacities are limited and life is short, wouldn't the better course be to locate an effective *upaya*, limited though it may be in intellectual terms, and follow it to the End?

CHAPTER FIFTEEN

Furthermore, only an apprentice esoterist could be "keenly aware of the limitations of religions as providential salvific forms," since he is still struggling with one of the more rudimentary lessons of metaphysics, namely that God is not imprisoned in the form He has mercifully provided for us, leaving Him free to express Himself through other forms. The more seasoned esoterist sees religious forms as doors to the Absolute, and consequently understands the limitations of his or her own chosen form precisely as a necessary *key* to that Beyond, without which he or she would become lost in the multiplicity of God's possible Self-Revelations, not immersed in the necessity of the Divine Essence Itself. And how can someone who is keenly aware of the limitations of religions and their salvific forms, and who even goes so far as to characterize them as "profanations of the Divine," be in any way be called a Traditionalist, given that the essence of Tradition is God's merciful provision of limited spiritual forms that, due to the fact that they are directly addressed both to terrestrial humanity and to fallen humanity, have the power to enlighten and save, and that one of the principles found in every version of Traditional metaphysics is that God as the Source of Truth is situated beyond all forms? I can think of no clearer example than passages like these of the intrusion of what can only be called the subversive spirit of Antichrist into the works of one of the greatest explicators and defenders of religion of the 20th Century, as well as into the writings of some of his followers. If we do not detect such glaring contradictions on the first or second reading, this should probably be put down to the paralyzing shock they produce, on a largely unconscious level, due to their unexpected and radical nature—a shock that seems designed, by someone or something, to darken the human mind.

CHAPTER FIFTEEN

Laude says many true and useful things in this chapter about Buddhism, particularly in terms of its recognition of the provisional and "methodical" nature of its own doctrines, but it seems that when he imports this notion into the sphere of the Abrahamic religions he can't help translating the notion that "the dharma-body is void" into a morally nihilistic antinomianism that suggests various Christian or Muslim heresies more than it does the prudent Buddhist vigilance that is careful not to create mental attachments by reifying ideas. Likewise he shows Frithjof Schuon as defining Christianity and Islam more in terms of their collective prejudices—that is, almost as caricatures of themselves—than as self-sufficient dialects of the Primordial Tradition, although Schuon (or Laude) immediately redresses this one-sidedness by going on to present them in terms of their metaphysical universality. These two tendencies—to illegitimately interpret one religion in terms of another and to assume the kind of false objectivity that results in a more or less condescending caricature of a particular sacred worldview—are inseparable from the act of viewing the religions from the outside, as a non-participant, no matter how subtle and sophisticated such an outsider's views might be. This chapter is nonetheless highly useful in defining the two inherent aspects of any true religion: the provisional yet necessary nature of the means of realization and the Absolute Truth to be realized. Would that Schuon, who was very clear on the second of these aspects, had been less contrary and impatient when dealing with the first!

Chapter Four, "The Nature of Things and the Human Margin," deals with the relationship between the principles of the metaphysical order and the relativities of contingent manifestation,

CHAPTER FIFTEEN

particularly with regard to the world of human contingencies: history, culture, race, politics, the limitations and potentialities of particular civilizations, theological schools and intellectual trends, etc. As such, "the human margin" is necessarily more involved with the vicissitudes of history than are the principles of metaphysics and cosmology per se.

The author goes on to present Schuon's "social criticism" with regard to religion over a scale of centuries, as well as his agreements and differences with René Guénon. Given the pace of historical change, however, this critique desperately needs to be updated—if time enough remains to update it!—to include such trends as the wholesale destruction of the Christian Tradition and major aspects of the Islamic one, the devolution of much of Hinduism into a collective ethnic identity, the degradation of the natural environment, the globalist co-optation of the world's religions, the acceleration of technological change leading to the deconstruction of the human form itself through transgenderism, transhumanism, etc. To give only the barest outlines of "the human margin" of today—if not the transhuman or subhuman margin—would take a whole book in itself.

Chapter Five, "Trinitarian Metaphysics," presents us with a dizzying multiplicity of perspectives from which the Trinity can be viewed: according to the three dimensions of space; to Schuon's triplicity of Divine hypostases, the Absolute, the Infinite, and the Perfect; to the Hindu Sat-Chit-Ananda; to a "horizontal" perspective of equality vs. a "vertical" one of gradation; in terms of a triangle with apex pointing upward and another pointing downward, etc. The trinitarianisms of Dionysius the Areopagite, Thomas Aquinas, and Meister Eckhart are also surveyed, particularly with regard to their differences. All of these perspectives have something to recommend them, especially the identification of the higher, metaphysical, horizontal, hypostatic Trinity, as Schuon conceives of it (as opposed to the lower, vertical, ontological Trinity) with Sat-Chit-Ananda, "Being, Consciousness, and Bliss," in which the Principles "later" to become the Persons are not yet differentiated. Yet all these views more or less act to relativize and/or replace the orthodox dogmas of the Christian Trinity, which—according to the criteria of Laude's *Chapter Three*—would be the only doctrinal *upaya* capable of making the "Supreme Ternary" spiritually operative within the Christian universe. Schuon tends to make a hard-and-fast separation between the theological and the metaphysical Trinities, the lower theological one corresponding to the orthodox dogmatic conception and the higher metaphysical one to Schuon's own conception, as well as distinguishing between the Trinity viewed objectively or metaphysically and the same Trinity considered subjectively or epistemologically. Yet it is clear, to me at least, that the orthodox Trinity can be subjected to a metaphysical exegesis without the theological and the metaphysical levels, or the horizontal/metaphysical and the vertical/ontological levels, or the metaphysical perspective and the epistemological perspective, first being as sharply separated as Schuon has done, and that a number of examples of this kind of exegesis can in fact be found in the writings of the Christian theologians, saints and Church Fathers. Schuon himself actually draws upon these writings, though without entirely overcoming his impatience in the face of the orthodox dogmatic conceptions of the Trinity that are partly based upon them; it almost seems as if his objections are not so much due to metaphysical issues as based on a fundamental resistance to the *authority* of orthodoxy. Laude expresses the essence of these objections as follows:

> Christian trinitarianism reveals its weaknesses by confusing ontological levels of consideration. The problem with (such) trinitarianism, from Schuon's 'absolutist' point of view, is that it introduces the differentiations inherent to the ontological Trinity into the supra-ontological Essence which is, by definition, incompatible with any notion of multiplicity.

In other words, the root of Schuon's problem with orthodox Trinitarianism comes down to its dogmatic tendency to "absolutize the relative" by baldly asserting that "The Trinity is the Essence," which Schuon sees as "abusive." When considered in strict isolation, this formulation admittedly presents difficulties; nonetheless orthodox Christian theology provides innumerable ways out of this dilemma, which Schuon is loathe to recognize since he is overly enamored of his own formulations—formulations that are often profound, though not uniquely so. In **Understanding Islam**, for example, Schuon says: "The concept of a Trinity seen as a *tajalli* (deployment) of Unity or the Absolute is in no way opposed to the unitary doctrine of Islam"—or, I would add, to the *Credo in Unum Deum* of the Nicene Creed; "what is opposed to it is solely the attribution of absoluteness to the Trinity alone, or even to the ontological Trinity alone as it is envisaged exoterically." But such dogmatic "literalization" is precisely the role and right of exoterism, especially in view of the fact that Christianity (in Schuon's terminology) is an "eso-exoteric Revelation." The question is, do we see this theological paradox and/or contradiction as "abusive," as Schuon does, after which we may be moved to "fix" it on the basis of this or that relatively heterodox formulation, or do we see it as a challenge to carry on a metaphysical exegesis *without departing from orthodoxy*, which is not only possible but which accepted Christian authorities—Dionysius the Pseudo-Areopagite for example—have repeatedly accomplished? In other words, are we heterodox Perennialists pursuing non-traditional speculations and private revelations, or are we Traditionalists whose object of meditation is the esoteric core of the orthodox faiths? Personal intellection and/or inspiration need not bind itself to, or measure itself against, explicit orthodox formulations at every point, but to openly rival such formulations is in itself "abusive."

Chapter Six, "Necessary Sufism and the Archetype of Islam," covers Schuon's critique of Sufism, which was (at least in name) his own spiritual Path. Laude points out that Schuon's one book on the subject, **Sufism: Veil and Quintessence**, has much to say on Sufism as "a religious phenomenon"—what Schuon called "average" or "possible" Sufism—as opposed to "necessary" or "quintessential" Sufism, which he saw as nothing less than "the archetype of Islam." Average or possible Sufism is characterized by an overabundance of sentimentalism and "voluntarism"—an excessive reliance on the will as opposed to the Intellect—while quintessential or necessary Sufism is *gnostic* in essence. Unfortunately, Schuon clearly had an intermittent but unwarranted tendency to equate *gnostic* Sufism with Sufi antinomianism.

Laude distinguishes gnostic or intellective mysticism from voluntaristic mysticism in this highly enlightening passage:

CHAPTER FIFTEEN

> "Truth ... makes us conscious of an absolute and transcendent Reality—at once personal and suprapersonal—and the will ... attaches itself to it and recognizes in it its own supernatural essence and its ultimate end" (*Esoterism as Principle and as Way*). Thus the universal Truth is a priori the initiating subject or agent of discernment within human consciousness, while the individual attaches himself to the Truth through his efforts of assimilation and concentration. In contemplative disciplines, the striving of the will results ultimately in the recognition of its own essential identity with the Self, therefore with the Truth ... by contrast, voluntaristic mysticism places its main emphasis on the individual dimension of the will, its perspective giving pre-eminence to actions and to the acquisition of merit through action ... from a gnostic point of view ... Knowledge can only be an outcome of actions indirectly, as it were, inasmuch as the latter constitute a symbolic allusion to it, or insofar as they facilitate removing the veils that prevent it from being actualized.

I agree with this description entirely—and one of the darkest of the veils to be removed is the veil of self-will. The central virtue of the *shari'ah*, like the injunctions of one's shaykh, is that it is obligatory, and therefore allows us to renounce self-will through obedience. When self-will is mortified it loses its power to produce obscuring turbulence in the spiritual Heart, with the result that (*insha'Allah*) the Eye of the Heart opens: this is *gnosis*. The will does not recognize its identity with the Self through spiritual ambition, but through its willingness to submit to God's Will. When the will is fully submitted to God, it is recognized that only God is the Doer—and that, secondarily, His Action encompasses, and is expressed by means of, the actions of the individual; in the words of the Qur'an [37:96], *Allah created you and that which you do*. This, however, is not the "voluntaristic mysticism" so often criticized by Schuon that sees God, and the human response to God, only in terms of the will. Rather, correct submission, by pacifying the will, removes it as the central object of consideration and struggle, allowing the purified Intellect to directly witness the Divine not as Will but as Truth, even though this Truth must express itself as a Divine Will when interacting with the created universe and the individual soul. This is the essence of normative Sufi practice, in which character development and the acquisition of virtue are not primarily directed toward amassing merit so as to gain a higher station in the next world, but toward realizing *Ma'rifa* or *gnosis* in this very life.

There are indications, however, that Schuon did not always clearly understand this principle. Laude says: "While Schuon considers (*shari'ah*) as a 'symbolic' manifestation of *haqiqah* or *gnosis*, he still rejects Ibn 'Arabi's notion of their conjunction. For him, this equation results from a legalistic emphasis that he sees as incompatible with gnosis." And again: "The exoteric limitations of esoterism"—that is, the limitations placed on the sort of "average" Sufism that considers adherence to the *shari'ah* to be a *sine qua non*— "include a voluntarist view of the Divine, whereby the Divine Essence is erroneously conflated with a dimension of the Divine Will that is 'relative' to the created order, and where an obedientalist understanding of humanity reduces the latter ... to its dimension of relative will in submission to the Divine Order. These two tendencies overlook what constitutes the Essence of God and the human being, precisely inasmuch 'God and man are defined as will.'"

This is indeed one of the possible reductionist influences of adherence to the *shar'iah* upon a realization of the *haqiqah*, but it is not a necessary reduction, particularly in the case of the gnostic, the *arif*; Schuon's own shaykh, Ahmed al-'Alawi, is a case in point. And is *disobedientalism* really any closer to *gnosis* than "obedientalism"?

Frithjof Schuon's shaky grasp on the gnostic significance of obedience to the Will of God in Sufism brings us to the question of his view of Sufi antinomianism, and of antinomianism in general. Laude says:

> Schuon's ... spiritual universe was utterly immune from any "religious nationalism" or "confessional bias" ... in this, he followed in the tracks of Guénon ... who also considered esoterism as being utterly free from religion, indeed as belonging to a radically different order of reality ... in particular, [Schuon] is keen to affirm that the religion of the Heart—which is none other than the *haqiqah*—is independent of the Law. This independence, however, pertains more to the realm of principles than to that of facts. This means, in practice, that antinomian Sufism remains the exception that proves the rule.

—or perhaps, as in the case of Schuon's own *tariqah*, the object lesson that proves the wisdom and prudence of the rule. And

Laude's claim that René Guénon "considered esoterism as being utterly free of religion" is totally wrong, as witness Guénon's chapter "The Necessity for a Traditional Exoterism" from **Initiation and Spiritual Realization**. "The quintessential Sufism propounded by Schuon," says Laude, "is not antinomian but, rather, supranomian, in the sense that its principles lie beyond the realm of the Law." It is the rare antinomian, however, who styles himself a criminal who loves to break the law; your average, everyday antinomian will usually present himself not as a defiant rebel against the *nomos* but simply as occupying a "supranomian" position above it. The defiant rebel defines the condition of being "beyond good and evil" simply as indicating that he can do whatever he wants, while the *arif*, rather than seeing the transcendence of good and evil as a personal liberation from the strictures of sacred law, understands it as something that pertains intrinsically to God alone, given that the Absolute, being the ultimate Performer of all action and the sole Reality that is reflected in all the qualities and processes of created existence, is not bound by the laws under which He places His creatures, which are equally the designs according to which He has created them.

Chapter Seven, "The Divine Feminine," is possibly the best treatment of Sophianic spirituality I have ever read; of its relationship to the essence of gender; and of the significance of gender, and indeed of polarity on every level, to both cosmic and metaphysical realities. As such it stands as a telling critique of the contemporary demotion and ultimate suppression of gender that threatens in our time to deconstruct the human form itself. The only serpent in this paradisiacal garden is the denigration of "moralism" so common in Schuon's writings. Laude says:

CHAPTER FIFTEEN

> Positively, religious outwardness is a principle of integration.... However, it is also a source of strife, if not destruction, as its limited emphasis on what to do and not to do (i.e., arguments about orthopraxy) are bound to impede the flowering of spiritual realization.

Certainly morality can become blind, heartless, and destructive—but is not a chaotic or rebellious contempt for questions of "what to do or not to do" equally destructive? Does this not also impede spiritual realization? The essence of morality is not the arbitrary imposition of external rules but the defense of human integrity, and thus of the *Imago Dei* that constitutes the human essence. If you objectify other people by failing to acknowledge them as subjects in their own right, you veil the *Imago Dei* in yourself as well. If you hurt others, you destroy your affinity with the Sovereign Good; if you lie, you set up a barrier between yourself and transcendental Truth, you blind the Eye of the Heart—which is to say that proper morality is an *upaya* with profound metaphysical implications. To believe that moral rectitude and moral turpitude have no effect on esoteric realization—if indeed this is what Patrick Laude is implying—is one of the commonest and most fatuous errors of the antinomian mindset.

Chapter Eight, "The Yin-Yang Perspective and Visual Metaphysics," is where Laude expands Schuon's metaphysics of polarity by surveying the Chinese metaphysical cosmology of Taoism from a Schuonian perspective, delving more deeply into the *I Ching* than Schuon himself did (if indeed he ever mentioned it), and providing many illuminating parallels with other traditions, notably Buddhism.

CHAPTER FIFTEEN

Chapter Nine, "The 'Tantric' Spiritualization of Sexuality," takes a detailed though rather abstract look at many of the possible forms of the union of sexuality and spirituality that appear in Schuon's writings—the Tantric, the Krishnaite, the example of the Prophet Muhammad, etc.—and provides us with many illuminating insights. Both the positive aspects and the potential pitfalls of these forms are considered. In view of the contemporary attempt, foredoomed but nonetheless profoundly destructive, to marginalize heterosexuality, a rediscovery of the metaphysical roots of Man and Woman, such as Schuon posits, is crucial. Unfortunately, Laude leaves Christianity, defined almost exclusively in terms of the anti-sexuality of Augustine, virtually out of the picture, ignoring both the elevation of matrimony to the status of a sacramental, quasi-initiatory rite and the immensely influential tradition of spiritual romance within Christianity that culminated in Dante. This leads the author to seriously misrepresent not only Christianity but Islam: "A Muslim sensibility will tend to assess the traditional Christian outlook as being contrary to nature and … to divine law and intent." Never mind that the Qur'an speaks highly of Christian monks, that it sees the Virgin Mary as the pinnacle of womanhood, that it presents itself as confirming the Gospels, that Muslims accept the reality of the virgin birth of Christ, and that Muhammad, in his Covenants with the Christians of his time, referred to them as *mu'minin*, "believers." Certainly there was to be "no monasticism in Islam," but to accuse Islam of asserting that the traditional Christian outlook is contrary to divine law is to seriously misrepresent Islam in order to slander Christianity, as if the intent behind it were to kill two birds with one stone. *This* is Traditionalism?

CHAPTER FIFTEEN

Furthermore, when considering Schuon's view of "sacred sexuality", we must take into consideration Laude's definition of "left-hand" Tantra as "an ascesis of antinomian behavior" that is "deliberatively transgressive" of socio-religious norms, while at the same time maintaining that such Tantra is "not . . . what Schuon primarily has in mind when referring to Tantrism." In order to objectively evaluate the reliability of this statement, the serious researcher will likely have to embark on the perilous course of attempting to evaluate Schuon's own practice in this regard. As first step on this road I refer the reader to **Revolt Against the Modern World** by Mark Sedgwick, whose perspective I have my own disagreements with—especially since he attempts to evaluate Traditionalism with almost zero reference to metaphysics!—and which a number of Schuon's followers have done their best to refute, but which nonetheless presents certain common criticisms of Schuon's *praxis* that need to be taken into account, and whose factual truth or falsity will hopefully someday be solidly established.

Nonetheless, speaking in general terms and with no specific reference to Frithjof Schuon, much of what passes for "sacred sexuality" in our time attempts, legitimately or otherwise, to raise eros from a personal to an archetypal level; the Krishnaite form—more appropriate for gods than for mortals—can be taken as emblematic of this tendency. Group sexuality, however gross or subtle—whether or not we take Krishna and his *gopis* as our model for it—inevitably acts to objectify and depersonalize those who engage in it; if someone claims that objectification and depersonalization are elements of sacralization, I am eager to hear his or her arguments. When Muhammad liquidated the pagan orgy culture in Mecca that characterized the pre-Islamic "time of ignorance"—a culture in which public nudity figured prominently—and when Jesus said "whoever has looked with lust upon a woman has already committed adultery with her in his heart," they were not fundamentally suppressing eros but rather opposing erotic *depersonalization*, working to sacralize sexuality by *humanizing* it. This spiritual impetus was further developed within Christendom, partly under the influence of elements of esoteric Muslim spirituality, in the traditions of Courtly Love and the Fedeli d'Amore that so influenced Dante. Courtly Love as a spiritual discipline is designed to purify and elevate sexual desire from the level of lust to that of True Love by the spiritualizing power of Romance, in which archetypal eros and personal affection are united. But if there is anything less romantic in the erotic field than group sex, it does not immediately come to mind. Without personal love, care, and compassion—of which Schuon writes hardly one word, though he often refers to the archetype of Divine Mercy, of which personal love is one of the human expressions—any attempt to spiritualize sexuality on an aesthetic or archetypal/symbolic level alone is worse than useless.

Chapter Ten, "Esoteric Ecumenism," has many interesting things to say about the affinities and oppositions between the religions in the exoteric dimension and their similarities and affinities in the esoteric one, and posits esoterism as the only perspective capable of both defining a true common ground between the faiths and restoring them to the fullness of their own traditions in the face of the continuing deconstruction of their exoteric dimensions, while fully respecting their providential differences as against the relativizing and homogenizing tendencies emanating from the world of "mainstream ecumenical sensibilities." I applaud this position. Such a restoration, however, could only be for an increasingly-marginalized "remnant" from each of the faiths, not for the intelligentsia of an "increasingly globalized world" that Laude apparently wishes to appeal to. The author, in line with my own call for a "united front ecumenism" in *The System of Antichrist* (2001), envisions Schuon's "esoteric ecumenism" as "forming a common front of traditional religions against scientific ideology and 'organized irreligion'" and "the pervasive influence of secularism," in order to promote "the integrity of exoteric dogmatic orthodoxy, the opposition to atheism, and the extent and means of affirmation of exclusivism." These are my hopes exactly. However, when Laude quotes a passage from Schuon's *The Transcendent Unity of Religions* which he sees as "the characterization of religion as a sort of profanation of the Divine," and then goes on to maintain that "The Christian 'Word made flesh' is probably the most direct expression of this profanation," he sabotages the very "common front of traditional religions" that he claims to support, expressing a virulent animus against Christianity that is perfectly in line with the "organized irreligion" of contemporary secularism. On the first page of his book he calls for a *philosophia perennis* that would constitute "a conceptual synthesis of the world's wisdom traditions ... without claiming to supersede their respective doctrinal integrity"— and then goes on to call Christianity "a profanation of the Divine"! Is it possible to conceive a more radical contradiction? Before taking defensive action against the *dunya*, the Darkness of This World, we must first recognize exactly what that World is, and make a clean break with it in our own souls.

CHAPTER FIFTEEN

In conclusion—to return to Laude's placement of Schuon's teachings in the context of "intellectual globalization"—I believe that, rather than attempting to establish a syncretistic conceptual unity or a hegemonic political unity of the religions, the least problematic use of the Transcendent Unity of Religions, one that avoids the negative influence of globalism, is to posit the *existential* unity of the religions on a plane transcending form, simply by recognizing that all true Revelations, whatever their similarities or differences, spring from the same Divine Source. Patrick Laude's version of the TUR, on the other hand, serves the very horizontal, political unification of religions that the globalist elites are laboring to create, and does so in two ways. First, it weakens these religions in their vertical dimension by positing a "quintessential esoterism" that transcends their own deepest and highest links to the Transcendent God, thus beginning the process of reducing them to mere ethnic or socio-cultural "sectors" capable of being politically unified by some outside force. Schuon's doctrine of the "relatively Absolute," to which Laude devotes one whole chapter and major sections of others, might have worked against this denaturing of the Traditional faiths by making it clear that each revealed religion is pre-eminent and incomparable, in line with Schuon's declaration in **From the Divine to the Human**: "A given religion in reality sums up all religions . . . all religion is to be found in a given religion, because Truth is one"—and therefore that it need not and cannot be amalgamated with one or more equally incomparable Revelations. However, Laude's error in positing Frithjof Schuon's quintessential esoterism as the equivalent of a separate quasi-religious dispensation on the plane of form, one that supersedes the "merely confessional" faiths rather than giving us a way to witness them in their metaphysical transparency, has

CHAPTER FIFTEEN

succeeded in transforming Schuon's "relatively Absolute" into a condescending demotion of all other religious forms in favor of the universal superiority of his own—and there is no denying that Frithjof Schuon himself prepared the way, though not without the judicious placement of various disclaimers, for this unfortunate development. That Schuon defined his quintessential esoterism (at least from time to time) as a spiritual *form* transcending the revealed religions, but nonetheless never claimed, at least openly, that he had received any new Revelation from God, is one of the central contradictions in his teachings.

The second way in which Laude's approach works to undermine the Traditional faiths is by providing those among the globalist elites who are doing research and development toward a One-World Religion—an institution that some believe is necessary to stabilize the New World Order, and one that, even if it is never in fact established, has already had a profoundly dissolutionary effect on the traditional faiths simply as an idea—with an ideology as if custom-built for the purpose, a "globalist theology" that articulates a true and profound metaphysic (though not entirely free of errors) while placing it in a false and non-Traditional context.

If, however, we can pass beyond the Symplegades of totally rejecting Schuon due to his errors, and accepting everything he said and did in the name of his deepest metaphysical insights, we will hopefully be able to subject his teachings, perhaps for the first time, to a sober, balanced, metaphysical assessment, rather than simply a moral, psychological, or sociological one. ***Keys to the Beyond*** presents us with an ideal opportunity to do this, allowing us to evaluate such statements as "error always implies a privation of knowledge, whereas sin does not imply a privation

355

of will" [*Gnosis: Divine Wisdom*]—which I see as an outright error—as well as dangerous mis-directions such as "Outward Beauty, even when combined with inner ugliness, testifies to Beauty as such" [*Survey of Metaphysics and Esoterism*]—in light of both "pure metaphysics" and the great wisdom traditions on which Traditionalism is based. If even the Holy Qur'an was assaulted (unsuccessfully) by certain "satanic verses," we must accept the possibility that Frithjof Schuon's profound metaphysical insights might have been distorted, on some occasions, by similar influences; what else is to be expected in these last days of the Kali-yuga?

Once Schuon's legacy is purified of its internal contradictions, metaphysical errors, and instances where it rejects the orthodox doctrine of a particular Divine revelation, we may find ourselves in the presence of an inspired exegesis of the inner dimensions of the world religions that works to support them, coupled with an exposition of the deeper aspects of the metaphysical principles they hold in common. If it is not subjected to this kind of purification, however, it may ultimately take the form of a heterodox and virtually Counter-Initiatory ideology that has no qualms about pirating whatever it needs from the God-given faiths, only to weaken, denigrate, and undermine them, after which it will make its plunder available (perhaps unwittingly) as a "higher doctrine" to those forces working to develop a One-World Religion—presuming that they think it worth their while to make use of Schuon's more wrongheaded efforts. And with the publication of **Keys to the Beyond: Frithjof Schuon's Cross-Traditional Language of Transcendence**, the parting of these two ways becomes clearer than ever before. Like no other

CHAPTER FIFTEEN

book I am aware of, ***Keys to the Beyond*** illuminates the immense complexity and comprehensiveness of Schuon's doctrines, but it does so partly at the expense of a sufficient sense of an operative spiritual Center—unless that center was Schuon himself, who unfortunately is no longer with us. In Prof. Laude's book it is as if the face of God were temporarily obscured behind the swirling cyclone of His Names. Be that as it may, for anyone interested in pursuing the academic study of Frithjof Schuon, this book is, or will shortly become, an indispensable resource.

ADDENDUM

A Last Word?

In my humble opinion, Frithjof Schuon was not "the Seal of the Sages" as some of his followers have maintained, but rather "the Seal of *Maya*," insofar as we define *maya* as the outward expression of Divine Reality which acts both to manifest and to veil its Transcendent Source, as well as the necessary and pre-existent potential for this manifestation as it subsists within the Divine Nature itself, a hypostasis that Schuon has named "All-Possibility" and "*maya-in-divinis*," and that is generally analogous to the Sufi term *wahadiyya*, denoting God's *synthetic* Unity. And inseparable from this *maya*, within the field of human experience, is the power of *glamour*, which the Merriam-Webster Dictionary defines as "an exciting and often illusory and romantic attractiveness; alluring or fascinating attraction; a magic spell"; in most sacred traditions, this glamourous power of *maya* is identified in one way or another with the Feminine Principle. In Hindu Shaivism, for example, *Mahamaya* takes the form of *Shakti*, the manifesting-and-reintegrating Power of the Divinity, analogous to the Jewish concept of the *Shekhina*, as well as to the figure of Holy Wisdom from the Book of Proverbs. *Shakti* is pictured as the feminine consort of *Shiva*, the Transcendent Absolute.

For our time, at least in the field of intellective spirituality, Frithjof Schuon was the quintessential epiphany of *maya* at its point of highest concentration—and in apocalyptic moments such as ours, this *maya* must take the form of Divine Judgment, precisely the sort of Judgment that is indicated by the Qur'an, surah 8, verse 30, *they plot but Allah also plots, and Allah is the best of plotters*—the One who both mercifully reveals the Truth to those who submit to Him whole-heartedly, and cunningly leads astray those who pridefully believe that they can ignore His revealed Word because they themselves know better. When Naked Truth is revealed, because the veil separating Heaven from Earth is torn in two from top to bottom, especially in times like ours that have collectively turned against this Truth, it must manifest at least partly in terms of illusion, which necessitates a radical act of discernment on the part of those witnessing the theophany in question, a true separation of the Sheep from the Goats, not only in the field of the human collective but within each human soul. In the face of such a theophany of *maya*, if any doctrine or human character is fundamentally oriented toward the Truth, then its very imperfections and errors will ultimately serve that Truth, whereas if it is oriented toward error, then even the truths it expresses will ultimately reinforce that error. The fact that *Vidya-maya*, the illusion that reveals the Truth, and *avidya-maya*, the revelation of Truth that ends by generating illusion, are both aspects *maya* per se is strictly analogous to the fact that, in Schuon's doctrine, "evil highlights the Good *a contrario*." Nor are we justified in easily assuming that the chosen messenger of this theophany of *maya* necessarily remained unaffected by it, given that *maya*, like God Himself and insofar as it subsists as a manifestation of God Himself, is no respecter of persons. Even Shiva, as I've already alluded to above, was led a merry chase at one point by the power of His own *Shakti*. Therefore, insofar as we are tempted to judge Frithjof Schuon, or anyone or anything else in this perishing world, we must realize that, in abandoning "judge not lest ye be judged," we have come into the field of "you will be required to judge precisely so that you *will* be judged," thus making sure that the Judgment of God, the definitive separation of the Sheep from the Goats, the final purgation, will be entirely satisfied on all levels, in ways that even our highest and most intellectually-informed spiritual discernment has never conceived of.

> *Allah guides aright whom He will and leads astray whom He will.* [Q: 16:93]

In the words of Shaykh Ahmed al-'Alawi from his **Munajah**, which anyone must heed who presumes to do a critical evaluation of so great a metaphysician as was Frithjof Schuon—just as he himself was required to heed them on pain of placing himself in the gravest spiritual danger:

> I seek refuge in ALLAH against the entrapments of the *nafs* and of Shaytan.
> I seek refuge in ALLAH against the evil of men and Jinns.

ADDENDUM

I seek refuge in ALLAH from ALLAH's punishment.
I seek refuge in ALLAH from ALLAH's wrath.
I seek refuge in ALLAH from ALLAH's stratagem.

~~ August 8, 2024

www.ingramcontent.com/pod-product-compliance
Lightning Source LLC
Chambersburg PA
CBHW071108160426
43196CB00013B/2506